D0567450

ESSAYS ON BRECHT

UNIVERSITY OF NORTH CAROLINA
STUDIES IN THE GERMANIC LANGUAGES
AND LITERATURES

Initiated by RICHARD JENTE (1949-1952), established by F. E. COENEN (1952-1968)

Publication Committee

SIEGFRIED MEWS, EDITOR   JOHN G. KUNSTMANN   GEORGE S. LANE

HERBERT W. REICHERT   CHRISTOPH E. SCHWEITZER   SIDNEY R. SMITH

For other volumes in the "Studies" see pages 239 ff.

Send orders to: (U.S. and Canada)
The University of North Carolina Press, P.O. Box 2288
Chapel Hill, N.C. 27514

(All other countries) Feffer and Simons, Inc., 31 Union Square, New York, N.Y. 10003

NUMBER SEVENTY-NINE

UNIVERSITY
OF NORTH CAROLINA
STUDIES IN
THE GERMANIC LANGUAGES
AND LITERATURES

Essays on Brecht

Theater and Politics

Edited by

Siegfried Mews and Herbert Knust

CHAPEL HILL
THE UNIVERSITY OF NORTH CAROLINA PRESS
1974

PT
2603
.R 397
Z 763

© University of North Carolina

Studies in the Germanic Languages

and Literatures 1974

Library of Congress Cataloging in Publication Data

Mews, Siegfried
  Essays on Brecht: theater and politics.

  (University of North Carolina studies in the Germanic languages and
literatures, no. 79)
   Bibliography: pp. 227-229.
   1. Brecht, Bertolt, 1898-1956. I. Knust, Herbert, joint author. II.
Title. III. Series: North Carolina University. Studies in the Germanic
languages and literatures, no. 79.
PT2603.R397Z763   832'.9'12   74-5262
ISBN 0-8078-8079-5

Manufactured in the U.S.A.

Augustana College Library
Rock Island, Illinois

Contents

PART III

ABBREVIATIONS

I. Works by and on Brecht, special issues of periodicals:

AJ — Brecht, Bertolt. *Arbeitsjournal.* 3 vols. Ed. Werner Hecht. Frankfurt am Main: Suhrkamp, 1973. I: *1938-1942.* II: *1942-1955.* III: *Anmerkungen.*

BBA — Bertolt-Brecht-Archiv, Berlin

BBA-B — *Bertolt-Brecht-Archiv. Bestandsverzeichnis des literarischen Nachlasses.* Ed. Herta Ramthun. Berlin, Weimar: Aufbau-Verlag, 1969-1973. I: *Stücke*; II: *Gedichte.* III: *Prosa, Filmtexte, Schriften.* IV: *Gespräche, Notate, Arbeitsmaterialien.*

BH — *Brecht Heute-Brecht Today. Jahrbuch der Internationalen Brecht-Gesellschaft.*

Brecht (D) — *Brecht. A Collection of Critical Essays.* Ed. Peter Demetz. Englewood Cliffs, N.J.: Prentice-Hall, 1962.

Brecht (E/1) — Esslin, Martin. *Brecht: A Choice of Evils. A Critical Study of the Man, His Work and His Opinions.* London: Eyre and Sprottiswood, 1959.

Brecht (E/2) — Esslin, Martin. *Brecht. The Man and His Work.* Anchor Books. Garden City, N.Y.: Doubleday, 1961.

Brecht (E/3) — Esslin, Martin. *Brecht. The Man and His Work.* New rev. ed. Anchor Books. Garden City, N.Y.: Doubleday, 1971.

Brecht (Ew) — Ewen, Frederic. *Bertolt Brecht. His Life, His Art and His Times.* New York: Citadel Press, 1967.

Brecht (G) — Grimm, Reinhold. *Bertolt Brecht.* 3., völlig neu bearbeitete Auflage. Sammlung Metzler. Stuttgart: J.B. Metzlersche Verlagsbuchhandlung, 1971.

Brecht (M) — *Brecht.* Ed. Erika Munk. New York: Bantam Books, 1972.

Brecht (W) — Willet, John. *The Theatre of Bertolt Brecht. A Study from Eight Aspects.* 3rd rev. ed. New York: New Directions, 1968.

Brecht-Chronik — Völker, Klaus. *Brecht-Chronik. Daten zu Leben und Werk.* Reihe Hanser. Munich: Hanser, 1971.

Brecht on Theatre — *Brecht on Theatre. The Development of an Aesthetic.* Ed., trans. John Willett. New York: Hill and Wang, 1964.

CP — Brecht, Bertolt. *Collected Plays.* Ed. Ralph Manheim and John Willett. Vols. I, V, IX. Vintage Books. New York: Random House, 1971-1973.

Gedichte — Brecht, Bertolt. *Gedichte.* 9 vols. Frankfurt am Main: Suhrkamp, 1960-1969.

GW — Brecht, Bertolt. *Gesammelte Werke in 20 Bänden.* Frankfurt am Main: Suhrkamp, 1967. I-VII: *Stücke.* VIII-X: *Gedichte.* XI-XIV: *Prosa.* XV-XVII: *Zum Theater.* XVIII-XIX: *Zur Literatur und Kunst.* XX: *Zur Politik und Gesellschaft.*

SF/1 — *Sinn und Form. 1. Sonderheft Bertolt Brecht* (Berlin, 1949).

SF/2 — *Sinn und Form. 2. Sonderheft Bertolt Brecht* (Berlin, 1957).

Stücke — Brecht, Bertolt. *Stücke.* 14 vols. Frankfurt am Main: Suhrkamp, 1953-1967.

SzT — Brecht, Bertolt. *Schriften zum Theater.* 7 vols. Frankfurt am Main: Suhrkamp, 1963-1964.

TuK — *Text und Kritik. Sonderband Bertolt Brecht I.* Ed. Heinz Ludwig Arnold (Munich, 1972).

Versuche — Brecht, Bertolt. *Versuche.* 15 vols. Berlin: Kiepenheuer, 1930-1933; Berlin, Frankfurt am Main: Suhrkamp, 1949-1956, 1959.

II. Periodicals

CL	*Contemporary Literature*
CLS	*Comparative Literature Studies*
DR	*The [Tulane] Drama Review*
GQ	*The German Quarterly*
GR	*Germanic Review*
GRM	*Germanisch-Romanische Monatsschrift*
MD	*Modern Drama*
MfdU	*Monatshefte für deutschen Unterricht*
MLN	*Modern Language Notes*
NYT	*The New York Times*
PMLA	*Publications of the Modern Language Association of America*
RLC	*Revue de Littérature Comparée*
SF	*Sinn und Form*
SR	*The Saturday Review of Literature*
TA	*Theatre Arts*
TdZ	*Theater der Zeit*
TH	*Theater Heute*
ZfdPh	*Zeitschrift für deutsche Philologie*

INTRODUCTORY NOTE

There is no need to belabor the obvious by attempting to expound the significance of Bertolt Brecht for literature in general and theater in particular. On the one hand, no justification would seem to be needed for publishing a collection of essays on a playwright who has been heralded as "the most important figure in 20th-century drama." On the other hand, it is legitimate to ask why the editors would wish to add to the apparent *embarras des richesses* of Brecht criticism. The answer to such a question is that both general and specific problems of Brecht research remain unresolved, as Reinhold Grimm pointed out in the third edition of his indispensable *Bertolt Brecht* (1971). Actually, it was precisely because the editors were aware of the manifold and varied research activities carried on by Brecht scholars in the United States that they conceived of the plan to publish *Essays on Brecht*. They were able to solicit and edit contributions which—apart from two revised essays which had been previously published in German—are the results of current research. Hence the editors are of the conviction that the thirteen essays they ultimately selected will either help advance knowledge in certain areas of Brecht scholarship or stimulate discussion by offering new and possibly controversial interpretations of Brecht's works. In keeping with the spirit of Bertolt Brecht, the proponent of *experiments,* the editors did not deem it necessary to impose restrictive rules on the individual contributors as to the approach chosen or method followed. Rather, they selected thematically related essays dealing with two major aspects of Brecht research, i.e., theater and politics, and arranged them somewhat loosely in three parts.

The three essays of Part I deal with Brecht's theory of drama by concentrating on his dialectic reception of the theoretical contributions to epic theater by naturalism, and on his literary affinities to and personal relations with individual playwrights and theater directors. Part II focuses more specifically on individual plays from Brecht's early period (*Drums in the Night, In the Jungle*) to those of his mature style (*Life of Galileo, The Good Woman of Setzuan*). Apart from exploring personal and literary relations between Brecht and other prominent figures of world literature in comparative studies or advancing new readings of specific plays, most of these essays also discuss the two facets so very closely and, ultimately, inseparably linked to any investigation of Brecht the man and his work: his dramatic theory and practice and his political views. Part III deals with Brecht's politics proper or rather with the interrelationship between ideology, politics, and art in general and with his reception in the U.S. in particular. As such a topic is most likely to stimulate debate and thought-provoking controversy, it may serve as a fitting conlusion in a volume dedicated to a man who attempted to demonstrate productive contradictions in his dramatic theory and practice.

A few remarks about some technical aspects of this volume are in order. The essays were written by scholars residing in the U.S. and Canada. They are addressed primarily (but not exclusively) to an English-speaking reading public; thus quotes are given in English. Only in cases where it was felt that a translation would not adequately render the meaning of the original (e.g., in poetry) has the German text been given. Although a considerable part of Brecht's *œuvre* is extant in English translation, many authors preferred to provide their own renderings. Hence, unless specific reference is made to the use of a particular translation, it may be assumed that the translations are those of the respective contributors. In general, the text for the quotations from Brecht's works is that provided in *Gesammelte Werke in 20 Bänden* (Frankfurt am Main: Suhrkamp Verlag, 1967). For the convenience of those readers who wish to resort to renderings in English, a Select Bibliography of Brecht's works in English has been added. Further, all titles of Brecht's plays, poems, prose writings as well as the titles of works by authors reasonably well established in the English-speaking countries in general and in the United States in particular have been given in English. An Index of Brecht's writings listing the titles in the original German has been provided to facilitate the checking of individual works. For reasons of economy works, periodicals, etc. frequently referred to have been cited by abbreviated title. The complete titles may be found in the list of Abbreviations (pp. x-xi).

Finally, the editors wish to gratefully acknowledge the financial aid they received from the University Research Council of the University of North Carolina at Chapel Hill and the Research Board of the University of Illinois at Urbana-Champaign. Without the help of these institutions the publication of the present volume would not have been possible.

PART I

NATURALISM AND EPIC DRAMA*

Reinhold Grimm

> On ne sait jamais au juste où un
> mouvement commence, parce
> que ce mouvement vient d' or-
> dinaire de fort loin, et qu'il se
> confond avec le mouvement
> précédent, dont il est sorti.
> (*Zola*)**

In a radio interview at the end of the twenties Bertolt Brecht declared, "Yes, it is true that this theory of the epic drama is ours. We have also tried to produce several epic dramas." And Brecht enumerated: his own play *A Man's a Man,* Arnolt Bronnen's *Ostpolzug* and the Ingolstadt dramas of Marieluise Fleißer. Brecht continued:

> But the attempts to produce epic drama were present much
> earlier. . . . They began in the previous century when science
> became so prevalent. The beginnings of naturalism were the begin-
> nings of the epic drama in Europe. . . . The naturalistic drama
> developed from the bourgeois novel of Zola and Dostoevski, which
> itself announced the invasion of science into the domains of art. The
> naturalists (Ibsen, Hauptmann) tried to bring the new subject matter
> of the new novels onto the stage and found no other form for it ex-
> cept that of these novelists: an epic form.[1]

It would seem that this statement is entirely clear. From it one deduced that Brecht, as a theorist at any rate, was undeniably, indeed even solely, dependent on the naturalists. "As far as the theory is con-cerned," asserts Helge Hultberg, "there is only one literary movement which provides an acceptable basis for comparison: naturalism as it is theoretically formulated in the writings of Zola." According to Hult-berg, Emile Zola (1840-1902) is "the only real predecessor" of Brecht; his most important theoretical work, *Le Roman expérimental* of 1880, was the "essential model" for the theory of the epic drama or, to use Brecht's later term, the epic theater.[2]

Of course Hultberg, whose book appeared in 1962, is not the first to devote attention to Brecht's relationship to naturalism in general and to

---

* This essay, translated by Siegfried Mews and Carolyn Ann Wellauer, is a revised and
  enlarged version of "Naturalismus und episches Drama," which first appeared in
  Reinhold Grimm, ed., *Episches Theater* (Cologne, 1966; 3rd ed. 1973), pp. 13-35.
** Cf. p. 27, and n. 132.
[1] GW, XV, 151-52.
[2] *Die ästhetischen Anschauungen Bertolt Brechts* (Copenhagen,1962), pp. 23, 155. For
  my critique of Hultberg, see the review in ZfdPh, 84 (1965), Sonderheft, 90 ff.

Zola in particular. In 1957 the Italian philosopher Galvano della Volpe published an article entitled "Da Zola a Brecht,"[3] and in 1961 Paolo Chiarini's studies on avant-garde and realism appeared,[4] both of which concern themselves, if only briefly, with these questions. Without exaggerating his importance, della Volpe definitely classifies Zola among the forerunners of the epic theater, whereas Chiarini maintains that Zola's theory of the experimental novel has nothing whatsoever to do with Brecht's drama theory. He rejects the influence of naturalism on Brecht as vehemently as Hultberg asserts it.

Chiarini, too, can base his argument on statements Brecht made at the end of the twenties. On another occasion, Brecht calmly proclaimed that naturalism had in no way been "a revolutionary change" but "merely a trifling and basically an inconsequential, casual influence on the drama by the international bourgeois novel." Further, "this movement produced no important works, gave the theater no new subject matter and failed completely after several attempts." With the grim pathos of an ideological convert Brecht even declared: "Naturalism reveals its naive, felonious instincts in its name." The word itself is a crime, and on the stage it signifies a pure *Menschenfresserdramatik.*[5]

Which of these two assertions, both made during the incubation period of the epic theater, is correct? With which of the critics should we agree, with Hultberg or with Chiarini? Or is one interpretation as mistaken and unsuccessful as the other—due to the fact that the contradiction is inherent in the matter itself?

Not only are the remarks of Hultberg and Chiarini incomplete, but also those of della Volpe. In order to be able to outline Brecht's relationship to naturalism, a far more comprehensive study is needed. It cannot, for example, be limited to *Le Roman expérimental* as it is in Hultberg's treatment but must also make use of Zola's other theoretical writings, particularly those on the theater, for purposes of comparison. Furthermore, it is definitely necessary to examine the German as well as the French theory of naturalistic drama. It is amazing to discover that in 1892, six years before Brecht was born, a pronouncedly non-Aristotelian drama theory was in print and was the cause of lively discussion. One cannot, therefore, ignore the reactions of those contemporaries who regarded naturalism skeptically. In fact, Brecht apparently studied one of them, Friedrich Spielhagen, very carefully. Spielhagen's *Neue Beiträge zur Theorie und Technik der Epik und Dramatik,* which deals thoroughly with the naturalistic dramas, is still in Brecht's library today. As expected, the seven volumes of Brecht's

---

[3] *Il Contemporaneo,* 4/5 (1957), 3; also available in G. della Volpe, *Crisi dell'estetica romantica* (Rome, 1963), pp. 113 ff.

[4] *L'avanguardia e la poetica del realismo* (Bari, 1961), especially pp. 88 ff.

[5] Cf. GW, XV, 139, 170-71, 207, 214, n. l.

writings on theater, which have appeared since 1963, provide an abundance of further information.[6]

I

Let us proceed step by step and first devote our attention to Emile Zola. Like Brecht, the French writer was in the habit of including theoretical comments with the printed versions of his dramas or dramatic adaptations. In these statements he took issue with the vehement and often malicious objections raised by his opponents. For example, he wrote: "According to certain critics I have a disordered mind which does not accept any rules; I dream of setting the works of Scribe on fire, I openly scorn convention, I nurture I do not know what plan for an abominable theater."[7]

Faced with such criticism, Zola took the only step possible—he turned the tables by mercilessly demasking the conventional theater of the time as an empty cardboard world populated by puppets.[8] The cause of these provocative assertions reflected not only clever rhetorical strategy but, from the beginning, an impassioned artistic conviction as well.

Emile Zola wrote his most important contributions for the plays *Thérèse Raquin* (1873), *Les Héritiers Rabourdin* (1874) and *L'Assommoir* (1885). The first play is patterned after Zola's early novel of the same name. The second drama (in German, *Die Erben Rabourdin*) is an adaptation of Ben Jonson's *Volpone,* and the third is a famous dramatization of his novel of 1877 which, under the title *Die Schnapsbude,* caused passionate reactions in Germany.[9] In the preface to *Thérèse Raquin* Zola's naturalism is already fully evidenced. Traditional drama theory and practice are becoming extinct, he says, and the time has come to create "works of truth." Zola leaves little doubt about the direction which must be taken. He proclaims: "I am of the profound conviction that the experimental and scientific spirit of the age is going to conquer the theater and that this is the only possible means of renovating our stage." Hence, the entire practice of the

[6] SzT, now in GW, XV-XVII. However, little progress has been made in Brecht scholarship regarding this question. Merely R. Steinweg, *Das Lehrstück. Brechts Theorie einer politisch-ästhetischen Erziehung* (Stuttgart, 1972), pp. 184 ff., deserves to be mentioned here. Steinweg makes much of his statement that there is "a correspondence between Zola and Brecht as to their experimental approach," however, a correspondence of "a formal nature only." As will be shown in the following, Steinweg offers few new insights; rather he engages in pedantic hair-splitting, as is his wont in all his scholarly contributions—which are otherwise quite useful. Cf. also on Brecht's theory of the theater: *Brecht* (G), pp. 88 ff. Finally, special mention should be made of the excellent article by Klaus-Detlef Müller, "Der Philosoph auf dem Theater. Ideologiekritik und 'Linksabweichung' in Bertolt Brechts *Messingkauf,*" TuK, 45-71. Müller deals in passing with Brecht's relation to naturalism.

[7] *Œuvres complètes* (Paris, 1927 ff.) XXXVIII/XXXIX, 133/V.

[8] Cf. ibid., XLI, 109.

[9] Cf. R.F. Arnold, *Das moderne Drama* (Straßburg, 1908), p. 248, n.

theater—direction, stage design, production—would have to change completely. Zola refers proudly to his own theatrical experiments: "I have continuously attempted to bring the stage back to the ordinary occupations of my characters in such a way that they don't 'play' but 'live' before the public." Only his new drama would allow this kind of a production by doing away with any sort of plot in order to give full rein to milieu depiction and character portrayal. The new drama had its origins in the modern novel, "this incessantly expanding, both social and individual study of so flexible a design," which had gradually absorbed all literary genres of the past.[10]

In his two later prefaces Zola advances the same theses; however, he develops them more fully. Thus, e.g., he writes about the eighth scene of *L'Assommoir:* "Here, in this exact reproduction of life, all of my ideas are manifested. The actors no longer act; they live their roles. The production is a miraculous reality—these people, who come, go, sit around drinking at the tables or leaning on the bar, transplant us into a real pub." Hence the complete identification of the actors with their roles in combination with a realistic, life-like stage set was to produce that effect which Zola cherished most—"total suspense of disbelief." Yet the French writer does not leave any doubt that without profound changes in dramatic structure all efforts would have been in vain. One necessarily had to reach the decision, Zola says, to stage several pulsating scenes "cut out" of the huge mass of material of a novel rather than an impressively unfolding five-act play. "If one pulls a play out of a novel, it must suffice to have a sequence of isolated scenes unravel without worrying about inventing a plot. There is the emancipation of the theater—I mean the abandonment of the wearisome stories, the ridiculous complications, the hackneyed pieces of work which drag on tiringly." Only this liberation of the theater, which was, at the same time, its "literarization" (*Literarisierung*), would make it possible to radically eliminate metaphysics, to destroy everything supernatural and irrational, and to subjugate the complete physical world, sensual and spiritual, to science. All this was to be accomplished "with the highly moral purpose of becoming master of these phenomena in order to control them."[11]

To be sure, Zola's distinction between two fundamentally different types of drama in the preface of *L'Assommoir,* i.e., plays consisting of a loose sequence of scenes on the one hand, and well-constructed plays with closely interrelated, tension-producing scenes on the other,[12] was hardly a novelty in 1885. Similar reflections are to be found not only in the preface of his *Volpone* adaptation but also in his other theoretical writings; e.g., in the volume *Nos auteurs dramatiques* (1881). It is ob-

[10] Cf. *Œuvres complètes,* XXXVIII/XXXIX, 47/II f.
[11] Ibid., L, 209 ff.
[12] Cf. ibid., 205.

vious that the close correspondence is of prime importance. Above all, the following phrase from his early writings is significant: "The primitive stages of the jugglers at fairs are wider and more epic (*plus larges et plus epiques*) than our wretched stages, upon which life is suffocating."[13] If this thought occurred in an isolated context, one might consider it a provocation. However, Zola expresses the same idea when discussing French classicism.[14] In his opinion the theater of Molière also stems from the shows presented at fairs. Significantly, he calls *Le Misanthrope* a character study in which, as he puts it, "the action is made fun of, all turning points are dispensed with, there is a broad (*large*) development without regard to the division into acts." Actually, Molière had not composed a drama at all but rather a "story" or, to be precise, "three stories": "because each act is a new story on the same subject matter."[14] Sneeringly, Zola asks how theater critics whose favorite invective is the term *romancier* are going to react when faced with this classical work in which there is, in total disregard of all traditional rules, leisurely narrative, description and depiction—a drama, moreover, which does not even have a proper dénouement but could just as well continue beyond its ending.

Zola responds to his own rhetorical question in unmistakably clear terms: "This proves that 'the theater' does not exist. There are 'theaters,' modes of treating the dramatic subjects according to the epochs, modes which change continuously and which cannot be determined by any code."[15] Art is conceived of as a function of history. Depending on conditions of time and place, a special form of theater as the reflection of each particular society would originate almost within each successive generation.[16] Whereas the Paris audience at the time of Louis XIV experienced a sublime pleasure when viewing Racine's "dissertation dialoguée" *Iphigénie,* the bourgeoisie of the Second Empire and the Third Republic would only derive satisfaction from frivolities and the grossest effects. "De l'action, de l'action, de l'action"—for Zola these words were not only the slogan of the contemporary theater audience but also that of their playwrights, who were only too subservient to their tastes. He realized that a "chasm" separated seventeenth-century epic theater from the present day hyper-dramatic plays. "These are two completely different art forms, two types of theater which don't have any resemblance to each other, neither in rules, in form, nor in spirit."[17]

Zola's recognition of the historicity of drama did not cause him to resign, however. On the contrary, Zola draws the conclusion that

---

[13] Ibid., XXXVIII/XXXIX, 133/IV.
[14] Cf. ibid., XLIII, 9 ff.
[15] Ibid., 18. Cf. also ibid., XLII, 30: "I understand the theaters, I do not see the [i.e., one] theater. There are never absolutes in any art."
[16] Zola goes even further: "Each generation has its [own] theater, that is the truth"; ibid., 31. Cf. also 18 ff.
[17] Cf. ibid., XLIII, 23 ff.

everything is possible in theater, even a change in the public's taste. Whatever one wanted could be tried out on the stage; for art knows no limit other than the inaptitude of its devotees. "Art is free. Since forms change, everyone is free to search for tomorrow's new formula which is to replace yesterday's outmoded one."[18] In such a fashion the theater of external suspense had once done away with that of inner logic. In the same way the new drama would, in its turn, administer the overdue *coup de grâce* to the boulevard drama, with its mindless exaggeration of plot at the expense of character portrayal.[19] The supposedly well-made play (*la pièce bien faite*) of a Sardou, Scribe, Dumas *fils* is realistic in appearance only. In actuality, it strangles reality—"il tord le cou à la réalité."[20] According to Zola, only the naturalistic drama, patterned after both the old epic theater[21] and the modern, scientifically-based experimental novel, can do justice to reality: "In a word, the classical formula appears fine to me, on the condition that one will employ the scientific method to study present-day society. . . ." Yet, the French writer does not only openly admit that this type of theater is by no means anything "absolutely new." He also seems to realize that his own theatrical efforts can, for the time being, be considered only as experiments. He exclaims: "When will the Corneilles, Molières, Racines appear to found a new theater for us?" And he continues: "One must hope and wait."[22]

II

The German *Reichstag* did not wait. The warning it issued as early as 1880 about the corrupting influence of Zola, though incorrect, was not unfounded.[23] The following phrase from *Le Roman expérimental*—"I want life itself with its excitement, its amplitude, its force. I want life in its entirety"[24]—also expressed the demands of the young naturalists in Munich or Berlin. They likewise desired the new novel and the new theater with their uncompromisingly truthful depiction of life. Whenever they did not base their claims on Zola, they referred, as is well known, to Henrik Ibsen (who did not seem to be less dangerous to official Germany). After all, it was Gerhart Hauptmann who, in a significant confession of 1889, stated that he was "an ardent admirer of Zola and Ibsen" and that he considered both of them to be "great

---

[18] Ibid., 18 f.
[19] Ibid., 36; XLI, 109.
[20] Ibid., 108, 111.
[21] Whether and to which extent Zola's classification is applicable, is a question which does not concern us here.
[22] Cf. *Œuvres complètes,* XLI, 122; XLII, 17, 20.
[23] Cf. Arnold, *Das moderne Drama,* p. 152, n.
[24] *Œuvres complètes,* XLI, 126.

writers."[25] Indeed, both Zola and Ibsen are the fathers of German naturalistic drama and its dramaturgy.

Above all, the correspondence between Zola's theses and those of the German naturalists is striking throughout. I shall quote rather at random a number of statements which are taken from the collection *Literarische Manifeste des Naturalismus* (1962). Michael Georg Conrad, e.g., who can be called Zola's direct follower, wrote in the first volume of the literary journal, *Die Gesellschaft* (1885): "The novel is influencing the trends in taste of the modern stage more and more vigorously. The result is that several conventional standards are being broken, many concepts which have been preserved by academic diligence are being thrown out, and pedantic aesthetic categories are being scattered about most disrespectfully." In the second volume of the same journal Julius Hillebrand declared: "Art is just as much a product of contemporary conditions in society as are ethics or politics. There is, therefore, no absolute aesthetics." Conrad Alberti merely offered a variation of this thought when he wrote three years later: "There is not an art for all times; rather, every period has its own art. . . . There is, therefore, no fixed theory of art with eternal rules and truths." Finally, in 1892, Leo Berg summarized the theoretical positions, again following Zola carefully: "Art must become science. It must become a new means of expressing and aiding science. Its techniques must be developed into a scientific method."[26] To be sure, this is to be accomplished with a "highly moral purpose,"[27] as Berg puts it, borrowing directly from the preface to *L'Assommoir.*

Of course, the German naturalists did not want to do away completely with tradition either; but, just like Zola, they wanted to examine it critically. The *Freie Bühne,* for example, which had been founded in emulation of Antoine's Paris *Théâtre libre,* did not turn against tradition in general but, according to its program, against "dead tradition," against the "rigid rules and the outdated criticism." Tradition "which is still alive" was explicitly recognized as valid.[28] These are truly admirable maxims; regrettably, they were not often adhered to. The normal procedure was rather to sweep the entire history of the theater under the rug with Teutonic thoroughness.

The theoretician Arno Holz behaved in a particularly rabid fashion. He was of the firm opinion that his own theory of art would not only deal the death blow to traditional aesthetics but also repudiate Zola's doctrine "beyond salvation"—an almost grotesque idea. "It will sweep away all the aesthetic theories which are the rage—including yours,"

[25] Cf. *Die Kunst des Dramas. Über Schauspiel und Theater,* ed. M. Machatzke (Berlin, Frankfurt, 1963), p. 94.
[26] Cf. *Literarische Manifeste des Naturalismus,* ed. E. Ruprecht (Stuttgart, 1962), pp. 58, 64, 132, 171 f.
[27] Cf. n. 11, above: "dans le but hautement moral."
[28] Cf. *Literarische Manifeste des Naturalismus,* p. 156.

Holz wrote in his "Open Letter" to Zola, which appeared in his pamphlet *Die Kunst. Ihr Wesen und ihre Gesetze* (1891).[29] The following passage demonstrates how ill-founded Holz's arrogant presumption was.[30] He considered these sentences the expression of one of his ingenious, trail-blazing, entirely novel discoveries: "The people on the stage are not there because of the plot; rather, the plot is there because of the people. It is not the end but only the means, not the primary but the secondary matter. In other words, the law of the theater is not the plot but character portrayal."[31] At least from 1873 on—when Holz was only ten years old—Emile Zola had been teaching his "fundamental law" of the primary importance of the characters and of the dramatist's complete renunciation of plot in favor of the depiction of milieu and character.[32] Moreover, if one casts a glance at the development in Germany, similar considerations can be found in the works of Otto Ludwig[33] and J.M.R. Lenz.[34] In fact, they reach as far back as the middle of the eighteenth century. After all, it was Lessing who had remarked that "the characters must be more sacred to the writer than the facts."[35]

So much for Arno Holz, the noisy proponent of the art which wasn't so new at all, its essence and laws. Gerhart Hauptmann, who was not a theoretician, was better informed about his artistic origins. He cited not only Zola and Ibsen in his support but also Lessing and Diderot.[36] But even he became quite rabid, indeed, *menschenfresserisch,* to quote Brecht, whenever he encountered Plot. Then he was likely to snarl in the following manner: "When will we finally witness, after the curtain is lifted, the hanging of the last carping German critic who discussed plot in drama?" Or he recommended in solemn bloodthirstiness that one should take "an ax, a club, or the first best stone at hand" to finish off the dramaturgical monster.[37] With or without metaphors of murder, Hauptmann's hatred breaks through again and again. One readily perceives that it is directed not only against the norms of "highbrow aestheticism" but just as much against the shallowness of the boulevard drama. Shortly before the turn of the century, in a diary entry of 28 March 1897, the poet castigated the mania for plots dealing with intrigues and the desire for a ";strange and magical knot of events," which caused drama to degenerate into a "cheap thriller novel." For what the

[29] Cf. ibid., pp. 212, 216.
[30] For the following, cf. also W. Kayser, *Die Vortragsreise. Studien zur Literatur* (Bern, 1958), pp. 222 f.
[31] *Literarische Manifeste des Naturalismus,* p. 225.
[32] Cf. *Œuvres complètes,* XXXVIII/XXXIX, 47/III, for the pertinent formulations: "The abandonment of all plots"; "the living drama with the double life of characters and milieus."
[33] Cf. *Gesammelte Schriften,* ed. A. Stern, E. Schmidt (Leipzig, 1891), V, 509.
[34] Cf. *Gesammelte Schriften,* ed. F. Blei (Munich, 1909 ff.) I, 252 f.
[35] *Hamburgische Dramaturgie,* 33. Stück.
[36] Cf. *Das gesammelte Werk* (Berlin, 1942), V, 494 f.
[37] Cf. *Die Kunst des Dramas,* ed. Machatzke, pp. 181, 186.

throng of "our zealous plot-fans," from the philological pedant to the shady author of run-of-the-mill plays, actually desired was nothing but highly trivial suspense.[38] However, Hauptmann, Zola's disciple, did not want any "Knalleffekte" (*coups de théâtre*)[39] but "life itself" with all its terror, all its power, and its almost inexhaustible epic breadth. Like Zola, he allocated the primary role to milieu and to the character, and he also considered complete empathy or, rather, illusion (*absolute Illusion*) the chief goal of the theater. "The illusion in a play is so great that one thinks he is seeing and hearing real people," Hauptmann declared. He composed dramas "as if the stage had four walls instead of three," and compelled his spectators "to become immersed," "to lose themselves," to let themselves become "absorbed totally" in what was happening on the stage.[40] In light of all these similarities, can it really be a coincidence that Hauptmann chose a formulation of Zola's which is most unusual in the German to characterize epic drama: "Epic composition is *larger?*"[41]

Only Hauptmann's devotion to truth and to the totality of life offer an explanation for his hatred of stage action, which he considered a sensational counterfeit. In the following sentence we notice a very clear, if surprisingly mild formulation of this idea: "In those instances when we cannot adapt life to the dramatic form, shouldn't we adapt the art form to life?"[42] This question could serve as the motto for the entire development of modern drama.[43] Apart from Zola's influence, it sounds like a clarification of what Henrik Ibsen wrote about the ending of his play *A Doll's House,* published in 1879. In a letter to Heinrich Laube written on 18 February 1880, Ibsen remarked: "You assume that this play does not fit into the category of a *Schauspiel* because of its ending. But, my dear Herr Doktor, do you really take these so-called categories so seriously? I, anyway, think that the dramatic categories are flexible and that they have to adjust themselves to the facts as they exist in literature and not the other way around."[44] It is rather noteworthy for Ibsen's special position and not at all contradictory that he chooses "literature" instead of Hauptmann's "life." For Ibsen, next to Zola the other great influence on naturalistic drama in Germany, was always a superior master of dramatic technique. As far as his stage experience and his sound instinct for theatrical effects were concerned, he even surpassed the French trio Scribe, Sardou, and Dumas *fils*. This "genius of the stage," as he was rightly called, achieved his overpowering effects

---

[38] Ibid., p. 193.
[39] Ibid., p. 26.
[40] Cf. ibid., pp. 41, 94, 202, 26.
[41] Ibid., p. 37.
[42] Ibid., p. 183.
[43] Cf. especially, P. Szondi, *Theorie des modernen Dramas* (Frankfurt, 1956).
[44] Cf. H. Schwerte, "Henrik Ibsen: Nora," *Das europäische Drama von Ibsen bis Zuckmayer,* ed. L. Büttner (Frankfurt, 1959), pp. 17 ff.

almost exclusively through the new subject matter of his dramas, hardly ever through new forms. Indeed, his dramatic technique proved to be traditional to such an extent and, at the same time, so mathematically perfected that even critics of a conservative bent to whom Ibsen's *Weltanschauung* was an abomination could be reconciled to him. "Everything is tied together in the most skilful way here. The final, hermetic ending. The most prudent, concise and expedient arrangement of the parts." Thus spoke Alfred Kerr in his famous essay on Ibsen, "Der Ahnherr" (1896).[45]

The only exception (and a rather decisive one) is the ending of *A Doll's House*. Kerr was thoroughly mistaken in calling it a "hermetic ending." It is, rather, a notoriously "open" ending similar to that which Zola seemed to discern in Molière's *Le Misanthrope* and similar to those which Gerhart Hauptmann employed at the beginning of the nineties. A definitive ending suits neither *The Weavers* (1892) nor *The Beaver Coat* (1893); both plays, although in a different way, have a "perspective which extends far into the clouds of the future." The contemporaries were not slow to notice this[46]; and what held true for the disciple was valid all the more so for the master. The "open" ending was not only characteristic of Hauptmann and Zola but of the naturalistic movement in general. To be sure, the conservative critics of the time—minds like Blumenthal, Lindau, Frenzel, etc.—cried endlessly, "Murder! Help!" in the columns of their papers.[47] A man like Paul Heyse, deeply concerned, generalized wildly before the illustrious, splendidly bearded fellows of the Goethe Society: "This art is no longer like that in the old emblem, a snake which bites itself in the tail, but one which coils itself around our chest and constricts us. Then, before it relaxes its grip, it bites us. . . . Instead of an uplifting, soothing catharsis the object is to get the impression of an unsolved problem and leave the theater in a disturbed state."[48] However, the younger *literati* triumphed and laughed at terms like *Erhebung* ("elevation") or *Beruhigung* ("calming"). The ending of a harmoniously rounded play seemed to them to be one of the shabbiest properties of the philistine aestheticism. Julius Hillebrand exclaimed: "Ibsen foregoes such cheap effects. He ends his dramas in a dissonant manner, just as dissonant as reality is."[49] But Henrik Ibsen himself had clarified matters long before. In a review from the year 1857 Ibsen wrote: "The play doesn't end when the curtain falls in the fifth act—the real ending lies outside of the theater. The playwright has indicated the direction we have to take, and

[45] A. Kerr, *Die Welt im Drama* (Berlin, 1917), I, 67.

[46] Cf. Arnold, pp. 198 f. For an interpretation of *The Beaver Coat* cf. R. Grimm, *Strukturen. Essays zur deutschen Literatur* (Göttingen, 1963), pp. 14 ff.

[47] Cf. the amusing report in Kerr, pp. 46 ff.

[48] P. Heyse, *Jugenderinnerungen und Bekenntnisse.* II: *Aus der Werkstatt.* 5th rev. and enl. ed. (Stuttgart, Berlin, 1912), p. 291. [The two sentences have been exchanged].

[49] *Literarische Manifeste des Naturalismus,* p. 69.

now it is our task to find this ending, everyone for himself."[50]

III

All in all, Kerr summarized, poor Nora had not been shown any more sympathy by the Berlin critics than by Helmer in the play. "Only one person had sympathy with her. He spoke about her fate in words which reveal his inner emotion and which are still impressive today. That was Spielhagen. With him Ibsen fared like Hegel with his students. Only one person had understood him. But alas, he had misunderstood him."[51]

Kerr is referring to Friedrich Spielhagen's review of 1881, which was printed in his collection *Beiträge zur Theorie und Technik des Romans* (Leipzig, 1883). However, it is debatable whether Spielhagen had really missed the point. Advocating the "complete division of the concept of the novel and that of the drama,"[52] Spielhagen was of the opinion that Ibsen's play represented "one of innumerable cases in which one could again see, this time with especially striking clarity, that a seemingly energetic drama is nothing other than a novel which has been stretched onto the dramatic (actually theatrical) bed of Procrustes. Therefore the result is necessarily a failure."[53] That was also the opinion of his friend Berthold Auerbach.[54] Both writers were apparently convinced that Ibsen's work would create an "extremely embarrassing impression,"[55] especially because of its ending. Both writers asked themselves, "How can one respond?" Spielhagen's answer was simple: "*A Doll's House* is not a genuine work of art. It is not an organic, self-contained, self-explanatory drama but a few chapters of a novel rendered into dialog. Its beginning lies much before the beginning of the play, just as its supposed ending lies much after the actual conclusion. From the very start of the novel all sorts of things involuntarily creep into these several chapters. Others are intentionally brought in by the playwright in order, he hoped, to help us understand the difficult situation and the puzzling characters. In reality, however, the situation is obscured and the characters are alienated to the degree of incomprehensibility."[56] Admittedly, there was a minimal chance of writing "full-fledged" dramas at the

---

[50] H. Ibsen. *Sämtliche Werke in deutscher Sprache* (Berlin, 1903 f.), I, 333.
[51] Cf. *Die Welt im Drama*, I, 57.
[52] *Beiträge zur Theorie und Technik des Romans*, p. 287.
[53] Ibid., p. VIII.
[54] Cf. ibid., p. X: "His essay on *Nora*, which I had read in its handwritten form, was not printed and, unfortunately, has not as yet been found among his literary remains. However, I remember that the result of our analysis was the same, even if we had reached the goal in different ways—as was customary with us."
[55] Ibid., p. 309. Julius Hillebrand seems to refer directly to this passage when he writes (*Literarische Manifeste des Naturalismus*, p. 69): "But that, e.g., Nora leaves her dear little children is too embarrassing."
[56] *Beiträge zur Theorie und Technik des Romans*, pp. 309 f.

present, Spielhagen says, because in contrast to earlier generations we "don't perceive with the naked eye anymore but always have to look through a microscope. Thus we see boundless diversity everywhere, whereas earlier one thought he saw a simple unity and in his way, really did." Spielhagen therefore advises the modern dramatist to follow "the sturdy tap-root of the tree of humanity" and not to pursue "the entanglement of the roots of every sprout into their smallest and most minute branchings and ramifications."[57] For the dramatist would never be able to project an all-encompassing view of man in the fashion of the prose writer, neither in a psychological nor in a sociological sense: "The catastrophe . . . closes in on him when he . . . attempts to reach a goal which is unattainable to him—the representation of an epic idea in its totality."[58] For these reasons Ibsen's play could not be called a "drama" but at best a deterrent for "the doom which hovers over modern dramatic production."[59]

It is readily apparent that Spielhagen judges and condemns quite in the spirit of traditional aesthetics; but, without a doubt, he has grasped the epic elements—the derivation from the novel, the dissolution of the closed form—far better than his critic Kerr. Spielhagen's illuminating exposure of the new elements in drama is of greater consequence today than his truly sympathetic analysis of Nora's character (omitted in our discussion), in which he strives for a just evaluation. It is not a question of "sensibility of the soul" (Kerr), for that is as outmoded as Spielhagen's rejection of A Doll's House. What remains of consequence is the negative outline of a theory of modern drama. This is not only to be perceived in the essay quoted above (programmatically entitled "Drama oder Roman?") but also in other places in Spielhagen's collected essays, occasionally even with a positive accent. Two samples will suffice. We read in his study Der Ich-Roman (1882) that "the current opposition to tragedy stems from yet another, better, and more justifiable motive than just fear. It comes from a democratic principle, I would say, the principle that no matter how wretched our human existence may be, we have to assume the risks and the responsibility by refusing to tolerate any forcible intervention. We must choose to do this, to the extent that it is in our power, no matter which side this encroachment comes from, from above or from below."[60] In a note further on Spielhagen says that the contrast between drama and epic actually existed "in full measure" only in the realm of the tragedy. In this respect comedy would require a separate investigation, "which would show a great number of correspondences between the two." That "hybrid," the

[57] Cf. ibid., pp. 297 f.
[58] Thus Spielhagen in his essay "Roman oder Novelle?" in which he deals with Georges Ohnet's novel Serge Panine (1881) and its dramatic adaptation—although he explicitly refers to Ibsen's A Doll's House. Cf. ibid., p. 286.
[59] Ibid., pp. 313, 310.
[60] Ibid., p. 165.

Schauspiel, has "so much of the epic substance" from which it developed that "most of the time one could change it back, form and all, without much trouble."[61]

Even more important than Spielhagen's *Beiträge* of 1883 are his *Neue Beiträge zur Theorie der Epik und Dramatik* (1898). As was mentioned before, Bertolt Brecht possessed this book and apparently studied it carefully. The volume contains, e.g., a thorough treatise taking issue with Zola's *Roman expérimental* and, in connection with it, with the drama and dramaturgy of naturalism. In his essay Spielhagen attempts to prove that the naturalistic theory of art can never be realized in drama. On the stage it must, of necessity, "fall to pieces." We hear that the approach of these dramatists is "essentially epic." However, they were prone to constantly confuse drama and epic; hence their "so-called dramas" turned out to be nothing but "dramatized novels, or, rather, last chapters of novels." Spielhagen would most of all like to implore the naturalists to "write novels and novellas to start with; there you can wallow in such epic details." His verbose verdict is:

> It is inevitable that respect for the dramatic hero and the dramatic plot, for which the hero is the main support, will suffer, if not perish, with this servile veneration of the all-redeeming milieu. And, in actuality, several of their plays exhibit only an external similarity to what one used to consider a drama. There is no longer a hero but, at best, a main character. One can no longer speak of a plot; at the most one can speak of events, which could happen in this or that order.[62]

Spielhagen not only recognized the independence, indeed, interchangeability of individual scenes around a "Monagonist,"[63] but he also described the modern principle of montage (reminiscent of Lesage's *Le Diable boiteux*) as it was put into practice by Ferdinand Bruckner in his play *Die Verbrecher* decades later.[64] Spielhagen continues:

> Sometimes these poets dispense also with the main character and rest satisfied with the events. In such a case one can certainly not speak of a pragmatic sequence of what happens on the stage, since there is no central focus. It is as if we are looking down on a city with a bird's eye view. The roofs of the houses have been removed so we can observe the activities of the inhabitants, whereby it makes no difference at all whether we begin our observations with Apartment No. I and stop with No. X, or the other way around.[65]

[61] Cf. ibid., p. 166, n.

[62] Cf. *Neue Beiträge zur Theorie und Technik der Epik und Dramatik* (Leipzig, 1898), pp. 227 ff.

[63] Cf. V. Klotz, *Geschlossene und offene Form im Drama* (Munich, 1960).—The decisive formulation is to be found in Lenz who simply reverses Aristotle's sentence: "A plot does not have unity, as some people think, simply because it deals with a single hero" (*Poetics* 8, 1) and writes: "With us *fabula est una si circa unum sit*"; cf. *Gesammelte Schriften*, I, 238.

[64] Cf. Szondi, pp. 103 ff.

[65] *Neue Beiträge zur Theorie und Technik der Epik und Dramatik*, pp. 227 ff.

15

The treatise climaxes with the ironic dilemma—"doctrinaire whim" or "dramatic impotence"? We realize that in this respect Spielhagen also anticipated a widespread criticism of modern drama, including that eventually leveled at Brecht.[66]

The general discussion is followed by quite a number of reviews containing the constantly reiterated phrase, "There is no point at all in mixing the various genres."[67] In addition to Gerhart Hauptmann's dramas, Max Halbe's *Jugend,* Hermann Sudermann's *Heimat,* as well as Otto Erich Hartleben's *Hanna Jagert* are treated. Most illuminating are Spielhagen's remarks about *The Weavers.* Here his prejudice on the one hand, and his recognition of the new movement on the other are in glaring contradiction. To begin with, Spielhagen writes that Hauptmann's work does not have a "hero"; therefore it cannot be called a drama but merely "a sequence of loosely connected dramatic scenes, variations . . . on an identical theme."[68] A little later Spielhagen completely reverses himself and declares the play to have "uniformity and powerful concentration," which left nothing to be desired at all. He even offers a distich:

> Heldlos erscheint euch das Stück? Wie denn? Durch sämtliche Akte
> Wachsend in riesiges Maß, schreitet als Heldin die Not.[69]

> (You think the play has no hero? What do you mean? Growing to huge dimensions, Misery, the heroine, strides through the entire play.)

However, such realizations do not prevent Spielhagen from raising a fundamental objection to the naturalist's claim of proceeding in a scientific manner. Anticipating the spectator's questions he asks:

> Was this really, even if nothing but truth, the entire truth, the truth which is pursued by science and which science alone can bring to light? Would science have been satisfied in its investigation to state the misery of these unfortunates? Or would it not have searched for the conclusive reasons and, in doing so, perhaps have found that the hard-heartedness of the employers was not at all the sole cause for

[66] Cf., e.g., A. Kerr, *Was wird aus Deutschlands Theater? Dramaturgie der späten Zeit* (Berlin, 1932).

[67] *Neue Beiträge zur Theorie und Technik der Epik und Dramatik,* p. 254. Cf. also Th. Mundt, *Kritische Wälder. Blätter zur Beurtheilung der Literatur, Kunst und Wissenschaft unserer Zeit* (Leipzig, 1833), p. 146: "The epic and dramatic elements of poetry should never be mixed. A playwright who puts an epic subject matter on the stage using dialogue and scenes and wants to persuade us that he has created a drama must be as much blamed for his abortive monster as [a painter] whose painting has been badly drawn, has untrue colors, or presents its subject in an unnatural position and is, hence, considered a monstrosity."

[68] Ibid., p. 250.

[69] Ibid., pp. 279 ff.

the weaver's misery in the forties [of the nineteenth century]? Rather, that this misery had to come about, even had they been the most humane of men, because of a trade recession and the irresistible changes which . . . took place in the textile industry and which caused the peremptory demand for the introduction of machinery instead of the customary manual labor, to the detriment of those who could not fulfill this demand. Or, often the workers refused apathetically and did not want to use resources offered them, even those imposed upon them in order that they might improve their lot, and thus they were exposed to misery, beyond help. In his drama Hauptmann knows nothing of this detached, objective view of things, which is sacred to science.[70]

IV

Friedrich Spielhagen also turned against total illusion on the stage.[71] To be sure, there was a meeting of the minds because the critically inclined among the naturalists soon began to reject the trite imitation of reality in order to again proclaim a "drama of the future." One of them was Richard Dehmel, who demanded in a half-orthodox, half-heretical "Declaration" (1892):

A new technique [should be created] which knows that the stage is not a place like that in the real world, but a place staged for the purpose of providing more powerful emotional stimuli of characteristic destinies. It is a concentrated, stilized place . . . for a hundred or a thousand invited guests, not for secretive eavesdropping through a key hole. This is a technique, then, which out of logical and psychological practicality dispenses from the start with the desire to give rise to an "illusion of reality," which is never possible anyway for both reasons of logic and psychology. Only a feeble-minded person could expect such a thing anyway.[72]

It hardly comes as a surprise that Dehmel mentions Frank Wedekind[73] as the first writer who had mastered the new drama, for Wedekind not only dismayed the bourgeoisie by daring to present "the sexual drive awakening in youth" (as Heyse lamented[74]), but he was at the same time the great model of Bertolt Brecht.

Finally, the "non-Aristotelian" dramatic theory mentioned at the beginning (and also published in 1892) does include both heretic and extremely orthodox views. Its author is the Bremen schoolmaster Henri Gartelmann (born in 1865), who has been completely forgotten by literary history. Gartelmann, in his work with the rather lengthy title

[70] Ibid., p. 285.
[71] Cf. *Beiträge zur Theorie und Technik des Romans,* p. 44.
[72] *Literarische Manifeste des Naturalismus,* p. 240.
[73] Ibid., p. 241.
[74] *Jugenderinnerungen und Bekenntnisse,* p. 106. Moreover, Heyse added with indignation, this happened "in individual scenes which are not connected by any kind of dramatic action."

Dramatik. Kritik des Aristotelischen Systems und Begründung eines neuen (Berlin, 1892), does not object to the theater of illusion but he does reject the empathy of the audience. "Every word in the drama which is directed towards the spectators breaks through the confines of dramatic form,"[75] we learn. "Since what is happening on the stage is supposed to be an imitation of reality, the characters must not be aware of the existence of spectators, except, of course, in cases when the spectators appear on stage and thus belong to the drama. . . ." At the same time, however, he says: "It is simply a ridiculous assertion that the spectator should have to identify with the characters on stage. The spectator is nothing but a spectator. The drama concerns him only to the extent that he is able to derive pleasure and, possibly, benefit from viewing it."[76] No one would contest the fact that these last sentences could have been written almost word for word by Brecht, the other critic of the Aristotelian system and the founder of a new one. Nor would anyone dispute the complete contrast between Brecht and Gartelmann's ideas about unbroken illusion.

In places like these the *Dramatik* is certainly no longer "consistent naturalism," as Richard Maria Werner points out.[77] Nevertheless, it definitely adheres to the naturalistic program. The exceptional deviations are made up for by the orthodox narrowness of its over-all conception. Certainly Gartelmann himself—he was sarcastically called the "Bremen Lessing" by a pamphleteer who wrote under the pen name of *Cerberus* (probably an envious colleague[78])—was firmly convinced of the uniqueness of his achievement. He informs us: "The content of the *Dramatik* is revolutionary, the form is precise and objective, the method is strictly scientific."[79] Further: "It [the *Dramatik*] lays down new rules about drama within a self-contained system. It refutes views which have enjoyed undisputed authority in philosophy for more than 2000 years. To this end it advances arguments and draws conclusions which hitherto have been completely unknown."[80] We are familiar with these supposedly new rules, arguments, and conclusions. We also know their false premise: "From Aristotle to Lessing and beyond him to our present time, 'action' in proper combination with 'thoughts and emotions' was considered to be the actual concern of the drama."[81] No, Gartelmann decrees: "The characters [are] the actual concern of the drama. . . . Drama is a kind of mimesis which portrays characters."[82]

---

[75] *Dramatik,* p. 166.

[76] Ibid., p. 83.

[77] Quoted from H. Gartelmann, *Zur Dramatik. Ein dramaturgischer Waffengang mit Professor Richard Maria Werner* (Berlin, 1896), p. 30.

[78] Cf. *Der bremische Lessing* (Bremen, n.d. [1893]).

[79] H. Gartelmann, *Sturz der Metaphysik als Wissenschaft. Kritik des transcendentalen Idealismus Immanuel Kants* (Berlin, 1893), p. 243.

[80] *Zur Dramatik,* p. 1.

[81] H. Gartelmann, *Streitschriften vermischten Inhalts* (Bremen, 1906), p. 62.

[82] *Dramatik,* pp. 56, 59.

Consequently, each character had to be "uniform."[83] Conversely, the plot, as merely a "means to an end,"[84] did not need such unity. "Unity of action, then, is not a rule of the drama."[85] Gartelmann, who had applied considerable acumen (as well as some nonsensical notions) in order to demonstrate the accuracy of his doctrine on the basis of the classical repertoire, advances the remarkable thesis: "I consider a drama 'epic' if the characters assume a lesser position than that of the plot, so that the plot, according to the intention of the poet, assumes the main role."[86] Later he added that he considered an "epic drama" to be the same as a "dramatized epic."[87]

What else our schoolmaster turned Herostratos (he had not only written an anti-Aristotelian but also an anti-Kantian treatise[88]) propounds does not deviate from the naturalistic norm. Above all, Gartelmann repeats the commonly known demand for a realistic, accurately imitative language which, of course, must be "prosaic."[89] "To employ verse and rhyme in a drama is like providing an eagle with the feathers of a peacock, which, to be sure, give him a beautiful appearance but which hinder the power of his flight."[90] Prologues and epilogues are likewise forbidden; monologues are only permissible if they are psychologically motivated.[91] Further, the admonition to use creatively subject matter taken from the present[92] (especially that drawn from the social realm) is a common theme of naturalism—not to mention the attacks against poor Gustav Freytag, who, in Gartelmann's opinion, had composed nothing but a dramaturgical "hodge-podge."[93]

Naturally, more evidence for such feuds, which were partially waged within the naturalistic camp itself, could be offered on the basis of a more exhaustive study of source material. To provide one last example—in 1889 Max Halbe took issue with an essay by Carl Bleibtreu, entitled "Ibsen und das moderne Drama der Zukunft." This discussion is instructive in several respects. For one thing, it shows how difficult it was even for some naturalists to dissociate themselves from conventional forms of drama. According to Bleibtreu, who approvingly cites Spielhagen's essay on *A Doll's House*, the playwright has "not only the right but the duty to speak a final, redeeming word to provide a hermetic, real [!] ending." We are told: "If a playwright slams the door in our faces and sends us home shaking our heads in dissatisfaction, we

[83] Ibid., p. 61.
[84] Ibid., p. 89.
[85] Ibid., p. 90.
[86] Ibid., p. 60.
[87] Cf. *Zur Dramatik*, pp. 27 f.
[88] See n. 79.
[89] Surprisingly, Gartelmann adds the qualification "in general." Cf. *Dramatik*, p. 125.
[90] Ibid., p. 141.
[91] Cf. ibid., pp. 167, 170.
[92] Ibid., pp. 173 ff.
[93] Ibid., p. 116.

may justifiably object to such puzzles because they are in flagrant violation of all rules of the drama, this most closed of all art forms."[94]

Halbe's reply demonstrates the dominating influence of Zola. Halbe not only declares (with ironic understatement) that whoever wanted to join the discussion must "have studied his Zola a little and have absorbed him"; he also postulates as the "ideal" the *"complete, inescapable illusion."* Indeed, he copies the French writer literally when he writes: "Pohl as Consul Bernick and Miss Karlsen as Lona Hessel [in *Pillars of Society*]—were not *acting,* they *lived* their roles." In support of his views and against the "straitjacket of rules" which Bleibtreu wanted to reimpose on the drama, Halbe quotes Zola's "immense jungle of life" and postulates: "There is no such thing as a special epic subject matter just as little as there is a special dramatic subject matter. Each subject, each slice of life is equally well suited for either the drama or the novel." About the relationship between drama and epic Halbe remarks in general: "There are countless ties which relate the drama to the epic, and vice versa."[95]

V

I believe that the question which was posed initially is as good as answered for everyone who is familiar with Brecht's works—and who is not? Both critics, Hultberg and Chiarini, are obviously right and wrong at the same time. Brecht's contradictory statements are by no means purely arbitrary; they simply reveal the complexity of the problem under discussion. I shall briefly summarize the essential points.

What Brecht and naturalism have in common is, first of all, the principle of the scientific attitude—the blunt rejection of any metaphysics, the striving for truth, and the "highly moral purpose" of dominating, guiding, changing all phenomena of our world. The basic concepts are *expériment* and *Versuch.* Zola develops an entire scale, which ranges from *essai* to *étude, expérience,* and *expériment*[96]; Brecht too, the author of *Versuche,* explicitly conceived of his theater as "experimental."[97] The abandonment of the powerful and tightly woven plot in favor of a "sequence of comparatively independent events,"[98] the famous "open endings" (*The Good Woman of Setzuan* comes to mind), as well as the realization that art is subject to historical change and

---

[94] Cf. Carl Bleibtreu, "Ibsen und das moderne Drama der Zukunft," *Monatsblätter. Organ des Vereins Breslauer Dichterschule,* 15/2-4 (1889), 24 ff., 45 ff., 55 ff. [the two quotes are taken from the last segment].

[95] Max Halbe, "Berliner Brief," *Die Gesellschaft* (1889/III), 1171 ff. [The quotes are to be found on pp. 1176 f., 1183, 1175, 1174, 1176; italics as given in the text].

[96] Cf. especially *Œuvres complètes,* XXXVIII/XXXIX, 133, VI f.; further, the title *Le Roman expérimental,* etc.

[97] As Brecht remarked himself, he used the naturalistic *Experimentaldramatik* as a starting-point. Cf. GW, XV, 288.

[98] GW, XVII, 1163.

hence cannot be subject to an "absolute aesthetics" are traits which Brecht shares with the naturalists. Like Zola, Brecht endeavored to "literarize" [*literarisieren*] the theater; both writers revived older forms of drama, and even admired the shows presented at fairs. It certainly would not be difficult to detect further correspondences. To mention one additional example, Zola writes that he again wants to make "great" everyday occurrences which we tended to consider "small" out of age-old habit.[99] What else is this process, I ask, but the procedure of "historicizing," which for Brecht was practically synonymous with the much discussed artistic device of *Verfremden*. In passing, attention may be called to the fact that one of the German naturalists, Wilhelm Bölsche, also demanded "historical works of art [which] take place both in the past and in the present."[100]

Especially the following sentences by Brecht are characteristic of that which distinguished him from naturalism: "Naturalistic performances created the illusion that one was in a real place. Looking into a room, the spectators seemed to smell the fragrance of the cherry orchards behind the house. Looking into the interior of a ship, they seemed to experience the force of the storm. . . . One saw as much of reality (and felt as much) as one saw (or felt) when he was actually on the spot, that is, very little." For Brecht this view "allows no genuine criticism." Under such conditions, he says, an "immutability," this unfortunate "perpetuity," prevails. Everything retains "such naturalness that one is no longer able to allow his judgment, his fantasy, and his impulses to intervene. Instead he lets himself be absorbed, empathizes, and thus becomes an object of 'Nature.'"[101] For reasons which are too commonly known to be mentioned here, Brecht fiercely rejected intoxicating empathy on stage as well as in the audience. Whereas Zola championed "total illusion" and enthusiastically extolled the naturalistic actor who did not seem to play his role but rather to live it, Brecht wrote of the actor in his theater (a greater contrast can hardly be imagined): "He doesn't let himself be totally transformed into the character for a minute. A judgment like: 'He did not play the role of Lear, he was Lear,' would be devastating for him."[102] Briefly, the naturalists tried to remove "the theater from the theater," as it was so aptly put. Brecht, on the other hand, prescribed succinctly: "The restoration of the reality of the theater as theater," that is, of its artistic nature, "is a prerequisite for realistic representations of people living together in society"—and hence for achieving insights and actions.[103]

If the Marxist Brecht rejected the "exact reproduction of life" and called instead for the representation of social antagonisms, he agreed in

[99] Cf. *Œuvres complètes*, XLII, 24.
[100] Cf. *Literarische Manifeste des Naturalismus*, p. 101.
[101] Cf. GW, XVI, 514 and 519; XVI, 921; XV, 251.
[102] GW, XVI, 683.
[103] GW, XV, 251. Cf. also Arnold, *Das moderne Drama*, p. 89.

this respect with the contemporary critique of naturalism by the liberal Spielhagen. This was true at least in principle, with which we are concerned at the moment. It is a similar matter with Brecht's assessment of plot. He does not want to hear about either overdone intrigue or a revelling in the atmosphere of milieu and psychological nuances. What he is concerned with are "connections of social interaction."[104] Forces and laws are to be shown, not the surface of life. Only on the basis of such a premise can it be understood that Bertolt Brecht, the decidedly anti-Aristotelian writer, agreed in the end with Aristotle by writing: "Everything depends on the plot; it is the heart of the theatrical production."[105] To be sure, it is a different matter that the concept of plot underwent a profound change. After all, Brecht's relationship to Spielhagen (if we may assume that it existed in this immediacy at all[106]) was of a rather contradictory nature. Brecht could have confirmed some of his convictions from several passages in the *Beiträge,* though others must have seemed totally antiquated to him and must have provoked him all the more. For example, Spielhagen's view that epic and comedy were closely related corresponds precisely to the teachings of the theoretician of the epic theater.[107] But, Spielhagen's formulation of alienation in his review of *A Doll's House* ("the events on the stage were 'alienated' [*entfremdet*] to the point of incomprehensibility") could only have been meaningful to Brecht if he turned around everything that Spielhagen had said. The verbal correspondence (between *verfremden* and *entfremden*) was undoubtedly provocative enough. It is, then, probably more than a mere curiosity that Spielhagen's close friend Berthold Auerbach, as far as we can determine, was the first to use Brecht's key term *Verfremdung.* He employed it both in an active meaning to denote behavior springing from alienation and in a passive sense to denote a state of being or becoming alienated.[108]

The same contradictions prevail in the relationship between Brecht's non-Aristotelian dramaturgy and the non-Aristotelian *Dramatik* by Gartelmann (which, surely, the playwright did not know). Although Gartelmann's attacks on the concept of empathy correspond to Brecht's thought, his interpretation of dramatics as pure character portrayal has

---

[104] GW, XV, 220.

[105] GW, XVI, 693. Cf. Aristotle, *Poetics,* 6, 19.

[106] There are, after all, two remarkable veiled references; cf. GW, XV, 214, where Brecht speaks, quite in the manner of Spielhagen, of the "novelists in disguise" of the naturalist stage; cf. further Brecht's remarks in reference to the stingy manufacturer in Hauptmann's *The Weavers.*

[107] Cf., e.g., *Bertolt Brecht's Dreigroschenbuch. Texte, Materialien, Dokumente,* ed. S. Unseld (Frankfurt, 1960), p. 134.

[108] Auerbach repeatedly used the term *Verfremdung;* cf. *Tausend Gedanken des Collaborators* (Berlin, 1875), p. 236. Further, *Briefe an seinen Freund Jakob Auerbach. Ein biographisches Denkmal.* Mit Vorbemerkungen von F. Spielhagen und dem Herausgeber [J. Auerbach] (Frankfurt, 1884), II, 260 (13 October 1875); 323 (4 September 1877); 354 (14 August 1878); 355 (14 August 1878).

little in common with that of Brecht. Above all, Gartelmann's definition of epic drama must be mentioned in this context. It is not only as reversible as the pertinent theses of Spielhagen; at the same time, it refers indirectly to Friedrich Nietzsche in connection with the formulation "dramatized epic." Nietzsche's *Birth of Tragedy* (1872) does, indeed, describe traits of the modern epic drama or theater in negative outline. At least the following passage is applicable here: "The writer of the dramatic epic cannot fully immerse himself in his scenes, just as the epic rhapsodist cannot. His is still the quietly passive, keenly observant perception which sees the scenes *in front of* it." Not even the actor, Nietzsche adds, could be completely transformed and absorbed in such a theater; even he had to remain "fundamentally a rhapsodist."[109] Needless to say, the author of *Birth of Tragedy* wants just the opposite of that to which Brecht aspired, though one might attribute these statements to Brecht. Nietzsche really proclaims the "Dionysian" ecstasy and decidedly rejects any "Socratic" theater of reason and knowledge.[110]

VI

Further questions which were raised in the foregoing discussion cannot be treated within the limits of this survey. One question, however, needs to be clarified. If the factors which separated Brecht from the naturalists were really as decisive as they appear to be, how can one explain the fact that both can claim the concept of epic drama for themselves, both with good reasons? How are we to evaluate such a contradiction?

There is only one answer to this question, namely, that there is a fundamental difference between "epic" and "epic." There are two entirely different forms of the "epic" which are associated with the concept of the drama or theater by Brecht on the one hand, and by the naturalists on the other.[111]

The kind of epic elements the naturalists had in mind should have become evident in the preceeding discussion. They are derived from the objective, impersonal, "scenic" novel of the last decades of the nineteenth century. It can be best characterized by the slogan "disappearance of the narrator."[112] One only has to think of Flaubert's im-

[109] *Werke in drei Bänden,* ed. K. Schlechta (Munich, 1954 ff.), I, 71.

[110] Naturally, Nietzsche proceeds from quite different premises than Brecht. Precisely because of this fact a comparative study, of which one does not find a trace anywhere, would be the more valuable. It is a similar matter with Brecht's relations towards Socrates. Cf. my remarks in the collection of essays, *Deutsche Dramentheorien. Beiträge zu einer historischen Poetik des Dramas in Deutschland,* ed. and intro. R. Grimm (Frankfurt, 1971), I, xxiii ff.

[111] The interesting definition attempted by Arnold remains necessarily in the realm of naturalism; cf. *Das moderne Drama,* p. 190.

[112] Cf. especially W. Kayser, *Entstehung und Krise des modernen Romans.* 3rd ed. (Stuttgart, 1961), pp. 32 ff.

passibilité, of Turgenev, Henry James, and, above all, Zola himself, who wrote: "The naturalistic novelist never intervenes, no more than the scholar." Rather, Zola continues, the novelist had become a recorder who emphatically refrained from "judging and drawing conclusions."[113] Zola continues consistently by stating: "Hence the novelist disappears."[114] How the disappearance of the narrator is effected is demonstrated in German literature by the prose collection *Papa Hamlet* (1889), in which dialogues play the predominant role. R. F. Arnold correctly said of it: "What the poet himself has to say is reduced to a piano accompaniment played with the left hand. In one instance this is even labeled as secondary and less important, as background or as a stage direction, by the use of a smaller print."[115] Clearly recognizing what was going on, Arnold continues: "It was only a step from *Papa Hamlet* to the application of the naturalistic doctrine to the drama."[116] Hermann Bahr summarizes the entire development as follows[117]: "Because it is in the nature of naturalism to require the stage if it is to be true to itself," it had become inevitable that naturalistic epics were staged. For naturalism wanted not just the "poor imitation of life" but the "true original." "The stage alone, no other manifestation of literature, can grant it that impersonality and objectivity." Only on the stage would naturalism receive its ultimate realization.[118]

Thus, the epic elements of the naturalistic theater are those of the "impersonal" novel (if we apply the categories of the theory of the novel).[119] Conversely, we find in Brecht's drama and theater the epic elements of the "authorial" novel, i.e., the type of novel which is characterized by the arrangement, interference, evaluation, and inferences of the omnipresent narrator. This narrator, who had been banished from the novel by the naturalists, takes over the stage in Brecht's plays. The omniscient, free-wheeling, reasoning first-person narrator (*das epische Ich*) dominates. *The Caucasian Chalk Circle* offers

---

[113] Cf. *Œuvres complètes,* XLI, 103 ff.

[114] With this sentence Zola anticipates the categorical *Exit author* which is supposed to characterize the development of the entire modern novel; in truth, however, it pertains to only a limited trend. Cf. J.W. Beach, *The Twentieth-Century Novel. Studies in Technique* (New York, 1932).

[115] Arnold, *Das moderne Drama,* p. 190.

[116] Ibid. It is also pertinent here that Hauptmann's drama *Before Dawn* originated from parts of a voluminous autobiographical novel. Cf. R. Hartogs, *Die Theorie des Dramas im deutschen Naturalismus* (Diss. Frankfurt, 1931), p. 46.

[117] Spielhagen, who was anything but a naturalist, helped further this development to a considerable degree. His theory and practice of the "objective" novel without a narrator and with its reliance on scenes as the structural principle led of necessity to drama. The "narrative freed from superfluous elements," as he formulated it hesitatingly, would gain in "dramatic and theatrical vivacity"; cf. *Aus meiner Studienmappe. Beiträge zur litterarischen Ästhetik und Kritik* (Berlin, 1891), p. 341. However, cf. *Beiträge zur Theorie und Technik des Romans,* pp. 293 f.

[118] Cf. *Literarische Manifeste des Naturalismus,* p. 232.

[119] F.K. Stanzel, *Narrative Situations in the Novel,* trans. J.P. Pusack (Bloomington, 1971).

the most impressive example. Here the narrator dissociates himself completely from the play and confronts the action in the role of a poet who recites an old story, an epic. He and his companions are constantly present on the stage. In this way he maintains the estranging (*verfremdend*) distance between the stage and the audience, which makes possible the critical reflection that Brecht desired. The narrator's possibilities are the same as in the classical authorial novel; he takes over the exposition, addresses the characters whose thoughts he expresses, and describes happenings which are being acted out in pantomime at the same time. From the very beginning, he also maintains close contact with the audience. His dominant position is probably most conspicuously demonstrated by the fact that he does not combine the actions centering around Grusha and Azdak in order to create a dramatic whole. Rather, he relates the two simultaneously occurring actions one after the other, developing them leisurely. There is no need to cite further examples; these matters are well-known and have been investigated sufficiently.[120]

In the meantime, the obvious counterpart of the epic drama has become known. It is the so-called "dramatic novel." As was almost to be expected in the case of this term, which played an important role as early as the eighteenth century,[121] one also has to distinguish between an impersonal and an authorial application. The term "dramatic novel" can denote both an impersonal, objective "scenic" narrative and a loosely connected drama of considerable breadth, interspersed with reports, reflections and lyrical elements (often occurring in the form of a "dramatized novel"). In the first instance, "dramatic novel" would be applicable to works like Klinger's and Meißner's novels or the recently rediscovered *Gustav Aldermann* by F.T. Hase.[122] In addition, Diderot's *Jacques le fataliste et son maître* and the English novel in dialogue form, *The Disguise* (1771), should be mentioned here. In the second instance, especially the plays of the Indians, Elizabethans, and Spaniards come to mind—I just refer to *Celestina*. Other pertinent examples include Goethe's *Faust*, the drama and dramaturgy of German romanticism

[120] Cf., e.g., W. Hinck, *Die Dramaturgie des späten Brecht* (Göttingen, 1959). R. Grimm, *Bertolt Brecht. Die Struktur seines Werkes* (Nürnberg, 1959).
[121] Cf. E.D. Becker, *Der deutsche Roman um 1780* (Stuttgart, 1964); further, the detailed discussion by Ernst Theodor Voss in J.J. Engel, *Über Handlung, Gespräch und Erzählung.* Faksimiledruck der ersten Fassung von 1774 aus der "Neuen Bibliothek der schönen Wissenschaften und der freyen Künste," ed. and afterword E. Th. Voss (Stuttgart, 1964).
[122] Cf. F.T. Hase, *Gustav Aldermann. Ein dramatischer Roman.* Faksimiledruck nach der Ausgabe von 1779. Afterword E.D. Becker (Stuttgart, 1964).

(Tieck, the Schlegel brothers[123]), Richard Wagner, and Eduard von Hartmann.[124] The foremost example is Shakespeare, whose works are conceived of as being dramatized epics. Even the plays of the Greeks are occasionally interpreted in this way; Herder[125] finds them "half-epic," Wilhelm von Humboldt[126] "epic to a great degree," and Alfred Döblin[127] still talks as a matter of course of Aeschylus' "novel-drama." Having mentioned Döblin, we have unexpectedly returned to Brecht, who, as has been said,[128] considered Döblin one of his "illegitimate fathers." Lion Feuchtwanger may rightly claim to be the godfather, at least as far as this paternity is concerned.[129] In 1919 he published a "dramatic novel" (thus the subtitle) called *Thomas Wendt*, which also influenced Brecht's concept of the epic drama or theater.[130]

VII

In conclusion, let the two writers with whom our discussion began, speak for themselves. Brecht stated shortly before his death: "I never was a naturalist, nor did I ever love naturalism. Despite all its shortcomings, however, naturalism marks the breakthrough of realism in modern literature and on the modern stage. It is a fatalistic realism. That which is of little consequence for historical progress stifles everything; the picture it presents of reality is not feasible; the poetic elements are somewhat stunted, etc., etc. Nevertheless, reality comes

[123] August Wilhelm Schlegel, e.g., was convinced "that the entire form of our dramas has to be judged according to the principles of the novel"; cf. A.W. Schlegel, *Vorlesungen über schöne Litteratur und Kunst. Dritter Teil (1803-1804): Geschichte der romanischen Litteratur,* ed. J. Minor (Heilbronn, 1884), p. 241. As to Friedrich Schlegel, cf. H. Schanze, "Shakespeare-Kritik bei Friedrich Schlegel," GRM, N.S. 15 (1965), 40 ff. Cf. also Mundt's criticism, *Kritische Wälder*, p. 149: "The dramatic form is used quite arbitrarily and frivolously if one writes novellas and novels with scenes and dialogue, as has been the custom more frequently in previous times than it is now, merely to achieve a more vivid effect and emotional upheaval—but still would like them to be considered novellas and novels. These are the so-called dramatic-historic-romantic works with which especially Schlenkert, at the end of the previous century, distinguished himself."

[124] *Aphorismen über das Drama* (Berlin, 1870), p. 9.

[125] *Sämmtliche Werke*, ed. B. Suphan (Berlin, 1877 ff.), V, 210.

[126] *Ästhetische Versuche über Goethe's Hermann und Dorothea*. 4th ed. Foreword by H. Hettner (Braunschweig, 1882), p. 128.

[127] Cf. E. Piscator, *Das politische Theater* (Berlin, 1929), p. 58.

[128] Cf. F. Sternberg, *Der Dichter und die Ratio. Erinnerungen an Bertolt Brecht* (Göttingen, 1963), p. 16.

[129] The other poet to whom Brecht refers in this context is Georg Kaiser.

[130] Cf. also U. Weisstein, "From the Dramatic Novel to the Epic Theater. A Study of the Contemporary Background of Brecht's Theory and Practice," GR, 38 (1963), 257 ff.

into view in naturalism." Naturalism was, he summarizes, "a great epoch of literature and the theater in spite of everything."[131] With remarkable fairness Zola adds—I think we are entitled to this little montage—"One never knows with certainty when a literary movement begins. As a rule, such a movement is a long time in the making and it combines inextricably with that other movement from which it originated."[132]

[131] *SzT*, VII, 79 [not included in GW].
[132] *Œuvres complètes*, XLII, 17 (cf. the motto of this essay).

EPIC STRUCTURES IN THE PLAYS OF BERNARD SHAW AND BERTOLT BRECHT

Karl-Heinz Schoeps

I. Introduction

In his book *Theorie des modernen Dramas*[1] Peter Szondi discusses, among other aspects, increasing epic trends in modern theater. One significant modern playwright not dealt with in Szondi's pioneering book is Bernard Shaw. Further, in one of the most comprehensive studies on epic theater, *Episches Theater*,[2] Shaw is only mentioned peripherally. Yet it is precisely Shaw whose work can lend considerable support to Szondi's observations as well as to the theory and history of epic theater. At the same time, strong affinities can be noted between Bernard Shaw and the most outstanding representative of epic theater, Bertolt Brecht, who "again and again referred to dramatists like Shaw and Kaiser and to directors like Piscator, Jeßner and Engel who had already created preliminary forms of epic theater."[3]

At first glance, neither the men, Bertolt Brecht and Bernard Shaw, nor their works seem to have much in common. Shaw was an apostle of the "Life Force," a puritan vegetarian and somewhat of a loner who had something to say about practically every topic from vivisection to the creation of a new alphabet (for which purpose he left part of his estate). Brecht, on the other hand, was a gregarious and epicurean Marxist who basically had only one topic—the creation of a society based on Marxist-Leninist principles—and who cared little for alphabets and grammar. When one compares works like Shaw's *Candida* with Brecht's *Mother Courage*, the only similarity would seem to be that both protagonists are women. The times in which the two playwrights lived and the audiences for which they wrote were also quite different. At the end of the nineteenth century Shaw's Britannia still ruled the waves, while in young Brecht's war-ravaged Germany bourgeois society began to disintegrate—a process which was hastened by the defeat of 1918. Shaw directed his works mainly towards the British middle-class society, whereas Brecht envisioned a more proletarian, anti-bourgeois audience. In 1898, when Brecht was born, Shaw was already 42 years old; moreover, he was a successful literary critic who had just achieved his first recognition as a playwright. In short: Shaw's literary concepts were largely formed in the nineteenth century, whereas Brecht profited from new literary developments in the twentieth century.

But it was precisely in the twenties that Shaw's plays were most

[1] Peter Szondi, *Theorie des modernen Dramas* (Frankfurt, 1963).
[2] Reinhold Grimm, ed., *Episches Theater* (Köln, Berlin, 1966).
[3] Werner Hecht, "Brechts Weg zum epischen Theater," *Episches Theater*, p. 53.

popular in Germany, especially in Berlin, where Brecht, after frequent visits, had finally taken up residence in 1924. His friend, Arnolt Bronnen, reports in his memoirs how he and Brecht studied theatrical life in Berlin and absorbed everything "from Shaw to Shaw."[4] During his brief period as *Dramaturg* at the Deutsches Theater (1924-1925), Brecht followed the rehearsals for Shaw's *Saint Joan* with extreme interest. In 1926, the S. Fischer Publishing Company asked Brecht to contribute to a congratulatory address in honor of Bernard Shaw's seventieth birthday. The result was the somewhat ambiguous "Ovation for Shaw" which appeared in the *Berliner Börsen-Courier* on 25 July 1926.[5] The ambiguity results mainly from ideological differences. Brecht wrote the "Ovation" while he was in Vienna to collect material for his play *Wheat*. These efforts led him to the intensive study of Marx. Consequently, Shaw's "theory of evolution" to which Brecht vaguely refers in the "Ovation" (GW, XV, 101) had little or no value for him. This becomes quite clear from Brecht's response to a query, published in *Filmkurier* (11 July 1927). He had been asked what had caused him to laugh hardest in his life, and he replied: "When I heard that Shaw is a Socialist."[6] Yet in the realm of form, dramatic technique, and history of drama, Brecht assigns Shaw an important position. The "Ovation" bears testimony to this, and it is significant that it was written when Brecht was beginning to talk and write about his epic theater.[7] It is in their dramatic concepts that the two playwrights, in spite of all their other differences, do have many things in common. I will therefore direct my attention to some of those similarities in the form and structure of their works from which certain conclusions as to influence and affinity can be drawn.

II. The Comic Spirit and the Estrangement Effect

After a rehearsal of *Baal* in February of 1926, Elisabeth Hauptmann, Brecht's closest associate in those years, noted: "If Brecht takes no pleasure in the things he has done, he immediately sets about to make changes."[8] Fun and pleasure were very important to Brecht, and at a time when writing seemed to him to be a pretty "melancholy business" (GW, XV, 100) he praised precisely those elements in Shaw's work: "He furnishes the theater with as much fun as it can take. And it can take a lot" (GW, XV, 98). But through the comic elements, a deeper relationship between the works of the two playwrights can be established. As

[4] *Tage mit Bertolt Brecht* (Munich, 1960), p. 33.
[5] Reprinted in GW, XV, 96-101. The translation used here is that by Gerhard H.W. Zuther in *G.B. Shaw: A Collection of Critical Essays* (Englewood Cliffs, N.J., 1965), pp. 15-18.
[6] Hans Mayer, *Bertolt Brecht und die Tradition* (Munich, 1965), p. 41.
[7] See Werner Hecht, *Brechts Weg zum epischen Theater* (Berlin, 1962), p. 4.
[8] *Brecht-Chronik*, p. 39.

Reinhold Grimm points out in his definition of *Verfremdung*,[9] there is a close affinity between the comic spirit, satire, and the estrangement effect; the elements of contrast, distance and surprise are characteristic of all three. How closely related the estrangement effect and satire really are is illustrated by Brecht's definition of estrangement as "negation of a negation" (GW, XV, 360), and Wolfgang Kayser's definition of satire as a "negative presentation of something negative."[10] Like Shaw, Brecht often uses humor or satire to achieve estrangement effects. An article in a Swedish newspaper entitled "Det finska undret" ("The Finnish Miracle"—GW, XX, 11*-15*), e.g., shows Brecht's indebtedness to Shavian techniques rather clearly. This article is a satiric treatment of the war in Finland in the winter of 1940. It is signed "Sherwood Paw." Knowing Brecht's inclination to play with names, one can easily derive the name of Bernard Shaw from this pseudonym.

Both playwrights regarded the theater as a forum, a platform for propaganda, and the comic spirit as well as the estrangement effect as means to an end: namely, to instruct and entertain at the same time. They also attempted to show the interaction of private and business life in their plays. Shaw complained in his article "Meredith on Comedy" that people keep the world of business and the world of theater nicely separated because "they realise the immense commercial advantage of keeping their ideal life and their practical business life in two separate conscience-tight compartments which nothing but 'the Comic Spirit' can knock into one."[11] As Shaw points out in the same article, "The function of comedy is nothing less than the destruction of old-established morals" (p. 41). At the same time, he deplores the attitude of the British theatergoers who tolerate an attack on established conventions only "when it is done seriously, or even grimly and terribly as they understand Ibsen to be doing it" (p. 41). Like Brecht, he stresses the importance of levity, which, however, the general public scorns as being too cynical: "But that it should be done with levity . . . is too scandalously wicked, too cynical, too heartlessly shocking to be borne" (p. 41).

Brecht recognized the same problem in the German theater in which business life and art were carefully kept apart because art was considered to be too serious to be contaminated by such base matters as business: "In these sacred halls the world of business is unknown," as Brecht paraphrased Sarastro's famous aria from Mozart's *The Magic Flute* (BBA, 328/134). In his struggle with the "ewige Meiningerei" (a type of staging which stressed pomp and seriousness), he found an ally in Shaw: "If one adds to this his exploding of the thoughtless, habitual

[9] "Verfremdung: Beiträge zu Wesen und Ursprung eines Begriffes," RLC, 35 (1961), 230.
[10] Wolfgang Kayser, *Das sprachliche Kunstwerk*. 11th ed. (Bern, 1965), p. 382.
[11] Quoted from John J. Enck et al., eds., *The Comic in Theory and Practice* (New York, 1960), p. 41. Further references by page number in the text.

assumption that anything that might possibly be considered venerable should be treated in a subdued manner instead of energetically and joyously; if one adds to this his successful proof that in the face of truly significant ideas a relaxed (even snotty) attitude is the only proper one, since it alone facilitates true concentration, it becomes evident what measure of personal freedom he has achieved" (GW, XV, 97-98). Brecht's statement about Shaw's work, which could be supplemented by many remarks of a similar nature in his own work (e.g., "But it is especially necessary to treat serious matters in a light vein"; GW, VII, 2992), reveals Shaw's as well as his own dialectic method. Both playwrights invert generally accepted modes of thinking; they "take delight in upsetting our habitual prejudices" (GW, XV, 99), and hope that the audience replaces its worn-out convictions with theirs. To achieve this, the theatergoer "must not hand in his brains along with his coat at the cloakroom" as Brecht pointed out (GW, XV, 189). Shaw expected the same of his audience: "And so effective do I find the dramatic method that I have no doubt I shall at last persuade even London to take its conscience and brains with it when it goes to the theatre, instead of leaving them at home with its prayer book as it does at present."[12]

III. Adaptation and Inversion of Literary and Nonliterary Subjects

One method of upsetting oldfashioned concepts is to give a new interpretation of well-known subjects and to use topics which are commonly known but regarded as nonliterary or even unliterary. Creative originality in the Aristotelian sense of *inventio* meant nothing to either Brecht or Shaw. Accusations of plagiarism were brushed aside with remarks such as, "Shakespeare was a thief, too" (Brecht),[13] and "I do not deny [the charge] as I possess in a marked degree that characteristic of Shakespeare . . . which is described as picking up a good thing when you find it" (Shaw).[14] One familiar literary topic both playwrights employed was the Saint Joan theme. Here again, what Brecht writes about Shaw with reference to Saint Joan is also true for his own works: "These complications can never be old and familiar enough to suit Shaw" (GW, XV, 99). Examples of nonliterary and un-literary topics which Brecht and Shaw exploited for their own purposes are the Salvation Army, boxing and prostitution.

Brecht was so fascinated by the Saint Joan theme that he used it three times: in *Saint Joan of the Stockyards* (1929-1931), *The Visions of*

---

[12] Bernard Shaw, "Preface to *Mrs. Warren's Profession,*" *The Complete Prefaces of Bernard Shaw* (London, 1965), p. 221. The page numbers in the text refer to this edition.
[13] *Brecht* (W), p. 124. For another instance of Brecht's borrowing, see the essay by James K. Lyon, "Kipling's 'Soldiers Three' and Brecht's *A Man's a Man*" in this volume.
[14] See Archibald Henderson, *George Bernard Shaw: Man of the Century* (New York, 1956), pp. 704-705.

Simone Machard (1941-1943), and in an adaptation of Anna Seghers' radio play, *The Trial of Joan of Arc at Rouen, 1431* (1952). Bernard Shaw's *Saint Joan* was written in 1923 and soon became one of his best known plays. In 1905, Shaw gave his interpretation of the role of the Salvation Army in a capitalist society in *Major Barbara*. Brecht's *Saint Joan of the Stockyards* combines the Saint Joan theme with that of the Salvation Army; his Saint Joan is an officer of the Black Straw Hats, as he called this Christian organization.

Brecht's *Saint Joan* differs from Shaw's *Saint Joan* first of all in the setting. Shaw leaves his Saint Joan in the medieval world (with the exception of the Epilogue), whereas Brecht transfers her to Upton Sinclair's Chicago. Moreover, Shaw lacks Brecht's proletarian viewpoint. But both Johanna and Saint Joan progress from naive belief to clearsighted recognition; both become a threat to the ruling class through their activities, yet both are carefully used as pawns in the powerplay by those who are in control. Their real message to the world is drowned out by praise from those they criticize. However, there is neither romanticism nor one-sided propaganda. Both playwrights avoid painting in black and white: they recognize weaknesses in their "heroines," and human traits in their "villains." They also pursue a similar objective with their plays: they take the familiar subject of Joan of Arc in order to demonstrate the need for social change. Their interest in the topic of Joan of Arc reveals yet another similarity, namely their historical and dialectic approach in the tradition of Hegel and Marx. Hegel had pointed out that history advances through clashes of contradictory forces. Brecht and Shaw, who knew their Hegel well, illustrate these dialectics of progress in the conflict between Joan and the ruling classes.

Neither Brecht nor Shaw sees the Salvation Army as a charitable organization which strives to improve the lot of the poor; rather, they consider it the complete opposite. Its activities only help to sustain a corrupt system by pacifying the impoverished masses with promises that the meek shall inherit the earth. For both writers the Salvation Army and all other religious organizations are instruments of capitalism. The industrial tycoon Mauler proposes to support the Black Straw Hats on a large scale if they speak for the system:

> If we promoted your Black Straw Hats
> grandly in your work, would you then—
> provided with soup and music and
> suitable Bible quotations, even with shelter
> in extreme cases—spread the word
> for us that we are good people? Planning good things
> in a bad time? . . . (GW, II, 770)[15]

[15] Bertolt Brecht, *Saint Joan of the Stockyards,* trans. Frank Jones (Bloomington, 1969), p. 112.

Major Barbara breaks down when she hears that she is not acting because she is in the power of a benign God, but rather because she is in the power of the ruthless industrialists Bodger and Undershaft: "Yesterday I should have said, because I was in the power of God, but you came and showed me that I was in the power of Bodger and Undershaft."[16] In the preface to this play, Shaw is—as usual in his prefaces—more outspoken: "The Salvation Army . . . has almost as many weaknesses as the Church of England itself. . . . It is even more dependent than the Church on rich people . . . Churches are suffered to exist only on condition that they preach submission to the State as at present capitalistically organized" (pp. 126, 131). The real gods of the capitalist society are money and profit. Thus money occupies a central role in many of Brecht's and Shaw's works, particularly in Brecht's *Saint Joan* and Shaw's *Major Barbara.* Undershaft, who is "not one of those men who keep their morals and their business in watertight compartments" (*Major Barbara,* p. 468), recommends that one "choose money and gunpowder" if confronted with the choice between them and "honor, justice, truth, love, mercy and so forth . . . for without enough of both, you cannot afford the others" (*Major Barbara,* p. 478). This was, and still is, a shocking statement for a bourgeois audience, just as Mauler's confession that without money, human society is doomed to chaos and destruction (see GW, II, 730). Yet neither playwright condemns material possessions for the sake of a blissful state of innocence in poverty. Poverty is "the vilest sin of man and society" (Preface to *Major Barbara,* p. 122), and in order to abolish it, a redistribution of income is essential. According to Brecht and Shaw, this change will not be brought about by peaceful means. Undershaft recommends gunpowder, Brecht's Black Straw Hats call for tanks, cannons, planes, and warships (cf. GW, II, 702).

Two further topics which Brecht and Shaw used to counter the traditional concepts of *belles lettres* were boxing and prostitution. The boxing motif achieved two purposes: it brought some freshness into an otherwise sterile atmosphere, and it served as a metaphor for the fight for survival in a capitalist society. For one of his early novels, *Cashel Byron's Profession* (1882), Shaw chose a boxer with the suggestive name of Byron as a hero. In this novel, Shaw applies the Darwinian principle of the survival of the fittest to Victorian society. Cashel points out to wealthy Lydia: "What is life but a fight? . . . You were born with a silver spoon in your mouth. But if you hadn't to fight for that silver spoon, some one else had."[17] In 1926, Brecht wrote a short story, "The Uppercut" (GW, XI, 116-20), a poem about boxing,[18] and he started to write the biography of the German middleweight champion Samson-

---

[16] Bernard Shaw, *"Major Barbara," The Complete Plays of Bernard Shaw* (London, 1965), p. 497. The page numbers in the text refer to this edition.

[17] Arthur Zeiger, ed., *Selected Novels of G. Bernard Shaw* (New York, 1946), p. 504.

[18] "Memorial for 12 World Champions," GW, VIII, 307-10.

Körner (GW, XI, 121-44). Moreover, in the Bertolt-Brecht-Archiv in Berlin there are some fragments of a novel on boxing with the working title *The Reputation* (BBA, 424). It was to be based on the world championship fight Dempsey-Carpentier and was supposed to expose the interaction of business, publicity, society and sports, and to show "how a man is made" (BBA, 424/31). Brecht wrote those works at a time when he advocated that elements of the circus and the sports arena be introduced to the theater and he condemned the contemporary production of lyrics as a collection of "pretty pictures and aromatic words" (GW, XVIII, 55). He recommended instead a poem entitled "He! He! The Iron Man!" about the racing cyclist Reggie McNamara—and by implication, some of his own lines from "Song of Mandelay," which dealt with "Mother Goddam's Brothel in Mandelay" (GW, VIII, 324-25). The desire to shock his audience still outweighed his social concern. But a few years after Brecht's wholesale condemnation of "400 (four hundred) young lyric poets" in 1927, he began to work on a play with a prostitute as the central character. Now his interest in social and political structures had gained the upper hand. This play, *The Good Woman of Setzuan*, completed in 1941, flies in the face of bourgeois morality when Brecht maintains that Shen Te, the prostitute, is the only decent person in the capital of Setzuan. Almost fifty years earlier, in 1893, Shaw, too, had made a prostitute the "heroine" of a play. His main intention in *Mrs. Warren's Profession* was to create a "counter-portrait to the general image of the romantic, sentimentally attractive courtesan of the stage."[19] Like Brecht, he based his play on economic realities. Through Shen Te and Mrs. Warren, both playwrights demonstrate that it is impossible to be decent in a society which is solely directed towards profit. Both of these women have to sell themselves in order to survive. But for Brecht and Shaw, the term "prostitution" is not restricted to these "immoral" activities. For them, marriage in its traditional form as the sacred institution of bourgeois life is also a sort of prostitution. In *The Philanderer,* Shaw talks about "the grotesque sexual compacts made between men and women under marriage laws" (Preface to *Plays Unpleasant,* p. 726). In a poem Brecht follows Kant and defines marriage as: "The pact made for mutual use/ of fortunes and sex organs" (GW, IX, 609; cf. also *The Tutor,* GW, VI, 2384).

Yet prostitution takes on an even more general meaning; it becomes a key word for the capitalistic society in general. Shaw maintains that ". . . we have great prostitute classes of men . . . who are daily using their highest faculty to belie their real sentiments: a sin compared to which that of a woman who sells the use of her person for a few hours is

---

[19] Martin Meisel, *Shaw and the Nineteenth Century Theater* (Princeton, 1963), p. 146.

too venial to be worth mentioning, for rich men without conviction are more dangerous in modern society than poor women without chastity" (Preface to *Plays Unpleasant,* pp. 726-27). With the term "prostitute classes of men" Shaw describes rather accurately the type whom Brecht in *the Tui-Novel* and in *Turandot or The Whitewashers' Congress* labeled "Tuis," i.e., "the intellectuals of the era of markets and merchandise," who offer their services as "whitewashers," "hired heads," "renters of intellect," "formulators," and "dealers in excuses" (cf. GW, XII, 3*).

IV. Adaptation and Inversion of Language and Structural Patterns

The concept of prostitution illustrates particularly well how both playwrights use a traditional mode of thinking and turn it into a club to castigate conventional bourgeois society. According to Grimm, this device of inversion or counter-convention in Brecht's works can be detected even in the details of language and word formation.[20] Anthony Abbott shows that the same principle is also characteristic for Shaw's language: "One of Shaw's favourite habits was the use of common words in an uncommon manner; he particularly enjoyed inverting the ordinary usage of terms."[21] Thus Brecht talks about "hired heads" (*Kopflanger*) and Shaw about "the son of a downstart gentleman" (Preface to *Buoyant Billions,* p. 891). The inversion of ordinary usage of language points out the wrongs in society in the following quote from *The Caucasian Chalk Circle:* "Terrible is the seductive power of goodness" (GW, V, 2025), and from *Mrs. Warren's Profession:* "But Lord help the world if everybody took to doing the right thing!" (p. 92). Sudden unexpected turns run counter to expectation and thus create distance. Mother Courage claims: "I won't touch Army stuff. Not at that price" (GW, IV, 1369). Undershaft does not exactly flatter politicians when he says about his son, Stephen; "he knows nothing and he thinks he knows everything. That points clearly to a political career" (*Major Barbara,* p. 490). Well-known quotations, especially from Shakespeare, the Bible and the German classics, provided both playwrights with an abundance of material. In Brecht's *Saint Joan,* e.g., Graham's description of the stock market echoes the familiar lines of Hölderlin's "Hyperion's Song of Fate":

> Unto prices it was given
> to fall from quotation to quotation
> like water hurtling from cliff to cliff
> deep down into infinity. They didn't stop before 30. (GW, II, 767)[22]

---

[20] See Reinhold Grimm, *Bertolt Brecht: Die Struktur seines Werkes.* 5th ed. (Nürnberg, 1968), p. 26.
[21] Anthony S. Abbott, *Shaw and Christianity* (New York, 1965), p. 73.
[22] Brecht, *Saint Joan,* trans. F. Jones, p. 109.

After Sir Ralph Bloomfield Bonington has "experimented" Dubedat to death in Shaw's *The Doctor's Dilemma,* he proclaims:

> Tomorrow and tomorrow and tomorrow
> After life's fitful fever they sleep well
> And like this insubstantial bourne from which
> No traveller returns
> Leave not a wrack behind. (p. 541)

The principle of inversion is also at work in larger structural units. It even determines the structure of whole plays in those cases where the dramatists base their play on a well-known theme or another play. Examples of Brecht's "counter-plays" are *Baal* (to Hanns Johst's *Der Einsame*) and *The Days of the Commune* (to Nordahl Grieg's *Die Niederlage*). Shaw is less radical in his inversions—he often remains within the structural confines of the theatrical convention he attacks, which is mainly the nineteenth-century "well-made play." But, as Martin Meisel points out in his excellent book on Shaw, he nevertheless uses inversions quite effectively: "Even in his primary phase of 'bluebook' drama, Shaw turned to the popular genres of the nineteenth-century theater to provide the vehicle for his social and intellectual concerns. The simplest way of exploiting a popular genre for revolutionary purposes was by the method of systematic counter-convention, by the creation of a genre anti-type."[23] According to Meisel, *Mrs. Warren's Profession* is anti-type of the courtesan play in general, and of Pinero's *The Second Mrs. Tanquery* in particular; *Captain Brassbound's Conversion* is an anti-type of the adventure melodrama, and *Arms and the Man* an anti-type of romantic comedy and the military melodrama.

Brecht's *Saint Joan* re-forms German classical elements—particularly Schiller's romantic tragedy, as Hans Mayer indicates.[24] And, as Shaw informs us in the preface to his *Saint Joan,* his version of The Maid is directed against her treatment in other literary works, especially Schiller's: "When we jump over two centuries to Schiller, we find Die Jungfrau von Orleans drowned in a witch's cauldron of raging romance. Schiller's Joan has not a single point of contact with the real Joan, nor indeed with any mortal women that ever walked this earth" (p. 616).

V. Other Structural Forms which Create Distance

Other structural forms which both playwrights used to create their type of drama are parables, contrast of form and content, prologues, epilogues, interludes, play within a play, intrusion of the author, comments on the action by one of the characters, and trial scenes. They all help to create distance and to prevent empathy. Parables are especially suited to Brecht's and Shaw's didactic theater in that they demonstrate a

[23] *Shaw and the Nineteenth Century Theater,* p. 141.
[24] *Bertolt Brecht und die Tradition,* p. 50.

moral truth by transposing it to a different milieu, time or place. Thus, Brecht's Setzuan and his Chicago stand for the world of capitalism and exploitation, and in Shaw's "Unexpected Isles" and the nameless tropical country in *Too True to be Good,* we recognize his native Britain. Prologues as in Brecht's *Herr Puntila and His Man Matti* and Shaw's *Caesar and Cleopatra,* epilogues as in Brecht's *The Good Woman of Setzuan* and Shaw's *Saint Joan,* and interludes as in Brecht's *A Man's a Man* and Shaw's *Man and Superman* are instrumental in destroying theatrical illusions of reality. The play within a play is a particularly effective means of making the audience realize that they are witnessing a play and not reality. They see their position as an audience watching a play repeated on stage. In Brecht's *The Caucasian Chalk Circle,* members of the collective farm Rosa Luxemburg perform the play of the chalk circle for the entertainment and instruction of the collective farm Galinsk on the stage as well as for the audience in the stalls. In Shaw's *Fanny's First Play,* Count O'Dowda's daughter, Fanny, puts on a play for the benefit of four eminent critics who discuss its merits in the epilogue. This structural device provides Shaw with an excellent opportunity to present his technique of a discussion play and to show the reactions of contemporary critics. Needless to say, the critics who condemn the play are thoroughly satirized. To increase the satirical effect, Shaw even introduces his name into the discussion. The critics are supposed to try to guess who the author of the play was. Gunn notices "the hackneyed old Shaw touch," but Vaughan opposes: "Rot! . . . Poor as this play is, there's the note of passion in it. . . . Now I've repeatedly proved that Shaw is psychologically incapable of the note of passion" (*Fanny's First Play,* pp. 682, 683). Brecht uses the same technique of introducing his name in *Roundheads and Peakheads* in which one of the landlords has a pointed head "because Mr. Brecht wishes it that way" (GW, III, 912), and in *A Man's a Man,* wherein Leokadja Begbick informs the audience:

> Mr. Bertolt Brecht claims: a man is a man.
> And that is something anybody can claim.
> But Mr. Bertolt Brecht then proceeds to prove
> That you can do almost anything with a man. (GW, I, 336)

A form closely related in structure to the play within a play is the trial scene. According to Walter Hinck, it can be regarded as "a central dramatic form of Brecht's theater."[25] In fact, his whole work can be understood as an indictment of the society in which he lived: "Just as with Kafka, the world of Brecht's characters is the legal world. Every one of Brecht's works could be called *The Trial.*"[26] Trial scenes also provide an excellent forum for argumentation and demonstration of conflicting ideas. They involve the audience intellectually, not emotionally. Even if

---

[25] Walter Hinck, *Die Dramaturgie des späten Brecht* (Göttingen, 1959), p. 74.
[26] Günther Anders, *Bert Brecht: Gespräche und Erinnerungen* (Zürich, 1962), p. 24.

a play contains no formal trial scene, judgment is passed on society, as in *Saint Joan of the Stockyards.* But in the majority of Brecht's plays, the trial either constitutes one part of the play, as in *Rise and Fall of the City of Mahagonny* or *The Exception and the Rule,* or it shapes the structure of the whole play, as in *The Measures Taken* or *The Trial of Lucullus.* Shaw uses the trial scene for similar reasons. *On the Rocks, Major Barbara,* and *Widowers' Houses* are indictments of the society in which he lives, without containing formal trials. In *Saint Joan* and *The Devil's Disciple,* the trial is actually a part of the play. In *Geneva,* the trial determines the whole structure.

Another important feature of both playwrights' anti-illusionary theater is their development of character—or rather the lack of it. Neither Brecht nor Shaw endeavors to present his characters in such a way that the spectators can identify with them. On the contrary, their characters are a "very real conglomeration of contradictory traits" (GW, XV, 99). These "contradictory traits" are particularly noticeable in Mrs. Warren and Shen Te, Undershaft and Mauler. There is no gradual, organic development, but an abrupt clash of opposites. Mrs. Warren and Shen Te, as well as Undershaft and Mauler, are victims and, at the same time, beneficiaries of the capitalistically organized society. The system forced Shen Te and Mrs. Warren into prostitution, but it also allowed them to become ruthless capitalists—Mrs. Warren the operator of an international call girl trust, and Shen Te/Shui Ta the boss of a big tobacco factory. Both Undershaft and Mauler are driven by the almost pathological fear of poverty, "the worst of all crimes" (*Major Barbara,* p. 498). These contradictions are not explained in psychological terms, but by sociological and political circumstances. The system, not the individual characters in the play, is the common target of both Brecht's and Shaw's attack. In the preface to his *Plays Unpleasant*, Shaw warns his readers that "my attacks are directed against themselves, not against my stage figures. . . . The guilt of defective social organization does not lie alone on the people who actually work the commercial makeshifts . . . but with the whole body of citizens" (p. 727). Similarly, Brecht's Saint Joan appeals to the audience to bring about change:

> . . . and nothing henceforth be considered honorable
> except what changes this world once for all: it needs it. (GW, II, 780)[27]

VI. Non-Aristotelian Theater

Because of their dramatic techniques and their antagonism to the dominating art forms of their time, both playwrights were accused of not being "realists." Both refuted these accusations with very similar arguments, thereby providing us with valuable insights into their own

[27] Brecht, *Saint Joan,* trans. F. Jones, p. 120.

views of what a drama should be. According to Shaw, it is the function of a playwright not simply to mirror the world, but to interpret it: "Holding up a mirror to nature is not a correct definition of a playwright's art. A mirror reflects what is before it. Hold it up to any street at noonday and it shows a crowd of people and vehicles and tells us nothing about them. A photograph of them has no meaning. . . . The playwright must interpret the passing show by parables."[28] Time and again Shaw emphasizes that it is the duty of responsible playwrights to point out social injustices and remedies for them: "If people are rotting and starving in all directions, and nobody else has the heart or brains to make a disturbance about it, the great writer must."[29] Only when the social problems are solved can the dramatists turn their attention to other subjects again: "When we succeed in adjusting our social structure in such a way as to enable us to solve social questions as fast as they become really pressing, they will no longer force their way into the theatre."[30] As a dramatic realist and social critic, Shaw sees himself in the tradition of Cervantes, Shelley, Swift, Gay, Beaumarchais and Samuel Butler. In his essay on "The Problem Play," e.g., he reveals his indebtedness to Shelley: "In short what is forcing our great poets to follow Shelley in becoming political and social agitators, and to turn the theatre into a platform for propaganda and an arena for discussion, is that . . . the political machinery . . . is so old-fashioned . . . that social questions never get solved."[31] Because Shaw wants to analyze rather than reflect reality, his dramatic technique comes close to what Brecht called *Experimentaldramatik:* "The dramas of Ibsen, Tolstoy, Strindberg, Gorki, Chekhov, Hauptmann, Shaw, Kaiser and O'Neill are experimental dramas. They are great attempts to capture the problems of the time in dramatic form" (GW, XV, 288). Shaw himself was quite aware of the experimental nature of his plays: "The drama progresses by a series of experiments made on the public by actors and actresses with new plays."[32]

By calling his plays "experiments" (*Versuche*), Brecht places himself in the very same tradition. Like Shaw, he emphasizes the didactic and dialectic nature of his definition of the art of the realistic playwright: "The term realistic means that the playwright is consciously influenced by reality and, at the same time, deliberately attempts to influence reality" (GW, XIX, 356). In explaining his concept of the realistic playwright, Brecht also uses the argument that a mere reflection of reality is meaningless: "The situation is so complicated that a simple rendition of reality has less meaning than ever. A photograph of the

---

[28] Quoted from Meisel, *Shaw and the Nineteenth Century Theater,* pp. 92-93.
[29] Bernard Shaw, "The Problem Play," *Shaw on Theatre,* ed. E. J. West (New York, 1967), p. 64.
[30] Ibid., p. 64.
[31] Ibid.
[32] "How to Lecture on Ibsen," ibid., p. 54.

Krupp works or A.E.G. reveals hardly anything about those institutions. . . . Thus it is indeed necessary to create something 'artificial'—to create art."[33] To support his concept of realism, he also points to some of the same writers Shaw mentioned as his literary ancestors, particularly Shelley and Cervantes. Shelley's ballad "The Mask of Anarchy" was the model for Brecht's poem "Freedom and Democracy" (GW, IX, 943-49); in this connection Brecht introduced "the reader to a writer of past ages who wrote differently from other bourgeois novelists but he must still be called a great realist. The name of this great revolutionary English poet: P. B. Shelley" (GW, XIX, 340). Cervantes' novel *Don Quixote* is called upon as witness to Brecht's view that "realism does by no means exclude imagination and invention" (GW, XIX, 371).

The dramatic devices described above allow the audience to rationalize and analyze the actions on the stage. In addition, many of Brecht's and some of Shaw's works have open endings which are designed to induce the audience to find solutions to the problems presented in the play along the lines suggested by the playwrights. Brecht's *The Good Woman of Setzuan* and Shaw's *Saint Joan,* for example, end with a passionate plea to the audience. But not only the plays, the stage, too, had to be changed to suit their purposes. The audience should be made comfortable and the "peephole" with the "fourth wall" should be replaced by a modern version of a Shakespearian stage. "I am in favor of making the playgoer comfortable," Shaw writes in his essay "Playhouses and Plays" and continues: "The auditorium must combine the optics and acoustics of a first-rate lecture theatre and a first-rate circus. There must be a forestage extending on occasion to the occupation of all the floor level."[34] The *Dramaturg* in Brecht's *The Purchase of Brass* also points to Shakespeare's theater: "People smoked in these theaters . . . the action took place in the closest proximity to the audience" (GW, XVI, 586, 587). Since neither Brecht nor Shaw wanted a spellbound spectator caught up in an illusion, but rather one who left the theater with a better understanding of the world around him, the Aristotelian tradition had little to offer them. They dealt with it in numerous articles, although Brecht was much more thorough and systematic in his discussion of the Aristotelian theater. They even brought the discussion of Aristotelian principles on stage in *Fanny's First Play* and in the dialogue fragments of *The Purchase of Brass,* respectively.[35] Their opposition is especially directed against the central purpose of Aristotelian drama: catharsis. Brecht's criticism of Aristotle's *Poetics* begins with an attack on the con-

[33] Quoted from Viktor Žmegač, *Kunst und Wirklichkeit: Zur Literaturtheorie bei Brecht, Lukács und Broch* (Bad Homburg v.d.H., 1969), p. 16.
[34] *Shaw on Theatre,* ed. E. J. West, pp. 179, 181.
[35] Brecht's untimely death prevented him from ever seeing *The Purchase of Brass* on stage, but his collaborators at the Berliner Ensemble staged it for the first time in 1963.

cept of catharsis: "The spectator's completely independent and critical attitude which is bent solely on the solution of problems here on earth is no basis for a catharsis" (GW, XV, 241). Shaw, too, is critical of the Aristotelian concept of catharsis: "In the old days Aristotle said that tragedy purged the soul with pity and terror; . . . I have never regarded that as a permanent definition."[36] Like Brecht, he argues that pity and fear only serve to obstruct the all-important social mission of the theater: "I do not want there to be any more pity in the world, because I do not want there to be anything to pity; and I want there to be no more terror because I do not want people to have anything to fear. . . . You may throw pity and terror to one side, and you can reveal life, and you can stimulate thought about it, and you can educate peoples' senses."[37] Like Brecht, Shaw topples the pyramidal structure of Aristotelian drama: "The writer who practices the art of Ibsen therefore discards all the old tricks of preparation, catastrophy, *dénouement,* and so forth without thinking about it. . . . Hence a cry has arisen that the post-Ibsen play is not a play; and that its technique, not being the technique described by Aristotle, is no technique at all."[38] Both writers discarded the Aristotelian unities of time, place, and action, as illustrated by Brecht's *The Caucasian Chalk Circle* and Shaw's *Saint Joan.* It should be noted, however, that Shaw had to be much more cautious since, in order to win a foothold in the theater of his time, he had to devise "certain expedients calculated to make his radically unconventional plays more tolerable to conventional people."[39] For Aristotle, epic elements had no place in a drama. Yet Brecht talked about his theater as epic theater and many of Shaw's plays obviously contain epic elements, such as his long prefaces and stage directions. Hans Mayer points out that Shaw's play, *Back to Methuselah,* is conceived as a dramatized epic modelled after the Pentateuch.[40] Shaw himself observes in "My Way with a Play": "The art of all fiction, whether made for the stage, the screen, or the bookshelf, is the art of story-telling. My stock-in-trade is that of Scheherazade and Chaucer no less than of Aristophanes and Shakespeare."[41] Brecht's and Shaw's characters do not suffer from a tragic flaw within themselves (*hamartia*), as Aristotle postulated. In the case of Brecht's Saint Joan, Shen Te or Grusha, and Shaw's Saint Joan, there is, indeed, an inversion of the Aristotelian *hamartia,* since trouble arises not from the vices, but from the virtues of the protagonist; the "flaw" lies in the prevailing social and political power structure.

However far both playwrights are removed from Aristotle's *Poetics,* their art and their techniques are new only to the stage of their

[36] "About Actors and Acting," *Shaw on Theatre,* ed. E. J. West, p. 197.
[37] Ibid., pp. 197-98.
[38] Bernard Shaw, *The Quintessence of Ibsenism* (New York, 1964), p. 183.
[39] Charles A. Carpenter, *Bernard Shaw and the Art of Destroying Ideals* (Madison, 1969), p. 18.
[40] Hans Mayer, *Ansichten zur Literatur der Zeit* (Hamburg, 1962), p. 125.
[41] *Shaw on Theatre,* ed. E. J. West, p. 269.

day—their roots lie in the tradition of rhetoric. In one of his major theoretical works, *The Quintessence of Ibsenism,* Shaw makes it quite clear which line of tradition he follows: "The new technique is only new on the modern stage. It has been used by preachers and orators ever since speech was invented. It is . . . a forensic technique of recrimination, disillusion, and penetration through ideals to the truth, with a free use of all the rhetorical and lyrical arts of the orator, the preacher, the pleader, and the rhapsodist."[42] As Ulla C. Lerg-Kill shows in her book on poetic language and party slogans,[43] Brecht, too, uses many rhetorical devices to convince his audience. His technique of estrangement—according to Reinhold Grimm the most characteristic feature of his dramatic technique[44]—can be regarded as an excellent rhetorical device to gain the attention of his audience and to persuade it to adopt his views. In fact, Aristotle himself suggested a very similar method in his *Rhetoric:* "It is therefore well to give to everyday speech an unfamiliar air: people like what strikes them, and are struck by what is out of the way."[45] The so-called *Verfremdungseffekt* therefore can be classified under the rhetorical category of *persuasio,* the art of convincing an audience. Of the subdivisions of the rhetorical device of *persuasio, docere* and *delectare* rather than *pathos* are the main purposes of Brecht's and Shaw's theater.

It should again be stressed that there are nevertheless considerable discrepancies between Brecht and Shaw. Some of them can certainly be attributed to differences in temperament. To a large extent, however, they are due to historical, political and sociological circumstances. Both playwrights had similar intentions and used similar dramatic techniques. One could almost say that exactly those things they have in common separate them from each other; they address a certain type of audience in a certain historic situation in order to change the political and social structure. Yet the numerous parallels and similarities in their dramatic techniques and intentions point to a close affinity; they belong to the same tradition: "The line of attempts to create better theatrical productions of social relations runs from the English Restoration Comedy via Beaumarchais to Lenz. The Naturalism (of the Goncourts, of Zola, Chekhov, Tolstoy, Ibsen, Strindberg, Hauptmann, Shaw) shows the influence the European labor movement has had upon the stage" (GW, XVI, 1*). Brecht saw himself as a successor to the writers mentioned, but he assumed a radically different point of view regarding social class.

---

[42] *The Quintessence of Ibsenism,* p. 184.
[43] *Dichterwort und Parteiparole* (Bad Homburg v.d.H., 1968).
[44] See Grimm, *Bertolt Brecht: Die Struktur seines Werkes,* p. 13.
[45] Aristotle, *Rhetoric,* trans. W. Rhys Roberts; *Poetics,* trans. Ingram Bywater (New York, 1954), p. 167 (1404b).

We can be sure that Brecht was influenced by some aspects of Shaw's work, not in a narrow, positivistic sense, but in the form of catalytic impulses originating from new and pioneering dramatic concepts. Although to a somewhat lesser extent than in the works of Wedekind, Kaiser or Shakespeare, Brecht found in the works of Bernard Shaw a confirmation and a reinforcement of his own ideas about drama, particularly during the incubation period of his epic theater.

PISCATOR AND BRECHT:
AFFINITY AND ALIENATION

Herbert Knust

> There was a sphere of brotherli-
> ness, of relatedness, of mutual ac-
> ceptance between us . . . in Berlin,
> in Moscow . . . in New York and
> once again in Berlin. But I never
> got over this disappointment. . . .
> *(Piscator* on *Brecht)*

Today no serious study of Brecht the playwright can deny that Erwin Piscator's theatrical experiments of the twenties considerably influenced Brecht's own theories and practice. Even before the publication of his voluminous *Writings on Theater* (1963-1964),[1] in which Brecht himself described Piscator's pioneering technical innovations and acknowledged his significance for modern political theater, some critics had already pointed to affinities between their "epic" dramaturgies; but especially in recent years—after Piscator's death in 1966 and the posthumous publication of his *Aufsätze, Reden, Gespräche*[2]—increasing attention has been paid to the connections between their work.[3] Some comparisons emphasize specific technical aspects (e.g., film projections) which several of their theatrical productions had in common[4]; others deal with their respective experiences and contributions at large in successive chapters, the titles of which might seem interchangeable[5]; some claim that Brecht profited more from Piscator than Piscator ever received credit for[6]; still others argue that there is indeed a relationship between the development of their experiments, but that despite similar

---

[1] SzT, now in GW, XV-XVII. Some of the theoretical essays had previously appeared in the *Versuche* series (Berlin, 1930 ff.).

[2] Part of Erwin Piscator, *Schriften* (Berlin, 1968), I: *Das politische Theater* [facsimile reprint of the 1928 ed.], II: *Aufsätze, Reden, Gespräche*. The Rowohlt publishing company issued a new edition of *Das politische Theater* (Reinbek, 1963) which had been revised by Piscator in collaboration with Felix Gasbarra. Further references to these works will be given as follows: S plus volume and page number for *Schriften;* PT for *Das politische Theater,* rev. ed.

[3] *Brecht* (G), p. 175.

[4] Marianne Mildenberger, *Film und Projektion auf der Bühne* (Emsdetten, 1961), pp. 141-205; 222 ff.

[5] E.g., "The Epic Theater of Erwin Piscator," "The Didactic Theater of Bertolt Brecht," Friedrich W. Knellessen, *Agitation auf der Bühne. Das politische Theater der Weimarer Republik* (Emsdetten, 1970), pp. 76-201; "Erwin Piscator or the Model of Political Theater," "Young Brecht or the Model of Epic Theater," Bernhard Reich, *Im Wettlauf mit der Zeit* (Berlin, 1970), pp. 201-271.

[6] E.g., Christopher D. Innes, *Erwin Piscator's Political Theatre. The Development of Modern German Drama* (Cambridge, 1972), pp. 189-200.

characteristics each man produced a distinct theater form of his own.[7] In the face of such an increasing amount of critical endeavor to assess the affinities and differences between these two important contributors to modern dramaturgy, it must come as a surprise to discover that Piscator himself, until a few years before his death in 1966, was actually in doubt and despair as to whether the world would ever recognize his significance in due relation to that of his more famous contemporary.

It is not my intention here to review or modify pertinent scholarship based on published evidence. Rather, I wish to preview hitherto neglected, unpublished sources that may lead to a fuller understanding of the complex and often complicated relationship between the two men and their respective work. These sources—letters, diaries, notes—have partly been collected in archives,[8] partly they are still in private hands. While some of these materials deal with personal matters, others contain significant information about artistic and professional concerns. Thus, for example, the Piscator Conference in Berlin (7-10 October 1971) placed considerable emphasis on the content of several Brecht letters then on exhibition; in them Brecht described the post-World War II situation in Berlin and urged Piscator to return, like Brecht before him, from American exile to Berlin in order to resume the joint struggle for a new theater. These letters, eagerly quoted by the newspapers as partial evidence for a desirable new appraisal of Piscator, do indeed testify to Brecht's respect for—and, possibly, need of—Piscator at a particular time; still, they constitute only a fraction of a more or less intensive and problematic dialogue covering several decades. This dialogue, which on Piscator's part often turned into an anguished monologue, must be seen as a whole; for inasmuch as it reflects—primarily from Piscator's side—a peculiar love-hate with many ups and downs, any assumptions based on a few letters, scattered diary entries and working notes, are likely to remain fragmentary and inconclusive. I do not pretend to give a full account of the personal relationship (which, of course, also includes the professional relationship) between Piscator and Brecht—that will be a task of future biographers. In my pursuit of the Schwejk theme,[9] which for a long time

[7] E.g., Günther Rühle, "Traum und Arbeit des Erwin Piscator," *Erwin Piscator, 1893-1966* (Berlin, 1971), pp. 8-21; Ulrich Weisstein, "Soziologische Dramaturgie und politisches Theater. Erwin Piscators Beitrag zum Drama der zwanziger Jahre," *Deutsche Dramentheorien,* ed. Reinhold Grimm (Frankfurt, 1971), II, 516-47; George Buehler, "Bertolt Brecht und Erwin Piscator: Ein Vergleich ihrer theoretischen Schriften" (Diss. Indiana University, 1972).

[8] BBA; Erwin Piscator Center, Akademie der Künste (West Berlin); Erwin Piscator Papers, Special Collections/Morris Library, Southern Illinois University.

[9] See my articles "Brechts braver Schweyk," PMLA, 88 (1973), 219-32; "Schwejk und kein Ende," *Germano-Slavica,* 1 (Spring 1973), 66-85; my critical edition *Materialien zu Bertolt Brechts "Schweyk im zweiten Weltkrieg,"* edition suhrkamp 604 (Frankfurt, 1974); and my collaboration with Hedy Landman, *Theatrical Drawings and Watercolors by George Grosz* (Busch-Reisinger Museum, Harvard University, 1973).

45

constituted both a common bond between and controversial issue for the two practitioners of theatrical art, I have investigated a sufficient number of unpublished sources to be able to present a tentative outline of their relationship based on hitherto unknown evidence. Four distinct phases of Brecht's and Piscator's relationship, which spanned the period from 1927 to 1956, may be discerned: their collaborative efforts with regard to theater productions in the late twenties in Berlin; their correspondence and occasional meetings during the years of their European exile in the thirties; their written and personal contacts in the U.S. during the forties; their uneasy relationship after their return to Germany in the late forties and early fifties respectively.

I. Early Association in Berlin

Having repeatedly visited Berlin, Brecht, in 1924, moved to that city which was then the center of theatrical life in Germany. It was here that he met the theater director Erwin Piscator, who, deeply disturbed by his experiences of World War I and the causes that led to it, had joined the Communist Spartacus Group. In his "Proletarian Theater," Piscator had radically replaced art by politics, and through his subsequent technical innovations for the stage, he attempted to develop a flexible "epic" dramaturgy aiming at the demonstration of complex but changeable socio-economic factors which condition modern man's existence. In 1927, Brecht, involved in numerous other activities,[10] joined Piscator's "dramaturgic collective" along with other young writers. He witnessed all of Piscator's productions, was a frequent guest not only at his rehearsals but also at those of other theater directors, and, no doubt, learned a great deal from Piscator's revolutionary techniques. However, Brecht's artistic and intellectual independence is confirmed by all the accounts we have. It may even be premature to claim that it was only Piscator who contributed to Brecht's development and that Brecht had no influence on Piscator whatsoever. This would seem to speak against the collective work which both Piscator and Brecht valued and practiced. Piscator himself, who attended Brecht's rehearsals just as Brecht attended his, mentions Brecht's cooperation as a member of the collective; he further states that the book *Das politische Theater* was a collective work, and, in his and Felix Gasbarra's revised 1963 edition of the volume, even adds episodic details emphasizing Brecht's contribution to the Schwejk project.[11]

---

[10] *Brecht-Chronik,* pp. 36-57.
[11] Gasbarra—who like George Grosz later renounced the Communist Party—was himself quite modest about his artistic significance. Even though he was frequently involved in theater productions and also wrote radio plays, he remarks in a letter of 12 November 1953 to Piscator (referring to his revision of *Das politische Theater*): "That I should be the one who is expected to stress the artistic side will cause all those to smile who know [about my limited abilities]." Gasbarra's correspondence with Piscator contains quite controversial views on Brecht.

Furthermore, from the sparse correspondence of their early association (1927-1928), written when they could not communicate orally, it appears that Brecht was in fact not too enthusiastic about the way in which Piscator directed his theater. To both Piscator and Herbert Ihering—the famous theater critic who had early recognized and publicly drawn attention to Brecht's talent—he made "farreaching" suggestions concerning the political nature of theater, or, rather, the literary nature of politics: he actually proposed to change what he called the "literary" character of Piscator's theater into a "political" one by founding a RED CLUB and by calling its theater the RED CLUB THEATER. The theater could be used for various political activities (such as meetings, production of pamphlets) of the political club. Not only writers, stage directors, actors, and critics were to become members of this club; but, significantly, the interested audience as well. Thus a new, real relationship between audience and experimental stage was to be achieved. While these thoughts foreshadowed Brecht's own "learning plays" (*Lehrstücke*) on which he was soon to embark, they also contain unmistakable reservations about the literary quality of the so-called "Piscator-Theater," and, apparently, misgivings about his own identification with the artistic style of this enterprise. His letters show that he was perturbed about a press notice in which Gasbarra—sent to Piscator by the Communist Party (S, I, 61)—was called the head (*Leitung*) of Piscator's dramaturgic collective. Brecht responded in characteristic fashion: he insisted that, while he did not mind Gasbarra's *political* guidance, he was not willing to work under Gasbarra's *literary* direction. Furthermore, while Brecht considered himself "perhaps" Piscator's comrade, he certainly did not think of himself as his dramaturgist: "ich bin vielleicht Ihr genosse aber ich bin bestimmt nicht Ihr dramaturg." In short, Brecht was sure of his own importance as a literary artist and stressed his independence. Piscator recalls how in connection with this issue Brecht shouted, "My name is a trade-mark, and whoever uses this trade-mark must pay for it" (PT, 141).

This dispute from their earliest association indicates a basic difference between Brecht and Piscator that was to strain their relationship more than once. No matter how similar their political interests, their use of certain stage devices, their theories on the pedagogical nature of future drama: Brecht was a great *literary* artist whereas Piscator—notwithstanding his occasional dabbling in poetry—was not. Piscator knew this although he apparently tried to ignore it. He even took it upon himself to "de-literarize" original works by radical reworkings of scripts—primarily cuts and simplifications—in order to emphasize their political impact and to pinpoint their topical interest; but he never really composed a play on his own. He needed playwrights to assist him, and there is considerable evidence that he valued especially Brecht's artistic contributions. During the theater season of 1927-1928 he wanted to stage Brecht's play *Wheat* (*Joe Fleischhacker*) [S, I, 127], but the project did not materialize. Brecht recalls that he himself reworked most of the important scripts for Piscator's performances, wrote additional scenes for these scripts, in one case a whole act, and that he did *Schwejk* all by himself (GW, XVI, 598). Piscator, having become very suspicious about Brecht's "thefts"[12] later denies this and writes in his diary[13] that Brecht, who received 5,000 Marks like every other collaborator on the Schwejk script, did not contribute more than the others. Yet, as we shall see, Piscator's desire for Brecht's literary, theoretical, and practical collaboration never ceases despite the later cooling of their relations.

One further example of their differing views on the literary style and effect of certain political subject matters might be mentioned. In a letter dated 1927 Brecht informs Piscator that after several unsuccessful attempts—and on the basis of theoretical considerations—he has to decline Piscator's request to translate Upton Sinclair's ballad "about the roses on the grave" because he discovered that the poem "is not good." As the recent bibliography of Sinclair's works does not list a poem by that title,[14] the text in question must have been part of another work in which Piscator was then interested. According to *Das politische Theater,* only Sinclair's play *Singing Jailbirds* would qualify—in the production or preparation of which Brecht, too, was involved. Indeed, at the end of the first act, a chorus takes up the song of the imprisoned workers:

Are you busy, fellow-workers,
Are your shoulders to the wheel?
    Get together for the cause
    And some day you'll make the laws;
It's the only way to make the masters squeal.[15]

Then the whole audience sings eight stanzas describing how everyone—police, judge, jailer, bed-bug flea, even God—is against the poor workers ("They go wild, simply wild, over me"), concluding with the lines:

Will the roses grow wild over me
When I'm gone to the land that is to be?
When my soul and body part in the stillness of my heart—
Will the roses grow wild over me?[16]

---

[12] On this point, the unpublished evidence definitely contradicts Piscator's published statement: "The question as to who voiced something first has always left me unconcerned—here I agree with my friend Brecht" ("Nachwort 1966," S, I, 266).

[13] Diary No. 21, p. 21 (November/December). The dating of the entries in Piscator's diaries is sometimes difficult. Further references to the diaries will be included in the text under D, either by date, or by number and page of the typed diary version.

[14] Ronald Gottesman, *Upton Sinclair. An Annotated Checklist* (Kent, 1973).

[15] Upton Sinclair, *Singing Jailbirds* (Pasadena, 1924), p. 27.

[16] Ibid., p. 28.

With this play by Sinclair, interspersed with numerous other songs, Piscator wanted to find out to what extent he could carry out political agitation within a specific audience. While he envisaged "a stream of songs through the whole house, the audience enveloped in songs, singing groups posted everywhere on the balconies, behind the stalls in the aisles" (S, I, 221), Brecht did not see much value in the experiment. Not that he lacked interest in Upton Sinclair—on the contrary; he had previously recommended Sinclair's *The Jungle* as an antidote to Schiller's *Don Carlos* (GW, XV, 9-11) and subsequently was to make use of Sinclair in his own works.[17] But he wrote Piscator: after some hard thinking he had arrived at the important conclusion that, while the above mentioned ballad was pretty and touching and, thematically, even contained some objective truth, there was "not one gram of revolutionary effect in it." Indeed, Brecht considered it as a typical example of "the worst kind of workers' song, appealing to compassion (*whose* compassion?)"; in an ironic mood he conjured up the vision of a whole house full of grown-up men, singing tearfully, in four voices, about the fact that all turn against them, even the roses on the graves.[18] Brecht calls the ballad an "historical genre painting with poetic expression and embarrassing effect" and sees in it (as also in Gerhart Hauptmann's plays *The Weavers* and *Drayman Henschel*) a certain undesirable tendency in socialist literature. As Piscator himself reports, his staging of *Singing Jailbirds,* particularly the intended agitation by chorus, proved a failure (S, I, 222).

This symptomatic detail—to which Brecht attributed great significance in his letter—hints at different conceptions about socialist literature at large. It shows that Brecht, while sharing with Piscator an interest in new social themes to be introduced into theater, distances himself from a style with direct emotional appeal to the working class, a style which Piscator had practiced in his "Proletarian Theater" and to which he continued to adhere even during his most "rationalizing" endeavors. Brecht began to develop his theory of intellectualizing estrangement about which, as we shall see, Piscator remained skeptical.

II. Exile in Europe

In 1932 Piscator left for Russia where, upon invitation of the film company Meschrapom, he began to produce the film "The Uprising of the Fishermen of St. Barbara." Brecht, wary of the Nazi threat, escaped in 1933 from Germany to Denmark, starting his long period of exile. To judge from their correspondence between 1933 and 1938 (in which year Piscator emigrated to the United States), the friendship between the two

---

[17] Reinhold Grimm, *Bertolt Brecht und die Weltliteratur* (Nürnberg, 1961), pp. 9-12.
[18] Possibly Brecht may have slightly misunderstood the last stanza (but not the poem as a whole), for the roses do not "go wild" (as all the other enemies do), but "grow wild" over the poor victims.

men continued. Over and over again they voice their desire for joint plans, but the need for collaboration—especially in literary matters—is expressed far more urgently by Piscator than by Brecht.

Piscator, apparently more experienced than Brecht in business connections, usually is the initiator. Repeatedly he asks for Brecht's plans and invites him to come to Moscow in order to collaborate on films and plays. During the period 1934-1935 he asks him for suggestions concerning an anti-Fascist film; he further requests and receives from Brecht the "United Front Song" (GW, IX, 652-53). He also asks for Brecht's contribution in writing in honor of Béla Kun[19] and indicates that he wants to stage *Roundheads and Peakheads*.[20] Having moved to Paris in 1936, Piscator reports that he encountered there a "fantastic political high tension and a tremendous spirit" (9 August 1936). Then, after his decision "to stay in the West for a while," Piscator bubbles over with plans and writes to Brecht: "You play a role in all my plans, and it is not a bad or minor one" (26 October 1936). In this connection, he mentions a Jewish theater of which he is to become director, several film projects, an invitation to take over a theater in Barcelona, and the possibility of working in Mexico. Apparently Brecht reacted favorably towards some of Piscator's plans; thus, e.g., he expresses his desire to go to Spain (18 January 1937) and remarks that "one could become professor in Mexico" (15 January 1937). Piscator tries to interest Brecht in a new form of satiric-dramatic dance ("accompanying the dance by a chorus, as in mickey mouse films") and invites him to Paris in order to work jointly with him "on many other plans." On 13 November 1936 Piscator asks Brecht for suggestions concerning a conference of famous dramatists that Piscator wants to launch as an anti-thrust against the recent "Nazi conference of war writers" (*als Gegenkonferenz der Nazi-Kriegsdichterkonferenz der letzten Wochen*). A film exposé sent by Brecht finds Piscator's praise (17 February 1937), as does Brecht's proposal for a Diderot Society (GW, XV, 305-309), aiming at the organization of a select group of theater and film practitioners (among them Piscator) who were to report to the society about the results of their inductive production methods. Piscator agrees with Brecht's proposal in principle and even sends a sketchy contribution on "film length" for discussion (31 March 1937); but he feels that the proposed organization would gain much more if Brecht were to come to Paris to work together with him on the various projects he is planning: "What is most important now: time and the dramaturgical work. That's why I want to ask you whether I can count on you" (25 March 1937). "Please answer my letter concerning your collaboration" (31 March 1937). At the same time Piscator has his secretary (F. Oliver Brachfeld)

[19] Cf. *Brecht-Chronik*, pp. 61 ff., and Reich, p. 370.
[20] Detailed news about the Copenhagen staging of *Roundheads* are included in Margarete Steffin's letter to Piscator of 15 November 1936.

write to Brecht, requesting an essay or commentaries by Brecht on Piscator that could be used as propaganda for Piscator's various activities in Paris and elsewhere (8 May 1937). What he has in mind is an essay similar to that published by Brecht in *The New York Times* during his 1935 visit to New York.[21] Piscator had read it in Moscow (where he had left all his materials) and apparently found Brecht's account of their respective previous work quite acceptable—a fact that needs to be borne in mind when one reads Piscator's later complaints about Brecht not having given due credit to Piscator's share in the development of epic theater.

In connection with Piscator's often-mentioned new *Schwejk* project, Brecht recommends on 21 April 1937 the film cartoon technique of his old friend Bartosch and also sketches another subject matter for a film, *Potato Jones* (*Kartoffel-Johns*). But it is especially with regard to a modernized, anti-Fascist film version of *Schwejk* that Piscator wants to have Brecht's advice and active help. This is not surprising in view of the fact that Brecht had substantially contributed to the success of the 1928 Berlin *Schwejk* performance, adapted from Jaroslav Hašek's famous novel, *The Good Soldier Svejk* (1921-1923). Brecht had also expressed some new ideas on how to perform *Schwejk*.[22] It is interesting to note, however, that the plans for a future collaboration on *Schwejk* contain the fear of rivalry which, in 1943, was to lead to a serious estrangement between Piscator and Brecht. As early as 1933 Piscator wrote that he wanted to make a film of *Schwejk* in Moscow and that he was afraid that Brecht might anticipate him by producing a *Schwejk* film of his own in Paris (1 August 1933). Brecht again wrote in 1937 when Piscator was closer than ever to realizing his favorite idea (i.e., a *Schwejk* film): "What about Schwejk? You simply must not under any circumstances tackle a production without me" (21 April 1937).

A tentative film script, prepared by Leo Lania (another collaborator from the Berlin period) and Piscator is sent to Brecht for his comments.[23] Piscator is quite apologetic about the literary shortcomings of the new version and tries to make clear that he only wanted to sketch the political "line along which Schwejk and the film are possible today." But it is obvious from his letter that, in working out the exposé,

---

[21] This essay must be "The German Drama: pre-Hitler" which appeared in the 24 November 1935 issue of NYT (9; 1,4) on the occasion of Brecht's visit to New York where he assisted in the production of *The Mother*. This would clarify John Willett's uncertainty about the date and occasion of this piece; he credits it to the London newspaper *Left Review* (July 1936), and included the text in his selection of Brecht's theoretical writings (*Brecht on Theatre*, pp. 77-81).

[22] See Fritz Sternberg, *Der Dichter und die Ratio. Erinnerungen an Bertolt Brecht* (Göttingen, 1963), pp. 13-14.

[23] The only extant copy of this particular script (BBA, 309) is discussed in Pavel Petr, *Hašeks 'Schwejk' in Deutschland* (Berlin, 1963), and in my edition of *Schweyk-Materialien;* several other versions of the film exposé are discussed in my essay "Schwejk und kein Ende" (cf. n. 9).

Piscator wants more than just polished style from Brecht: "Then I need you. That may be in approximately fourteen days, or even sooner—or later. Until then, I think we can solve some basic questions by correspondence. What is your opinion about the outline? Do you think the subject has been handled properly? Does the political line seem clear enough? Which anecdotes would you omit? Which would you advise to add?" (10 May 1937).

The plot of the film script is a mixture of episodes from Hašek's novel, the 1927 dramatic adaptation by Max Brod and Hans Reimann, and the subsequent 1928 version which was largely a product of Brecht's efforts. Piscator had updated the events by changing the murder of Archduke Franz Ferdinand in Sarajevo on 28 June 1914 into an unsuccessful (fake) assassination attempt on the "Marshal" (i.e., Hitler); however, the story is everything but documentary and concludes in a rather romantic vein: the "Marshal" is expelled from the country by the democratic powers, Schwejk happily finds his way back to his favorite saloon, and Lieutenant Lukáš finally gets his girlfriend Dora.

Brecht's polite but skeptical reaction, containing the most extensive comment he ever made on the Schwejk theme (10 June 1937), reveals once again that his and Piscator's views on the particular representation of political reality do not coincide. There is irony or perhaps poetic justice revealed in the fact that Brecht criticizes the film exposé in much the same vein in which Piscator had commented on the 1927 dramatization of Hašek's novel by Max Brod and Hans Reimann as unacceptable (S, I, 188 ff.): the subject matter (war) had not been dealt with seriously enough; the plot was not sufficiently political and revolutionary; Schwejk had not yet been characterized as a complex type but too much as an idiot of the usual kind appearing in comedies of military life. Piscator, while wanting to agree with Brecht's numerous suggestions, points out the difficult political situation in Paris and the compromises forced upon him. Wistfully he recalls the Berlin years when he did not have to bother about such considerations. While the project for the *Schwejk* film met with increasing difficulties, Piscator approached Brecht with plans for a new play. This play, *War and Peace*, he hoped to stage on a market place in the *Everyman* style. Again he asked Brecht about his suggestions with regard to the script: "Do you have any idea what such a play should look like? And would you be interested in tackling the matter? If I had a play, its performance in Belgium would not be difficult. But I don't have the play" (22 June 1937).

Considering the great importance which Piscator placed on Brecht's collaboration, it is regrettable that none of these ideas were carried out jointly. In general, Brecht showed interest in Piscator's many plans and, often enough, he offered specific assistance. But this interest is in no way substantive. Brecht must have realized that too many of Piscator's projects (which had also raised hopes in Helene Weigel for new roles) were too spontaneous and lacked the possibility of materialization. Besides, Brecht was occupied with his own projects. During his exile in Svendborg (1933-1939), where he worked with a team of close friends and associates and received inspiration from many guests, Brecht was extraordinarily productive. Furthermore, he had the opportunity to travel to London, Moscow, Paris, and New York in order to promote his professional interests. In Moscow and Paris he did meet with Piscator,[24] but there is no evidence of substantial development in any of the "joint" plans envisaged by the latter. Piscator never did visit Brecht in Svendborg, even though he was invited repeatedly. Piscator always received copies of Brecht's works and was informed about new performances of Brecht's plays in Copenhagen and in Paris; still, he seems to have felt somewhat neglected, particularly with regard to the performance of *The Threepenny Opera* in Paris. In a long letter (27 October 1937) he criticizes the production (prepared by Ernst Josef Aufricht), arguing that it was not at all adjusted to French conditions, and that the director, Francesco von Mendelssohn, was simply incompetent. Piscator also complains that Brecht had not informed him about his attempts to found an international theater troupe; but for some reason he did not mail this letter to Brecht. Their correspondence in 1938 reflects further joint plans (e.g., the staging of *Fear and Misery of the Third Reich*) for New York. But despite their continued contact in American exile the two men did not come closer to each other, neither personally nor geographically.

III. Exile in America

In 1939 Brecht retreated from Denmark to Sweden whereas Piscator, late in 1938, emigrated to the United States. His first letter to Brecht (3 March 1939) reflects a profound cultural shock; it shows his depression, his longing for their earlier time together, their language, their political struggle. Piscator's negative impressions about New York theater life, dominated by Stanislavsky and the box office, echo Brecht's own experiences expressed several years earlier in a letter to Piscator written from New York, where Brecht had tried to assist in the Theatre Union production of *The Mother*.[25] Referring to their Berlin years, Piscator remarks: "Our time, 1920-1930, appears to me like a massive block, an epoch, like something mythical—compared to this place here

---

[24] *Brecht-Chronik,* pp. 61-62; Reich, pp. 331-92.
[25] See Brecht's letter to Piscator (8 December 1935) concerning *The Mother,* reprinted in Eberhard Brüning, *Das amerikanische Drama der dreißiger Jahre* (Berlin, 1966), p. 61. In a letter dated July 1936, Brecht wrote Piscator: "I read Stanislavsky's 'my life in art' with jealousy and disquiet. That man has brought his system into order—consequently everyone in Paris and New York is a disciple of Stanislavsky . . . we really are romantic dreamers." For Brecht's continued concern with Stanislavsky, see his *Writings on Theater,* especially GW, XVI, 841-66.

[New York], where, after all, there is the liveliest theater excepting our [Brecht's and Piscator's] own." Yet, despite his apparent difficulties of adjustment, Piscator wants to found a "community of producers" (*Produktionsgemeinschaft*), mentions many other immigrants and common friends, and tries to persuade Brecht to come to the United States. In fact, he refers to a telegram that Brecht had sent in 1935 from New York to Piscator in Moscow, urging Piscator to take advantage of the professional opportunities in New York; Piscator now wonders why Brecht commits the same (i.e., Piscator's earlier) mistake by not coming (15 May 1939).

So far, little has become known about the extent of Piscator's assistance with regard to Brecht's immigration to the U.S.[26] As early as March 1939 Brecht had succeeded in having his name and the names of the members of his family placed on the American immigration quota list. During the long waiting period with its uncertainties about the "refugee papers" (*flüchtlingspapiere*) of Brecht's family, Piscator, who now resided in New York, was for Brecht not only one of the main sources of information about the American scene and about the activities of their joint friends there (such as Eisler, Grosz, Jessner, Toller, Kortner, Borchardt, Weill, Gorelik, Karin Michaelis, Zuckmayer, Viertel, Homolka), but he also offered practical assistance. In June 1939 he reported to Brecht that the New School for Social Research would set up an actors' workshop (*Schauspielschule*) for Piscator. "It is only an experiment, of course, but your presence here would have helped." Subsequently Piscator tried hard to get Brecht a position at the newly founded Dramatic Workshop, now under his direction. His motives were twofold: on the one hand, the offer of a job would speed up Brecht's immigration to the United States. On the other hand, he was eager to collaborate with Brecht, whose intellect and literary genius he greatly admired, and about whose activities and new works he had been kept informed, partly through Brecht himself or, more in detail, through Margarete Steffin and partly through mutual friends like Hanns Eisler. Brecht acknowledged Piscator's help most gratefully when he actually received an appointment (*lehrauftrag*) from the Dramatic Workshop. Having further retreated to Helsingfors, Brecht now was eager to leave Finland where he felt politically endangered and intellectually isolated. Repeatedly he expressed his expectation of working together with Piscator in the United States which he then considered to be one of the few countries where free literary work was still possible. When Brecht's departure was delayed, Piscator was able to provide for an extension of the contract with the Dramatic Workshop. But when Brecht attempted to obtain a visa for Margarete Steffin and suggested to Piscator that she, too, be appointed at the Dramatic

[26] Völker, who has had access to many private sources, mentions nothing about this in his recent *Brecht-Chronik*.

54

Workshop as Brecht's assistant, Piscator was unable to secure an additional position because of restricted funds.

In May 1941 Brecht finally received all the necessary immigration papers and left with his family, Margarete Steffin and Ruth Berlau for the United States. Had he been able to choose the Atlantic route, he would have disembarked in New York, and his American exile, including his affiliation with Piscator, might have taken a different turn. But as the Scandinavian ports were controlled by the Nazis, Brecht travelled via Moscow (where Margarete Steffin died of a lung disease), embarked in Vladivostok and entered the United States "comically" (*ulkigerweise*) at Los Angeles, where a colony of German emigrants had settled in nearby Santa Monica. Friends persuaded Brecht to stay, arguing that life in Los Angeles was cheaper and work—possibly in the Hollywood film industry—easier to obtain than in New York.[27] However, two weeks after his arrival Brecht indicated to Piscator his continued interest in working at the New School for Social Research if the School were willing to renew his contract which, in the meantime, had expired. He made concrete suggestions as to the activities envisaged; for a number of reasons he preferred seminar-type classes to theoretical lectures, and he proposed to work in the border area between dramatic structure (*dramenbau*) and acting style (*darstellungsstil*). He intended to remove some of the barriers between playwright and play director (*regisseur*), between play director and actor, between actor and rational man (*vernünftiger mensch*), etc., because the playwright usually is helpless vis-à-vis the theater, the actors are helpless vis-à-vis the playwright's dramaturgy, etc. As a start, Brecht proposed to experiment with suitable material he had brought along, e.g., the practice scenes for actors, from *Macbeth* and Schiller's *Mary Stuart* (GW, VII, 3003-3027), or scenes from *Fear and Misery of the Third Reich*. In short, Brecht planned to do exactly the kind of work that he was to undertake later (1949) at the East Berlin Theater am Schiffbauerdamm, work which brought world fame to the Berliner Ensemble. Curiously, Marlon Brando, Tony Curtis, Tennessee Williams and Arthur Miller, who are mentioned among Piscator's students and colleagues at the Dramatic Workshop,[28] might also have been trained or influenced by Brecht; one wonders whether American theater history might not look different today if Piscator and Brecht, once the two pioneering innovators of a "Berlin Dramaturgy," could have carried out their plans in New York.

But, like so many of their joint projects, this one did not materialize either. However, it is mistaken to state that while in the U.S. Piscator and Brecht did not have any contact or exchange of ideas (cf. L. Hoffmann; S, II, 359). Even though they were separated by the width of the American continent, Piscator continued to be interested in Brecht's

---

[27] *Brecht-Chronik*, p. 86; AJ, I, 290.
[28] *Erwin Piscator 1893-1966*, (Berlin, 1971), p. 39.

activities and wanted to have several of his plays performed in New York. As can be gathered from this correspondence, there emerged two problems: the difficulty of finding a good translator, and the question whether Brecht's plays were at all suitable for an American audience. These two concerns are already evident in Piscator's letters of 1939 regarding the first version of *Life of Galileo*. On the one hand, he praises the play highly: "Once again, I am full of admiration for the increasing clarity of constructive form, the spiritual-philosophical lucidity, the fantastic expressiveness of language, the power and beauty of logic and sound, the refreshing atmosphere of optimism, of faith in reason and progress without the narrow-minded sort of stupidity (*ohne Scheuklappen-Dämlichkeit*); in short: a real Brecht." On the other hand, Piscator expresses some reservations: "I am not sure as yet whether—in all due consideration of the epic form—certain things, especially in the second act, should not have led towards a more dramatic conclusion. If this were possible, the play would be better received in America. The views on theater here are antiquated; people want the good old drama—and one must oblige them (just as Galileo obliged the Pope)" (11 April 1939). It is noteworthy that the uncompromising promoter of the political epic drama of the twenties now, under the pressure of different circumstances, finds *Galileo* too epic (and not sufficiently dramatic) whereas Brecht himself considered *Galileo* one of his least epic plays and, technically, a regression toward Aristotelian (dramatic) principles.[29]

But despite his own apprehension and the opinion of Kortner and Eisler, both of whom liked *Galileo* but did not find the play suitable for Broadway, Piscator was eager to obtain a good English translation.[30] Thus, he endeavored to find a translator not only for this play (which Brecht together with Charles Laughton was to rework later in Santa Monica), but also for *The Good Woman of Setzuan*, *The Resistible Ascent of Arturo Ui* and for the old, joint *Schwejk* project, all of which he actually wanted to stage in New York in the early forties. In a letter to Eisler, Piscator hints that there is no money for a translation of *The Good Woman:* "The Theatre Guild cannot read German and doesn't want to commit itself without knowing the piece." Besides, Piscator finds the play (especially the first act) too long and asks Eisler for suggestions of how to make cuts "without stepping on the toes of our friend who is just about to arrive" (18 April 1941).

At the time, the translation of *The Good Woman* did not materialize, a fact which Piscator later regrets: "It was idiotic not to perform *The Good Woman of Setzuan* immediately" (October 1941). Yet Piscator does find a translator (Hofmann-Hays) for *Arturo Ui* and reports to

[29] AJ, I, 41; II, 747.
[30] According to a letter by Margarete Steffin (20 July 1939) Brecht had originally planned to entrust Ferdinand Reyher with the English translations of *Galileo* and *Furcht und Elend*.

Brecht that he will wait for his reaction and that of his (Piscator's) collaborators before deciding whether the play should be staged at once. He agrees with Brecht that Oskar Homolka would be eminently suited for the main role; in anticipation of Brecht's visit to New York, Piscator invites Brecht to stay at his home (23 September 1941). However, irritated by Brecht's failure to comment on the *Arturo Ui* translation right away, Piscator complains: "Why do you act against your own interests? Or does that have anything to do with epic theater? Or is your interest so tied up with the events in Moscow that you completely forget yourself? Please answer me and Hofmann-Hays immediately" (October 1941). A letter written a few months later still reflects the same kind of frustration on Piscator's part: "Dear Bert, please take a chair and a pencil and write out clearly, what is the matter with you. I simply don't understand the nature of our relationship. You are here in this country, I offer to stage your play, and then all comes to nothing. If we want to count on *The Good Woman of Setzuan* next year, then we must begin with the preparations now. If you plan to stage the play elsewhere, it would be nice and friendly of you to let me know. . . ." (21 January 1942).

It was not until late in 1942 that Brecht prepared to visit New York. In order to obtain the necessary travel papers he needed as an enemy alien he asked Piscator and Paul Czinner for formal invitations.[31] Piscator's reply (in English) still reflects resentment: "Dear Bert, Miss Berlau told me you needed a letter to come here to New York after Christmas. Is the enclosed letter alright? Otherwise, write me. In this case, I am sure, you will write. What do you need? As a matter of fact, I have a lot of things to discuss with you, which I think you will be interested in . . ." (1 December 1942). The formal invitation, attached to Piscator's letter, reads: "Dear Mr. Brecht, The Studio Theater considers your play *The Good Woman of Setzuan* for a performance in January, but it is necessary to have you here to discuss changes in the play and participate in a translation, which must be done to your satisfaction. The Dramatic Workshop is also preparing a lecture for you at the same time. The title is: 'What is the Theater Doing to Help Win the War?' This lecture has to be discussed also. Could you let me know as soon as possible when I may expect you? Sincerely yours, Erwin Piscator" (1 December 1942).

Whether Brecht actually gave such a lecture during his subsequent visit to New York is uncertain. But—as Völker reports—there was a Brecht evening in the Studio Theater of the New School for Social Research on 6 March.[32] Ruth Berlau confirmed that Brecht repeatedly met with Piscator for animated discussions. One of their topics—Schwejk—was soon to lead to Piscator's deep estrangement

[31] *Brecht-Chronik*, p. 98.
[32] Ibid., p. 99.

from Brecht. Ever since their collaboration on the famous 1928 production of *Adventures of the Good Soldier Schwejk* (during World War I), both Piscator and Brecht had repeatedly planned to rework the theme for an anti-Fascist play or film, and now they discussed the possibility of staging an updated *Schweyk in World War II*.[33] We know that during his stay in New York Brecht wrote a new plot outline for *Schweyk*, reread Hašek's novel on his return trip from New York to Los Angeles, and started to work on his own *Schweyk* version immediately upon his arrival in Santa Monica; however, there are conflicting reports as to who or what persuaded him to do so. Ernst Josef Aufricht, who together with Brecht and Weill had so successfully produced *The Threepenny Opera* in Berlin in 1928, claims that since Kurt Weill needed a subject for a Broadway musical, he [Aufricht] suggested that Brecht and Weill collaborate on a new version of *Schwejk*.[34] Brecht's entry in his diary seems to confirm Aufricht's story.[35] But Piscator almost exploded with wrath. He had made several attempts to repeat the success of the Berlin performance of *Schwejk* in New York and had asked Alfred Kreymborg to write an English version of *Schwejk*. (Actually, Kreymborg later did translate Brecht's version.) Since he had discussed his new *Schwejk* plans with Brecht, Piscator came to the conclusion that Brecht had betrayed him, taken the idea from him, and stolen the march on him with a new version of *Schweyk in World War II*.

Quite apart from the fact that the planned Brecht-Weill-Aufricht Broadway production of *Schweyk in World War II* never materialized, Piscator's keen disappointment about Brecht is noteworthy in that it tainted whatever he subsequently had to say about him. As can be easily gathered from Piscator's correspondence, he had an impulsive, self-righteous temper which once caused Hanns Eisler to remark: "You have a special gift for writing heated letters" (1 December 1936). Piscator's most scathing letter addressed to Brecht (14 August 1941), but fortunately not mailed in that form, recounts how they greeted each other in New York as emigrants and friends, and how Brecht then later disappeared without saying good-bye. "The explanation is soon at hand: a cowardly, unscrupulous fraud—a disgusting behavior which can be properly termed only as: Brechtian disgusting behavior (*Brechtsche Schweinerei*)." Piscator argues that surely Brecht could not excuse his behavior by "conditions"; for if a great mind must depend on such methods—how then is the little man to act? by means of robbery and murder? Piscator concludes that whatever is positive in Brecht's works becomes a lie by his very actions; he pities Brecht for having to stray so far from the principles he himself proclaims: "That isn't class struggle

---

[33] For further details, see the comments in my edition of *Schweyk-Materialien* (cf. n. 9).
[34] Ernst Josef Aufricht, *Erzähle, damit du dein Recht erweist* (Berlin, 1966), p. 256.
[35] AJ, II, 568.

or race struggle any longer—that is fratricide, theft from the open pocket of your host and friend."

Over a month later Piscator sent identical letters, far more moderate in tone, to Brecht, Aufricht, Weill, and Kreymborg, advising them that he "owned the rights to *The Good Soldier Schwejk*" and that he would take legal action if they proceeded without him. Soon after Brecht had completed the plot outline (GW, XVII, 1186-1196) or possibly a first draft of the play in the spring of 1943, Piscator must have gained access to a copy. It is interesting to observe that his criticism of the text is now much more severe than it was earlier regarding other plays by Brecht. Considering Piscator's stake in the history of *Schweyk* it is of course understandable that he tended to compare the new version with the famous Berlin performance of 1928 or with his own ideas as reflected in the 1938 film script. Piscator finds the first scene far too long, too garrulous, without action. He misses the episode in which Schweyk is drafted to the military, and he does not think that Baloun's voraciousness is sufficient motivation for the play. He criticizes that Baloun has, in fact, become the main character and that Schweyk is relegated to the background. He objects that the opposing forces (*Gegenkräfte*)—by which he seems to mean the established powers—play a minor role both in comparison to the original and in view of the present political situation. From the outset Schweyk appears to him to be "superior" to everyone else including Brettschneider and the Nazi functionary (*Scharführer*); it would have been better to show him as the underdog finding a way out. Piscator observes that the new play is neither Brecht nor Hašek: it lacks Hašek's Dadaist carelessness, formlessness, anarchy; it further lacks the constructive epic idea that one might expect from Brecht. The many vulgar expressions like "shit" and "piss" would be highly offensive to the Puritan taste of American audiences; Piscator adds that many of the similes and stories are failures (*nicht geglückt*). He concludes that the format of the Berlin performance (*die Berliner Form*) should have been chosen even if Grosz[36] were not available. The scenes should have been shortened, placed on the "conveyor belt" or turn table stage (*Drehbühne*), etc. Some of Piscator's handwritten remarks are hard to decipher, but it is obvious that he wholeheartedly disapproves of Brecht's play on somewhat dubious grounds.

There is no evidence that during Brecht's next extended visit to New York[37] the strained relations between the two men were in any way improved. On the contrary, the fact that Brecht now negotiated with Weill (who had had success on Broadway) rather than with Piscator about

[36] George Grosz, who with his satirical drawings and stage designs had greatly contributed to the success of the Berlin *Schwejk* production, had emigrated to the United States (New York) as early as 1932. Both Piscator and Brecht were in contact with him during their American exile.

[37] *Brecht-Chronik,* pp. 105-106.

The Good Woman of Setzuan and *The Caucasian Chalk Circle* probably only added to the estrangement. However, despite the Schweyk affair which Piscator was unable to forget, there was one more attempt at a collaboration in the United States—which once again led to insurmountable differences. In March 1945, when Berthold Viertel expressed his interest in staging *Fear and Misery of the Third Reich*—which had been translated by Eric Bentley and renamed *The Private Life of the Master Race*—Brecht apparently was uncertain as to whether the time was right for a performance of this play.[38] However, in May of the same year or earlier, Brecht agreed to a New York staging of *The Private Life* under Piscator's direction. On 29 May, less than two weeks before the scheduled opening performance, a frustrated Piscator turned down the job in a letter dictated in English because he and Brecht (who had just arrived in New York) could not come to terms: "Unfortunately, I cannot permit myself the luxury of an artistic failure . . . when I direct, I need the time for myself without your co-directing. And when you direct, you need the time without me. For my part I have conceived a different physical performance from yours, and we have greater difficulties in following your version, enough so that I suggest that you take over the direction and I withdraw." Brecht consequently turned the production over to Berthold Viertel, who apparently understood Brecht's intentions better than Piscator. In one week of concentrated work with day and night rehearsals, Viertel—assisted by Brecht—prepared the performance which opened on 12 June. As Brecht noted, "the press attacks the production but spares the piece. However, nowhere does it come to a discussion of the content."[39]

Not only the press attacked the production. In a long letter, dated 15 June 1945 and written in English, Piscator severely reprimanded Brecht, starting off with: "Dear Bert. At different moments the other evening I wanted to jump over the footlights, come back stage, and beat you." On the factual side, too, the letter is an interesting document, because it illustrates specific details of the production style on which Brecht's and Piscator's views differed. For example, Piscator claims that it was silly to render the "scene with the judge"[40] static and lifeless from the beginning—the judge simply sitting behind his desk; "the scene only starts to live in the last few moments when the judge gets up, and by his bewildered behavior creates in an instant the atmosphere you needed from the beginning. Had you opened the scene thus, it would have been tremendously successful. This alone proves how little you understand about the theater as far as staging goes: in *writing* it, you wrote it in such a way that every intelligent director was given an opportunity to stage it in this way. But the foolish, misleading intellectualism on your part

[38] *Brecht-Chronik*, p. 111.
[39] Ibid., p. 113.
[40] This apparently refers to scene vi: *In Search of Justice* (GW, III, 1103-1120).

steered it another way." Commenting on the scene *The Chalk Cross*,[41] Piscator criticizes that Brecht's sustained breadline [sic] generalizes the story, whereas in Piscator's opinion every episode should have been singled out and understood as such. "You did here what every amateur does—when he likes one bit of business, he expands it far beyond the limit of its potentialities." The Staircase and Box scenes[42] Piscator would have wanted to use as stepping stones to other scenes, not as short, realistic components between scenes: "When I formulated the Staircase scene—strong, almost stylized—I wanted to set the tone of the play; not keep repeating it, but have the following scenes develop and grow into a project. I wanted to stage the Box scene monumentally." But, Piscator continues, Brecht's staging of the scene was conclusive proof "that you had not an idea of an epic play as you put the scenes together, but in your mind it was nothing but un-epic, disconnected, disunified—a series of coincidental scenes written one after another and laid side by side." After an excursion on Brecht's "impertinent" personal behavior, Piscator gives further examples of Brecht's incompetency as a director: "How you used the speaker, how you used this S.A. group which never seemed to be able to convince us which side they were on—the torturers or the tortured [sic]; that buckles on a uniform should be placed in the center of the belt, instead of right or left or behind; that Nazi helmets don't have the tilt of a longshoreman's cap; . . . that they slithered with undulating movements as they marched toward their places—all these things are quite ridiculous. I would erase such blotches in five minutes." Piscator claims that he would have staged "sense" whereas Brecht staged "nonsense." In short: "The staging, stage design, scenery, and lighting were killing. . . ." Piscator assures Brecht that he writes all this not to hurt him but "to prepare an understanding"; he claims that as long as the playwrights dominate the theater, the theater as an institution will remain mediocre; the art of directing and of acting are just as important as the art of playwriting, and these arts must be unified in "a more spiritual theater"; after all this, Piscator concludes that together they could have achieved something which would have been more satisfactory to both Brecht and to him personally.

Although Brecht returned to New York in the fall of 1946, there seems to be no evidence of renewed contact between him and Piscator. However, early in 1947, Brecht—apparently undisturbed by Piscator's previous attacks—inquires what he thinks about doing theater work (*theatermachen*) in Berlin. Since the end of the war Brecht had repeatedly been asked to agree to performances of his plays in Germany. But because of the lack of suitable actors and of the "terrible ac-

[41] Scene iii (GW, III, 1079-1096).
[42] Possibly a reference to scenes xiv: *The Box,* and xi: *Winter Relief* (GW, III, 1153-54, 1159-61). However, inasmuch as the stage manuscript differed from the printed version in GW, this identification may not be entirely correct.

ting style" then current in Europe, Brecht had refused to give his permission—always with a view to returning to Germany himself, despite the depressing news that came from the post-War German scene. In discussing his possible visit to Berlin, Brecht had also raised the question of Piscator's return, without whom—so he writes—he could not imagine to carry on the fight against provincialism and empty emotionalism, and to work towards a great, politically mature theater. It was not his idea, Brecht adds, that they should start one theater together—even though he would continue to be available for almost any joint project; rather, they should work from two points (*man müßte zumindest von zwei punkten aus arbeiten*). If Piscator were interested, then they should work out a plan together and send it to Berlin (February 1947).

Piscator's reply, which was not available to me, must have contained reservations or objections; for in March 1947 Brecht wrote Piscator again, assuring him that of all the people who in the last twenty years had done theater work, none had been as close to him as Piscator. This statement was not contradicted by his plan to establish two theaters in Berlin; as Brecht explains, they would need two bases (*punkte*) to establish their joint (*gemeinsame*) ideas. The fact that for some of his theater work Brecht needed an acting style different from that of Piscator was the only reservation on Brecht's part—but he considers that a "productive" difference. He argues that Piscator certainly could not believe in a mechanical separation of playwright and director (*inszenator*). By having two theaters, they would still work along the same lines and enjoy the same opposition (*widerstände*). As if to appease Piscator, Brecht then proposed an Aristophanic revue (dealing with the return of the god of war, Ares) which they could best realize together. He invites Piscator to offer his own suggestions to be incorporated in a concrete plan, including the invitation of a sufficient number of emigrants (such as Rewalt, Roth, Neumann, Donath, Haas) to launch new endeavors in Berlin.

Piscator's reaction to this renewed invitation once again reveals his inclination to view the differences between Brecht and himself far less "productively" than Brecht did. On the one hand, Piscator expressed his conviction that he, too, had found no other author so far who had come closer to his own ideas of theater. But, Piscator regrets, it was precisely because he did not believe in the difference between author and director that Brecht and he could never really work together very closely. "That is why I was so disappointed with *The Private Life;* and that is why I wrote you about one theater and not two . . . for we all suffer from a disunion concerning matters of art (*künstlerische Zersplitterung*) which can only be resolved when not a foot of room is left which allows differences to creep in" (*wenn kein Fuß breit Platz mehr gelassen ist, in den sich Andersgeartetes hineindrängen kann*). Piscator claims that both of them could have profited more, if in Berlin during the twenties they had known each other better and thus been able to better serve each other's work. Quoting a letter from Friedrich Wolf, who condemned the post-War political conditions in Germany, Piscator on the one hand hints at his own qualms about returning there; on the other he indicates that he himself might soon be invited by the Volksbühne in Berlin. Whereas he finds Brecht's idea for the new "Ares" play excellent and inquires about his next trip to New York and his departure for Europe, Piscator's letter (29 March 1947) remains noncommittal and vague on the whole.

It is likely that Brecht saw Piscator in October 1947 in New York, where he stopped over on his way back to Europe after he had defended himself, one day before his departure, before the Committee on Un-American Activities in Washington. But while Brecht was never to set foot on the United States again, Piscator stayed in New York for another four years. He continued to express his interest in staging *The Good Woman of Setzuan, Mother Courage,* and *The Threepenny Opera* in New York; however, none of these projects came to fruition.

Then, early in 1949, Brecht reported to Piscator in two unusually long letters about his experiences in Berlin, hoping to persuade him to come for a visit, direct a play at the Theater am Schiffbauerdamm and examine the general situation. Brecht finds it both necessary and feasible to revive theater in Berlin. Even though there were few actors and almost no directors (*Regie fast gar keine*), he considered everything to be on a higher level than in New York. Trying to dissipate Piscator's apprehensions, Brecht emphasized that the audience as well as various military representatives come from *all* sectors in Berlin to see his *Mother Courage;* that the press in both parts of Germany had reacted favorably; that everything was peaceful in Berlin; that there were no transit difficulties; and that Piscator would be received very warmly. Brecht thought that the time was ripe: everything was still in flux (*im Fluß*), and new directions could be given by important people present (*die vorhandenen Potenzen*). But even though Brecht assured Piscator that once in Berlin he neither needed to feel committed nor was expected to make public statements, Piscator did not follow Brecht's repeated invitations.

IV. Back in Germany

Not until 1951 did Piscator return to West Germany. For the next ten years he directed plays in several cities, including West Berlin, where in 1962, six years after Brecht's death, he became director at the Freie Volksbühne. For the period 1951-1956 there does not seem to exist any noteworthy correspondence between Brecht and Piscator. No doubt, they met and exchanged political and professional views, but there is no immediate evidence of joint plans about which they had talked so often in the years of emigration, and for which their return to Germany, albeit divided, would have provided a unique opportunity, especially during the years 1955-1956 when both were in Berlin. It is all the more surprising therefore to observe that in his diaries and notes of the fifties, Piscator constantly took issue with Brecht, the man and the playwright.[43] On the one hand, he witnessed Brecht's rising fame, saw plays by him performed on several occasions and felt impelled to comment on them in long critical notes; on the other hand, he could not rid himself of the personal differences with Brecht that haunted his memory, leading him repeatedly and almost obsessively to accusations and self-justifications.

Only a few excerpts can be quoted here from the bulk of notes which—in part at least—Piscator apparently planned to turn into another book, if not together *with* Brecht (who had already digested Piscator's ideas and experiments in his own writings) then certainly *about* Brecht and himself. From one undated entry, "Brecht—cf. Cuckoo's Egg," one may easily gather in which roles he continued to cast himself and his more famous contemporary. "Nowhere does Brecht mention me," Piscator complains in 1955, "and yet: in everything he does there is part of me—witness his two letters to me" (D, XV, 24). Piscator is overjoyed when John Heartfield tells him that Brecht, disagreeing with Ernst Schumacher's book,[44] called Piscator his [Brecht's] teacher; but he adds: "never is this mentioned publicly." He indicates that in a special chapter of his contemplated book he wanted to prove point by point where Brecht got his ideas, for example: Schweyk's anabasis, Mother Courage's wandering on the turning stage, the masks in *The Caucasian Chalk Circle,* the whole idea of the "epic" which Brecht adopted as a name, but which Piscator had actually practiced "ever since Kliem's festival halls" (D, XV, 33).[45]

Apart from Piscator's repeated claims that Brecht had surreptitiously taken possession of his "heritage" (which, even in Piscator's own examples, amounts to nothing more than certain stage techniques), the diaries also contain detailed critiques which are especially interesting in that they point to the differences between Brecht and Piscator time and again. Commenting, for instance, on the performance of *The Caucasian Chalk Circle* by the Berliner Ensemble in 1954, Piscator observes that Brecht's style is not purely Brechtian, that it contains—besides Piscator—also elements of the Jiddish theater of Granovsky and

[43] This survey has, I think, made clear that Ludwig Hoffmann, the editor of Piscator's *Schriften,* is wrong when he states: "Unfortunately Piscator did only occasionally—and then only with a certain shyness—discuss similarities and differences between his conception and Brecht's theory. . . . with certainty we can assume that there are no extensive notes for a *Politisches Theater 2*" (S, II, 359-60).

[44] Ernst Schumacher, *Die dramatischen Versuche Bertolt Brechts 1918-1933* (Berlin, 1955), took a negative view of Piscator's "originality."

[45] "Kliems Festsäle" in Berlin-Neukölln were among the many localities in which Piscator's "Proletarian Theater" performed plays in 1920-1921 (S, I, 40).—Only a limited amount of this material (or of these views) has gone into volume II of Piscator's *Schriften* where occasional references to Brecht occur rather unsystematically.

elements of Meyerhold. Piscator dislikes the music ("second-rate opera à la Eisler and Weill") because it does not clarify anything but is confusing, and because it does not develop the action but interrupts it, thereby gaining an obnoxious independence without value. Before the actor Busch enters the stage, the play is "artificial, forced, farfetched." Nobody laughed, even though there were good Brechtian jokes and the audience seemed to be quite intelligent. In Piscator's opinion it is simply "old beard theater" (*altes Bart-Theater*), exaggerated make-up, nonfactual; not "estrangement" but simply repulsively "strange" (*nicht Verfremdung—sondern nur fremd bis zum Abstoßen*). Sometimes it is wild, unrestrained "character theater" à la Stanislavsky—"beards, beards, panting, fussy affectation, typification." Piscator cannot get over the fact that Busch has to wear three beards and a false bald head—considering that he was, after all, a human being—nor does he understand why the other characters have to be so "ugly." Something must be wrong with the principle of the performance (D, XV, 24). The structure, too, appears to him forced and unconvincing, for if the final verdict of the chalk circle scene (which, in Piscator's opinion, "is not the last and absolute decision since the mother is not really the mother") turned out differently, the structure would still remain unchanged. And so Piscator concludes that the moral is a lie and that *The Caucasian Chalk Circle* is Brecht's weakest play. He cannot agree with the simplified formula: the poor are good and the rich are evil; for, he argues, we have learned that the opposite is true: bad traits, especially evil in man, is a result of circumstances, hence man improves if circumstances improve. Brecht's play would seem to show that all of us are false, that we only need to become "poor" in order to become "good." Or did Brecht mean to say: Unfortunately people—including the poor—have not yet come far enough in order to make the noble world of Communism a reality? At this point Piscator actually begins to ponder what East Germany might have gained in the past ten years (since 1945) if he, Piscator, had been brought back to Berlin by the Government of the German Democratic Republic (D, XV, 28). Apparently he had forgotten that in 1949 Brecht had tried to persuade him to return.

A brief reference to one more example of Piscator's critiques from this period may suffice to show that there is a certain pattern in his attitude towards Brecht's plays. Mother Courage he calls a "female Schweyk," i.e., again he sees his own influence at work. "It is the anabasis of Schweyk, but expanded into lengthy hours," he observes. "The idea is marvelous, but the performance is drawn out and expansive, and the music actually is a hindrance and produces false opera; 'estrangement' really leads to bad acting and to the worst kind of dilettantism—and all the characters are so ugly, dirty, and tactless (kiss my ass, says a young soldier to Mother Courage—not just once as in our famous monologue in *Rasputin,* but many times, at suitable and unsuitable occasions)" (D, XV, 35). At another place he calls *Mother*

Courage a "play with many corpses—sometimes very silly, and dramaturgically half-finished . . . basically a sentimental piece" (D, XXI, 139).

These and many similar examples only confirm an obvious paradox: On the one hand, Piscator sees in Brecht a disciple who betrayed him, and on the other as someone who considerably differs from him and who thus does not really fit the role of disciple. In particular, they show that Piscator acknowledges as "epic elements" only those innovative stage techniques which Brecht supposedly borrowed from him, and that he completely misunderstands or disapproves of Brecht's practice of "estrangement" which is at the core of Brecht's own notion of the "epic theater" (or, as he would later call it, "dialectic theater"). These elements do not only pertain to certain stage techniques but also to the presentation of the plot, the play's structure, the style of performance, and even its poetic language. It is precisely this central technique of "estrangement" that made Piscator call Brecht a non-realist, a romantic, who fell back into practicing a poetic theater of illusion. He believed that Brecht turned towards "estrangement" because of the artist's fear of the politician's tendency to oversimplify. In this context, Piscator recalled that once in New York Brecht had accused him of such simplification and had disagreed with his staging techniques. But, as Piscator argued, Brecht himself did not have a solution either: "what nonsense if Schumacher writes there are developments; no—both of us were searching, and his estrangement of the subject, i.e., his method to project our problems into other countries and times simply doesn't work, and he knew that."[46] If in the forties Piscator had claimed that Brecht's theories fitted his (Piscator's) performances much better than Brecht's own plays,[47] he now states, in the fifties, that even though they had chosen similar paths, they had achieved different results, of which Piscator's—and not Brecht's—were pointing towards the future (D, XV, 99).

Brecht's sudden death in August 1956 brought into focus the contradictions, the self-torture, the love-hate which Piscator had expressed in the course of many years in numerous notes on Brecht, the man and his work. In his usual sketchy diary style—brief, sometimes disconnected and incomplete statements, occasional longer excursions, interspersed poems—Piscator reflects on the radio announcement of Brecht's death. The melody from "Mac the Knife" leads him to muse on Weill and Brecht, their erstwhile collaboration in Berlin, and the way in

---

[46] Quoted from an undated and unnumbered typewritten page from the materials in the Erwin Piscator Center, Akademie der Künste, West Berlin.

[47] "There is an incredible amount of practical material that is based on *my* work. Whenever I read Brecht's notes to his plays, I notice that the examples chosen by him correspond much more to the plays directed by me than to those authored by him." (From an undated miscellaneous note in a folder containing material from Piscator's American exile; Morris Library, Southern Illinois University).

which they later took advantage of each other and how both in turn used Piscator. The key word "Schweyk" once again throws Piscator into a turmoil of feelings: Brecht's death had only deepened the gap that had proved an insurmountable obstacle for any reconciliation. Piscator tries to ignore his personal feelings and to look objectively at Brecht's achievement—but again he is compelled to see him as the thief. Assuming a rare attitude of melancholic humor, Piscator exclaims: "And again he has stolen the march on me, even in death! He will already be playing epic theater in heaven—with the best ensemble—by the time I arrive there" (D, 16 August 1956).

Johannes R. Becher's telegram inviting him to attend the state ceremony in Brecht's honor in the Theater am Schiffbauerdamm raises conflicts in Piscator; he finds it peculiar that he receives his first official invitation on occasion of Brecht's death.[48] As if recreating a contrastive device of epic theater to obtain a comprehensive picture, Piscator weighs his decision by juxtaposing different perspectives:

shall I	shall I not
brother in spirit	not always a good one
gave help, nonetheless	when I was unsuccessful
	when I had success, he was far away
he stood to the cause	but never became a party member
a great poet	skeptical and romantic
simple, beautiful, best culture of language	
discovered "epic theater"	the word—after he saw its fundamental application in my theater
But he was able to develop the theory and write plays	too formal
then he was the "greater" one after all	
He was the only one who, through his art, succeeded to represent the unified Germany during its division. He has become influential across all borders. His plays are also performed in the West—one can only appreciate him.	

---

[48] Only in 1956 did Piscator become a member of the Deutsche Akademie der Künste in East Berlin (*Erwin Piscator 1893-1966*, p. 3).

But even after Brecht's death Piscator's comments on Brecht did not cease. In various archives there still exist hundreds of unpublished pages in which again and again Piscator takes issue with Brecht, the "beloved culprit" (*der geliebte Verbrecher;* D, XXI, 23) and with epic theater. He also ponders his own staging of *Mother Courage* and the dramatized version of *Conversations of Refugees,* which took place after Brecht's death, compares their respective works and reviews the unhappy history of their mutual relations. However, Brecht's death reminded Piscator, among other things, of the relativity and limitations of all professional ambitions and personal jealousies. The lines quoted above, which Piscator wrote on this occasion, may best serve to conclude our preliminary survey; for they culminate not only in an honest praise of Brecht, the artist, but they also honor Piscator, the man.

PART II

BRECHT'S *DRUMS,* A DOG, AND BECKETT'S *GODOT**

Hans Mayer

I

Ein Hund ging in die Küche
Und stahl dem Koch ein Ei
Da nahm der Koch sein Hackebeil
Und schlug den Hund entzwei.

Da kamen die andern Hunde
Und gruben dem Hund das Grab
Und setzten ihm einen Grabstein
Der folgende Inschrift hat:
Ein Hund ging in die Küche . . .
(Brecht, *Drums in the Night;* GW, I, 112-13)

      *   *

Un chien vint dans l'office
Et prit une andouillette.
Alors à coups de louche
Le chef le mit en miettes.

Les autres chiens ce voyant
Vite vite l'ensevelirent
Au pied d'une croix en bois blanc
Où le passant pouvait lire:
Un chien vint dans l'office. . . .
(Beckett, *En attendant Godot,* Act II)

A dog came in the kitchen
And stole a crust of bread.
The cook picked up a ladle
And beat him till he was dead.

Then all the dogs came running
And dug the dog a tomb
And wrote upon the tombstone
For the eyes of dogs to come:
A dog came in the kitchen. . . .
(Beckett, *Waiting for Godot,* Act II)

II

Every child in Germany knows the roundelay about the unfortunate fate of the dog who went into the kitchen and stole an egg from the cook. You can repeat it endlessly, and children love this because their aesthetic principle obeys an impulse to repeat things, not an impulse to create things eternally anew. Moreover, children are not disturbed by the light touch of obscenity in the horror story, whereas Brecht made conscious use of it: the stolen *Ei* ("egg") means much more than the simple product of a hen and rooster in German.

This story haunted Brecht his entire life. In the first version of *Drums in the Night* (Munich, 1923) the dog is already present in the text. To be sure, it is merely a brief play on words and recalls a story that is quite well-known. Kragler does not sing the ballad about the cook and the

*Translated by Jack Zipes. The translation is based on a slightly revised version of Hans Mayer, "Brecht, Beckett und ein Hund," TH, 13/6 (June 1972), 25-27.

dog but simply cites it in conversation with Glubb in the gin mill: "The cook picked up his chopper and chopped the dog in two."

It is no secret that Brecht loved to hear and recite popular stories filled with blood and sex. He also derived a great deal of pleasure from hearing about surprisingly harsh judgments which were meted out for disorderly conduct in an authoritarian society. During the period in which I knew him, he told me a certain story two times, and both times he laughed heartily at the end of the story: A father takes a walk with his small son. He places the child on a fairly high wall and demands that he jump down. The child is afraid, but the father calms him down. "I'm your father. You can trust me. I'll catch you. Nothing will happen." So, the small boy jumps, and the father lets him fall to the ground where he lies crying. Whereupon the father warns him: "That's so you'll never let yourself depend on anyone." Then Brecht laughed and laughed.

This could actually be Judge Azdak talking in *The Good Woman of Setzuan* or the worker Kalle. In *Conversations of Refugees,* Kalle reports about the teacher Herrnreitter who instructs the children of poor people that one cannot afford to have bad luck in life. Much later Brecht returned to the dog and the egg and the tombstone in the essay "Practice Scenes for Actors."[1] And the Berliner Ensemble appropriately included this horror ballad, which revolves around the same point and continually returns to the comically gruesome beginning, in its production of *The Purchase of Brass.*

In March 1954, Brecht finally allowed his early dramas to be reprinted, and he contributed a preface entitled "On Looking Through My First Plays," which revealed his distance from the early texts and also had a distancing effect. In this essay he expressed special irritation about his re-encounter with *Drums in the Night:* "In *Drums in the Night* the soldier Kragler gets his woman back, even though she is 'damaged,' and he turns his back on the revolution. This appears to be just about the shabbiest of all possible alternatives, especially since there is still a faint hint of approval on the part of the playwright" (GW, XVII, 945).

As a result, Brecht attempted to eliminate the political "shabbiness" of the original text by carefully retouching it. Kragler's proletarian counterpart, the nephew of the gin mill owner Glubb, who is merely mentioned and never appears, is nevertheless alluded to, and thus becomes the alternative to the petit bourgeois misery of Kragler and his kind. Aside from this, Brecht is more thoroughgoing as an adapter in Act IV of this new version where the dog originally appeared in a short quotation. Now, Kragler, drunk and malicious, sings the entire lamentable story through to the eternal repetition. In doing so, he demonstrates his petit bourgeois and fatalistic viewpoint—just as his author and adapter would have it.

When Brecht began work on the new version of his early drama, most

[1] SzT, V, 208. Cf. also GW, XV, 424.

likely during 1953, Samuel Beckett's *Waiting for Godot* was already extant. In fact, the German translation by Elmar Tophoven had been published, and Brecht had read it. An edition of the Beckett play with textual changes in Brecht's handwriting was discovered in his posthumous papers.[2] Originally Brecht had hoped to adapt the play by Beckett for himself and possibly for a production at the Berliner Ensemble. The notes and rough drafts allow us to see the direction that the adaptation was to take—toward social concreteness. The sham abstraction of the clowns in Beckett's play displeased the Marxist *Dramaturg* Brecht. He makes an "intellectual" out of Vladimir and a "proletarian" out of Estragon so that the play would have reverted to the Brechtian *Conversations of Refugees* between the proletarian Kalle and the intellectual Ziffel. The relationship between the master and his servant was also placed more exactly in its proper sociological context. Lucky was to be an "ass or policeman," while Brecht thought he could make an aristocratic landowner out of Pozzo, hence a new Herr Puntila.

As a consequence, the plans for a Beckett adaptation would have basically found their own natural ending. This projected reutilization (*Umfunktionierung*) of Beckett would not have produced anything new for Brecht, merely a repetition of *Herr Puntila* and *Conversations of Refugees*. However, in his attempt to adapt Beckett, Brecht once again came across his favorite story of the dog and the cook at the beginning of Act II; except this time he encountered it from the perspective of "negative infinity," to use Hegel's words. Didi is waiting for Gogo and tries hard to remember the story. Beckett took great pains to record this children's ditty as accurately as possible, first in the French version and then in his own English version. In the original French text, the sausage (*l'andouilette*) still suggests the obscene word play of the *Ei* in German. The English version has apparently abandoned this association.

It is evident that Beckett was familiar with the story about the dog and was not introduced to it by Brecht. On the other hand, Brecht was probably drawn to the dog, the cook, and the repetition once again as he *simultaneously* began adapting his own early dramas and Beckett's play. Of course, this cannot be proven, and on the surface it would seem to have significance only for philologists that Brecht was influenced by Beckett to include the entire children's song in his new version of *Drums in the Night* where it had originally been used only as a quotation and a fragment of memory. Yet, there is more to this than meets the eye.

Brecht was aware of the potential and meaning of the ballad from the very beginning. However, it was probably Beckett's conscious, metaphysical use of it that caused Brecht to adopt the same story with all its metaphysics and to use it for presenting a new interpretation of Andreas Kragler—as extreme alienation. If one compares the two plays,

[2] For details, cf. Werner Hecht, *Aufsätze über Brecht* (Berlin, 1970). pp. 118 ff.

Godot and the final version of *Drums in the Night,* from such a vantage point, then the dog becomes an important symbol in both cases. In fact, thanks to the dog, we can more readily gain insight into the differences of the dramaturgy of Beckett and the late Brecht.

III

The story of the dog and his tombstone assumes an aspect of eternal progress, for the story happens, then is reported on the tombstone in order to be continually and eternally presented as the report of a report, etc. The infinity here is also purely quantitative. In the first part of his *Science of Logics,* which is concerned with objective logics, Hegel makes the following remark: "Progress is consequently not a going away and going further but a repetition of rhymes and the like; positing, suspending, and positing again; this is the impotency of the negative which in its suspending allows for the return of that which is suspended as something continual."

Hegel consistently returned to this later in his *System of Philosophy* and consciously gave a sarcastic explanation about why one could not sense any emotion with such a form of infinity—an observation which, of course, was intended as an opposition to Kant. Indeed, after the first reading of the inscription on the tombstone, we know the story and are not disposed to continue presenting it eternally as a ballad. Hegel also explains why this is the case: "This much is now certainly correct, that we finally let it stay as it is, that we allow it to keep the same perspective and move forward continually, however, not because of the *sublime,* but because of the boredom of this business" (*System of Philosophy,* §94).

IV

Just how drastic the changes in Act IV of *Drums in the Night* were meant to be is revealed by the new title Brecht gave to it when he reworked it. In the original it is entitled *The Booze Dance.* Now the title is (*A Dawn Will Come*),· a quotation from the "Ballad of the Dead Soldier." The soft tones of a utopian melody are heard. But the quotation is placed between parentheses, and the dramaturgical arrangement is correspondingly changed. Brecht now works with the tried and tested instrument of the estrangement technique (*Ver-fremdungstechnik*) which he expressly regretted not having used in the original version of the play.

Of course, the original version of the play already contained elements of the parody of language. Brecht as Wagnerian and anti-Wagnerian set the language melodies in sharp contrast to one another at the very beginning of this play which was supposed to have the motto "Don't gape so romantically!" However, it was not until the new version was completed that the ideological contrasts were expressed by three different song-forms. Once this is understood, the ideological as well as the dramaturgical meaning of the ballad concerning the dog and the cook becomes more evident.

The original version stated: "The action takes place during a night in November, from the evening to dawn of the next day," i.e., during the November Revolution of 1918. In contrast, the new version sets the action in January 1919, in other words, at the time when Karl Liebknecht and Rosa Luxemburg were murdered. To be sure, Brecht kept the original reference to the time of the action in the adaptation without worrying about it. But now the drunk sings:

Meine Brüder, die sind tot	All my brothers now are dead,
Und ich selbst wär's um ein Haar	I came through, I don't know how.
Im November war ich rot	In November I was Red,
Aber jetzt ist Januar. (GW, I, 112)	But it's January now. (CP, I, 96)

Three contrasting positions, three monologues and confessions in song. The gin mill owner Glubb sympathizes with the Spartacists and the Revolution. His nephew evidently sides with Liebknecht and Rosa Luxemburg. Glubb sings—Brecht had already indicated this in the original version—the "Ballad of the Dead Soldier." In other words, he sings Brecht, and, accordingly, the following lines:

Die Sterne sind nicht immer da	The stars won't always be up there.
Es kommt ein Morgenrot.	The dawn is turning red.
Doch der Soldat, so wie er's gelernt	But the soldier goes off to a hero's death
Zieht in den Heldentod. (GW, VIII, 259)	just like the handbook said. (CP, I, 371)

The drunk was evidently a man of the Revolution in November 1918. But now he has withdrawn. Glubb seems to despise him. Perhaps the drunkenness is related to an inner wound which at one time had meant solidarity. However, now he no longer wants that. We see here the breaking asunder of the private and public spheres.

The third position is assumed by Andreas Kragler. His lyrical leit-motif—the ballad about the dead dog in contrast to Glubb's ballad about the dead soldier—is set to the tune of "the eternal recurrence of the same." Kragler, too, is drunk, and he lets the nickelodeon play. As a contrast to Glubb's song of solidarity and the drunk's renunciation song of November and January, he sings the roundelay about the dog and the egg and hops around the floor with Auguste.

The drunk brings his ditty to an end and makes his point even clearer:

> All my brothers now are dead, yes, dead.
> I've come through alive, I don't know how.
> In November I was Red, yes Red.
> But it's January now. (CP, I, 98)

There is a note of regret. The drunk still feels red inside, but in praxis he strives to become white, to fit in with the counter-revolution.

The position of the drunk is understood by Brecht to be that of the reform Social Democrats—red inside and white outside. Glubb and his nephew support the Revolution, but Kragler is the petit bourgeois, who takes the white position *without regret*. The drunk was still torn between revolutionary subjectivity and real non-action. Kragler chooses, and he decisively acts to reject the Revolution and denounce it as romantic humbug. In order to justify his ideological position, he uses the fate of the poor dog, who had rebelled and had been destroyed. The solidarity of the other dogs had no significance for the dead dog. Later in Brecht's opera about *Rise and Fall of the City of Mahagonny,* the men sing those beautiful lines: "Can't help a man who's dead" (GW, II, 563-64).

What remains when one transforms the story about the dog and the cook into praxis is the posthumous fate of the dead dog who once dared to take a bite. His fame runs through the history of all times, but as "negative infinity." Eternal, but boring. This is the way that the petit bourgeois Kragler wants to look at it. And because he found this interpretation of the ballad rather dubious, Brecht distanced himself completely from Kragler in the new version of this early drama. Kragler sings about the negative infinity and Nietzsche's "eternal recurrence of the same." However, the Marxist Brecht knows exactly just what to make out of all this.

The only reference to the dualism of the ballad about the dog in Brecht and Beckett is in the dissertation "The Dialectic and the Early Brecht: An Interpretative Study of *Trommeln in der Nacht*" by David Bathrick,[3] who has elaborated upon the meanings of the songs as ideological commentaries. In speaking about the dog and the cook, he states: "It is interesting that Act II of *Waiting for Godot* opens with the recitation of this same ditty. Beckett was obviously interested in the circularity of its structure (the last line of the second stanza introduces the first line of the first stanza like a round) as well as the horror of its message. Both are important for *Trommeln in der Nacht* as well."[4]

Of course, this reference seems to indicate that Brecht and Beckett take the same position in regard to that circular movement and negative infinity. In reality, it is right here—in *the contrasting function of the ballad* in Brecht and Beckett—that the *ideological antagonism* between the two playwrights becomes especially evident. Brecht's opposition to Beckett becomes even more explicit when one reads in his "Practice Scenes for Actors" how he wanted the stanzas about the dog employed. Brecht was of the opinion that these roundelays were a good exercise for actors of the epic theater. This is why he recommended that "the lines . . . be said in a different gesture, each time by different characters

---

[3] (Diss. University of Chicago, 1970).
[4] Cf. also David Bathrick, " 'Anschauungsmaterial' for Marx: Brecht Returns to *Trommeln in der Nacht,*" BH, 2 (1972), 136-48.

in different situations. The exercise can also be used for learning how to fix the manner of delivery."[5] The actors of his Berliner Ensemble worked this out in the production of the dramatized version of Brecht's dramaturgy—*The Purchase of Brass*.

The playwright Brecht recommends extreme gestic and mimetic activity in the presentation of a text which must explain all that happens as senseless. For Brecht the roundelay is an artistic device for learning the estrangement technique. Whereas the other exercises for actors posed the technical task of developing famous dramatic scenes from Shakespeare or Schiller for the epic theater, the actor here is supposed to learn from the roundelay how to "dramatize" an epic report. This must and is supposed to produce a comic effect. The impotent infinity of the roundelay fits perfectly into the dialectical concept. Also, the spectator learns something in the process, as Brecht assumed, namely the difference between real and theatrical "praxis."

VI

In Beckett's *Waiting for Godot* the dog already has a prominent position in the dramaturgical structure. The first words at the beginning of Act II are "A dog came in . . . " To be sure, there is also the important, silent activity by Vladimir after his entrance which preceded this. As is well known, this play is marked by its *repetition*— dramatically as well as dramaturgically. The angry and disturbed audiences at the first performances which were accustomed to traditional spectacles felt this to be an imposition: to be forced to continue to experience after the intermission what was seemingly only a reproduction of what had already been produced on the stage. This is why the stage directions for Act II begin with the words: "Next day. Same time. Same place." Didi is extremely active. He runs, stands, investigates, is ready for action and begins to sing loudly upon reaching the high point of his desire for action. Then there is the conventional misfortune of the clown who starts in too high a voice and must learn to control his artistic expression. Didi now lets loose with the song about the dog, cook, death, and burial. Here he falters for the first time, becomes contemplative, and begins once again. He recalls the solidarity of the other dogs and the burial. Again he runs straight through the story to the end. Didi is not disturbed by the fact that he now *reproduces* the story just as actively and smoothly as at the beginning, a story that he had already presented and sung. Obviously he does not distinguish between a first-hand report and a report about a report. For him, everything is on a single level.

Of course, he returns to the story of the tomb and the burial in the repetition. Once again it is the repetition of the repetition—con-

[5] SzT, V, 208.

templation and then a new beginning. However, this time it does not continue. He tries it once again but now sings "somewhat more softly." Yet, it will not go any further. The ending is the tomb, not the tombstone. He becomes quiet, stands immobile. Then he runs wildly and feverishly around the stage again. Act II is already reproduction in that the clown Vladimir begins it. He sets both the form and essence of this act to tune with a roundelay of endless reproduction according to Beckett's intention—and in the process, he sets the tune for the structure of the entire play. Activity is confronted everywhere by frozen situations—the same scenery, time, and place, whether it be product or reproduction. In the end it is always the same—the tomb. Only Didi is capable of disturbing it. He remains a man of action and an idealist to the end. He constantly has new hopes and is ready to wait for Godot. Nothing seems to lead him astray. Only sometimes he becomes contemplative again, and this is when he is struck by the thought that the dog is now dead and buried. The roundelay was for him merely a form of activity, production of art, and aesthetic superstructure up to that fateful sentence. He sang loudly because of his desire for activity. But the "work of art" had attached itself to reality. Didi surrendered himself too easily to empathy. Suddenly art spoke about death and the tomb and took on a disturbing element in "life."

It is clear that Beckett is once more concerned here with the opposition between an ahistorical view of history on the one hand and a subjective, affirmative view on the other. It could also be demonstrated that he may even have similar philosophical conceptions as those of the humanitarian Andreas Kragler. More important in regard to the remarkable similarity between Brecht's and Beckett's use of the symbolical dog is the remarkable way in which they differed in their use. Whereas Beckett ironically employed the roundelay about the dog, the cook, and the tomb to serve his dramaturgy of *empathy,* Brecht felt it to be an especially good example for demonstrating the dramatics and dramaturgy of *Verfremdung.*

THE *JUNGLE* TRANSCENDED: BRECHT AND ZUCKMAYER

Siegfried Mews and Raymond English

From our present-day vantage point it would appear that Bertolt Brecht and Carl Zuckmayer have not only nothing in common but are polar opposites in both dramatic theory and practice. In fact, at one point in his career Brecht felt compelled to take issue with one of Zuckmayer's popular dramas by obliquely attacking *The Merry Vineyard* in his *Gegenentwurf, Herr Puntila and His Man Matti,* as Jost Hermand has recently shown.[1]

Although there are certain similarities in both Brecht's and Zuckmayer's artistic careers and in their lives, they, in themselves, certainly do not give us reason to expect any close personal or literary relationship. Surprisingly, there is one specific instance in which a direct influence of Brecht upon Zuckmayer can be assumed. Concerning his second play, "Kiktahan oder die Hinterwäldler," which was performed under the title *Pankraz erwacht* (Deutsches Theater Berlin, February 1925),[2] Zuckmayer tersely states: "Brecht thought it was good—it was the only play I wrote under his influence" (AweSvm, 327).[3] No further elaboration concerning the exact nature of Brecht's influence on *Pankraz Awakens* is provided; moreover, so far hardly any critics have drawn attention to Zuckmayer's literary indebtedness to Brecht.[4] Therefore, the attempt to shed light on the hitherto neglected literary and personal relations between two dramatists who played so prominent a role in the German theater of the twenties seems to be an eminently worthwhile enterprise. Our discussion shall begin with a presentation of the external evidence of Zuckmayer's acquaintance with Brecht—both the man and his work—and then proceed to an examination of the most obvious common link between the two dramatists, i.e., their exoticism. It shall conclude with an analysis of internal evidence such as parallels in theme, structure, motifs, imagery in both Zuckmayer's and Brecht's pertinent works.

---

[1] Cf. Jost Hermand, "Herr Puntila und sein Knecht Matti," BH, 1 (1971), 120-27.

[2] "Kiktahan or the Backwoodsmen"; *Pankraz Awakens.* In the following, the drama will be referred to as *Pankraz Awakens.* All references are to the typescript (*Bühnenmanuskript*) circulated by the G. Kiepenheuer publishing company and will be given by abbreviated title (K = "Kiktahan") and Arabic page number.

[3] All references to Carl Zuckmayer's autobiography, *Als wär's ein Stück von mir,* Fischer Bücherei (Frankfurt, 1969), will be given by abbreviated title [AweSvm] and Arabic page number. The abridged English translation, *A Part of Myself,* trans. R. and C. Winston, (New York and London, 1970) has been partially used.

[4] Only very recently Siegfried Sudhof, "Carl Zuckmayer," *Deutsche Dichter der Gegenwart,* ed. Benno von Wiese (Berlin, 1973), pp. 69-70, has pointed out that more attention should be devoted to the affinities between young Zuckmayer and Brecht.

I

According to his own account, Carl Zuckmayer first came into contact with Brecht's works almost two years after the failure of his first drama *Kreuzweg* (Staatstheater Berlin, December 1920). As *Dramaturg* in charge of selecting new plays to be performed at the Kiel theater during the 1922-1923 season, Zuckmayer received from the Kiepenheuer publishing company the typescripts of *Drums in the Night, Baal,* and *In the Jungle.* He professes to have been immediately struck by Brecht's dramatic talent. Faintly echoing Herbert Ihering's effusive comment on occasion of the first performance of one of Brecht's plays, i.e., *Drums in the Night* (Kammerspiele Munich, 29 September 1922),[5] Zuckmayer enthused: "There is a poet! A new tone. A power of language and form which sweeps away all of this stale expressionism" (AweSvm, 309).

At this stage, *Baal* seems to have most attracted Zuckmayer's attention. Although the play was not performed until December 1923 (Altes Theater, Leipzig), it had been published by Kiepenheuer in an edition of 800 copies in October 1923, and in a second, larger edition shortly thereafter.[6] The publicity *Baal* received may have been a contributing factor to Zuckmayer's unsuccessful endeavors to have the play staged in Kiel. At any rate, the implied reason for his choice of *Baal*—i.e., that the play had not yet been performed—was an equally valid one for *In the Jungle.* A more important reason for attempting to have the play staged may have been Zuckmayer's affinity for the world presented in *Baal.* Even if one must discard any direct influence, there remains the curious coincidence that Zuckmayer had created a Baal-like figure in his "Lappenvogt Bal" who, in the fashion of his Brechtian namesake, indulges in an unrestrained life of alcoholic and sexual exploits.[7] In the spring of 1923 Zuckmayer's attitude of *épater le bourgeois* led to his dismissal from the post of *Dramaturg* in Kiel; he eventually found himself in Munich.

It was in Munich where Zuckmayer was to become more intimately acquainted with Brecht. In his autobiography he claims that he saw one

---

[5] Herbert Ihering, *Von Reinhardt bis Brecht,* I (Berlin, 1958), 273-74: "The twenty-four year old poet Bert Brecht has changed over night the literary face of Germany. . . . His dramas . . . are new poetical spheres." Zuckmayer also quotes Ihering verbatim (AweSvm, 317, 320).

[6] *Brecht-Chronik,* pp. 31, 32.

[7] "Die Geschichte vom Lappenvogt Bal" was published in Carl Zuckmayer, *Ein Bauer aus dem Taunus und andere Geschichten* (Berlin, 1927), pp. 98-115. According to Zuckmayer (oral communication on 17 June 1973 in Saas-Fee), a direct influence of Brecht upon this story cannot be assumed because he wrote the story under the stimuli provided mainly by his experiences in Norway (where he spent the summer of 1922 prior to going to Kiel). The fact that "Bal" was not included in subsequent editions of Zuckmayer's prose fiction suggests that the author considered the story an immature work.

of the only six performances of *In the Jungle* (AweSvm, 317), the premiere of which took place on 9 May 1923 (Residenztheater, Munich). In the middle of October of the same year, Zuckmayer came to know Brecht personally and fell temporarily under his spell. In addition to the three dramas mentioned before, poems, songs, ballads enlarged his knowledge of Brecht's work. But even more so than by his works Zuckmayer must have been impressed by Brecht's personality; he simply could not escape being fascinated by Brecht the man, poet, and singer of his own lyrics. Apparently not too long after they had become acquainted, Brecht presented Zuckmayer with a typewritten copy of *In the Jungle* and inscribed it: "It is right for a man/ To smoke/ And to struggle with metaphysics" (AweSvm, 322).

In the late fall of 1923, *after* having received a personal copy of *In the Jungle* from Brecht, Zuckmayer wrote his drama *Pankraz Awakens*. Several factors suggest that *In the Jungle* exercised a considerable—though not, by any means, exclusive—influence upon *Pankraz Awakens*. First, the only performance of a play by Brecht which Zuckmayer had seen was that of *In the Jungle*; second, Zuckmayer possessed a personal copy of the typescript; third, there is a strong likelihood that the two young dramatists discussed *In the Jungle*, which Brecht was revising for publication,[8] during this time of intense personal contact; fourth, Brecht took interest in Zuckmayer's play and sent it to his own publisher, Kiepenheuer, in order to have it distributed to stages in the hope of seeing it performed—an act which was surely based on Brecht's realization that here was a drama kindred in spirit to his own work.

From the sequence of events we may conclude that Zuckmayer was familiar with the first version of *In the Jungle* on which Brecht had begun to work in September 1921 and which was completed in the spring of 1922. It is this version (*Erstfassung von 1922*) as published by Gisela E. Bahr in 1968[9] which, although it may not correspond in all details to the presumably lost typescript which Brecht gave to Zuckmayer, will have to serve as the basis for the comparison of the two plays. It is reasonable to assume that at least some of the changes which Brecht had begun to make in January 1923, and then continued to make during the rehearsals for the premiere of *In the Jungle,* were reflected in the typescript Zuckmayer received from Brecht after the play had folded in Munich. It is even conceivable that the version Zuckmayer received from Brecht was closer to the *Drama in zehn Bildern* of the Munich performance (cf. D, 11) than to the sixteen scenes of the first version of 1922. As it is impossible to ascertain precisely of which version Zuckmayer possessed a copy, it may be noted that his extended ex-

---

[8] *Brecht-Chronik*, p. 35.

[9] Bertolt Brecht. *Im Dickicht der Städte. Erstfassung und Materialien*, ed. Gisela E. Bahr (Frankfurt, 1968). References to this edition will be given by abbreviated title (D) and page numbers in Arabic numerals.

posure to Brecht presumably resulted in a far more incisive (but also more intangible) influence than that exercised by any written copy. Apparently, Zuckmayer's contacts with Brecht did not cease once they had left Munich for Berlin. In fact, their common tenure as *Dramaturgen* at Max Reinhardt's Deutsches Theater offered a significant opportunity for cooperation—perhaps, a somewhat one-sided one. Thus Zuckmayer reports that soon after the premiere of *In the Jungle* at the Deutsches Theater (29 October 1924) the rehearsals for *Pankraz Awakens,* in which Brecht, Zuckmayer, and Caspar Neher participated, began.[10] However, the production of *Pankraz Awakens* in the regular program of the Deutsches Theater did not materialize; only a single performance of the drama by the experimental Junge Bühne took place in February 1925.

In a sense, the further development with regard to *In the Jungle* and *Pankraz Awakens* is rather instructive; whereas Zuckmayer abandoned his youthful play in order to steer a new course, Brecht, the "restless amender and modifier" (CP, I, xviii) continued to revise his play until a new version, *In the Jungle of Cities* (Berlin, 1927), emerged which differed markedly from the version which Zuckmayer had known. In comparison to the first version of 1922, the printed version of 1927 exhibited far greater emphasis on the city as expressed in both title, subtitle (*In the Jungle of Cities. The Fight Between Two Men in the Gigantic City of Chicago*), and the contrast between the prairies (*Savannen*) and the jungle of the city (*Dickicht der großen Stadt*).[11] The sixteen original scenes have been condensed to eleven, the vaguely expressionistic stage directions have given way to precise dates and times which are supposed to create the illusion of "objective reality," names have been changed ("Americanized") and some characters altered (Skinny and Manky), the references to the fight are more prominent than those to the jungle. In general, "a more urban, American, technological flavor [was] given" (CP, I, 425) in both the book and the Darmstadt production (December 1927).[12] There are also some plot alterations: Jane is not murdered, Garga's illegal reselling of Shlink's timber is newly introduced, the lynchers respond to Garga's accusations he made before he went to jail, and, in the end, Garga goes to New York.[13]

Unlike Brecht, who responded to the critics by continuing to revise his play and by repeatedly attempting to explain its meaning (cf. D, 134-44), Zuckmayer decided after the failure of *Pankraz Awakens* to shun

[10] Cf. Zuckmayer's unpublished letter to Mr. Korte (13 December 1972). For another instance of collaboration from the Munich and Berlin periods see below, p. 91.

[11] For a comparison of the two versions, cf. Gisela E. Bahr, *"Im Dickicht der Städte:* Ein Beitrag zur Bestimmung von Bertolt Brechts dramatischem Frühstil"* (Diss. New York University, 1966), pp. 1-100, and CP, I, 425-34.

[12] Cf. Günther Rühle, *Theater für die Republik* (Frankfurt, 1967), p. 564.

[13] GW, I, 193. Cf. also Bahr, *"Im Dickicht,"* pp. 1-100; CP, I, 425-34; Rühle, *Theater für die Republik,* p. 564.

dramatic experiments. In diametrical opposition to Brecht, he felt not called upon, " . . . to inaugurate a new epoch in literature, a new theatrical style, a new artistic direction" (AweSvm, 335). Rather, he wanted to come close to nature and life as he knew and saw it. The first product of his new orientation and determination was the enormously successful *The Merry Vineyard* (premiere: Theater am Schiffbauerdamm Berlin, 22 December 1925)—a play which decidedly marks the end of any artistic affinity between Brecht and Zuckmayer. *The Merry Vineyard* was, in fact, so un-Brechtian or even anti-Brechtian that Brecht could not but polemicize against it as late as 1940.[14]

It is clear then that one has to go back to the first version of *In the Jungle* (1922) to establish Zuckmayer's professed dependence on Brecht in *Pankraz Awakens*. Consequently, the *Druckfassung* of *In the Jungle of Cities* (1927), upon which most critics base their interpretations of the play, is only of peripheral interest for our purposes. Similarly, Brecht's own comments which extend from the play's inception in 1921 to the semi-apologetic essay "On Looking Through My First Plays" in 1954 (GW, XVII, 948-50) are of limited value for us because, for the most part, they lack consistency and reflect views which Brecht arrived at after both he and Zuckmayer had well established their separate artistic identities.

II

At first glance, there seem to be no really compelling similarities between *In the Jungle* and *Pankraz Awakens*. A cursory plot summary of Zuckmayer's play will suffice to demonstrate this point. The settler Pankraz, a former pirate, feels an incestuous desire for his younger daughter Alit who seems to respond to his advances after she has spent a night with the Indian Teton. But Pankraz's older daughter Judith, possibly motivated by jealousy, interferes. Later, when Alit joins Pankraz in a woodshed, Pankraz inexplicably kills her with an axe. Teton, the Indian, is murdered by a European outcast who pretends to be a priest. The false priest is then sentenced by a hastily assembled jury and hanged. Before he dies, the condemned man also assumes the guilt for the murder of Alit for no obvious reason. In the typescript version,

---

[14] Cf. n. 1. As far as can be ascertained, personally amiable contacts between the two dramatists persisted during the Berlin period and later, notwithstanding the fact that Brecht sharply rejected Zuckmayer's "corruptibility" in the face of success (cf. Brecht's undated remarks [1926]; BBA, 462/142). Further evidence for this dialectic relationship is provided by an anecdote related by Carl Zuckmayer on 16 June 1973. At the dress rehearsal for the premiere of *Herr Puntila and His Man Matti* in Zürich (premiere: 5 June 1948), Zuckmayer remarked to Brecht that he liked Puntila much better than the "ideological" Matti. Brecht replied that he had had Zuckmayer in mind when he was creating the character of Puntila. Cf. also Brecht's ambivalent response to Zuckmayer at the dress rehearsal of Zuckmayer's play *Barbara Blomberg* on 5 May 1949 in Zürich (*Brecht-Chronik*, p. 133).

Pankraz is killed by the Negro Kongo; in the stage version Pankraz apparently survived and began devoting his attentions to his older daughter Judith. Nevertheless, perceptive critics immediately noticed Zuckmayer's dependence on Brecht. Herbert Ihering wrote in his review of *Pankraz Awakens*:

> [The play] is an indication of the awakening productivity of the theater, resonant with the sound of the times. But it is also an indication of dangers: romanticism as an outlet, exoticism as an expedient. . . . While Brecht in his *Jungle* seldom succumbs to exoticism as romantic evasion and his language opens up the situation of his characters, Zuckmayer does not come to grips with the world, but rather flees from it. And the wilder it goes on stage, the weaker and thinner becomes his poetic personality.[15]

Ihering correctly observed that exoticism is the common denominator for both plays. This exoticism was particularly evident in the first version of *In the Jungle,* as the same critic somewhat nostalgically remarked when the *Druckfassung* was published in 1927: "Now he [Brecht] has transferred the *Jungle* out of the tropical climate of the first atmospheric versions into the cooler air of objective struggle. I like the colorful fullness of the old *Jungle.* Nothing seemed to me to testify so much to Brecht's wealth of ideas and talent as these scintillating, exotically pulsating scenes darting back and forth."[16]

Both Brecht's direct influence and the general vogue of anarchy and lawlessness—which were associated with America—were the potent ingredients which left their mark on *Pankraz Awakens.* The younger generation of those artists and writers who had undergone the shattering "experiences of war, revolution and economic collapse" formed a

> whole school of synthetic debauchery . . . , which set out in its own way to match the gangster and Western story, and took much of its inspiration from overseas. It was at once aggressive and frivolous . . . a combination of the new language of the dance-band with Rimbaud's notions of exotic adventure: a pungent flavour that recalled the great international sea-ports and the newly translated stories of Kipling, and even the traditional cowboy-and-Indian world of Fenimore Cooper and Karl May.[17]

More specifically, Brecht derived his notions about America in general and Chicago in particular (as well as some of his imagery, themes and motifs) from two literary sources: Upton Sinclair's *The*

---

[15] Ihering, *Von Reinhardt bis Brecht,* II, 95, 97.
[16] Ibid., 264.
[17] *Brecht* (W), p. 69.

Jungle and J.V. Jensen's *The Wheel*.[18] Brecht's remark of September 1921 that he was wondering why nobody had yet described the big city as a jungle (cf. D, 138) should not be taken too seriously because, by that time, he had read both *The Jungle* and *The Wheel*. Paradoxically, despite his self-proclaimed discovery, Brecht decidedly did not proceed to present Chicago as a jungle in the *Erstfassung*. Rather, the city and natural landscapes exist as separate entities. The place of action is given quite correctly as "Chicago and hinterland" (D, 12); five scenes of the original sixteen do not take place in Chicago proper,[19] among them the three crucial ones in the natural landscape of the "Jungle." The distinction is further enhanced by John Garga's implicit contrast between city and jungle.[20] Without doubt, the proximity of Brecht's early "Chicago and hinterland" was much closer to Zuckmayer's "Log cabin in the Far West" (K, title page) than one would be inclined to assume when examining the *Druckfassung* only. Not surprisingly, Zuckmayer avoided an urban setting altogether; in his more conventionally realistic stage description of a rustic, if exotic, milieu which does not convey inner landscapes as do the *Innenraum* scenes of *In the Jungle*[21] the future author of *The Merry Vineyard* shows his true colors. The similarity in the setting of Brecht's and Zuckmayer's plays should not induce us to conclude that Zuckmayer's choice of an American setting was due to Brecht's direct influence; rather, the general vogue of America as well as specific literary models provided the initial impetus for the selection of a certain milieu in both cases. Brecht's Chicago was vaguely patterned after Sinclair, Jensen (and Rimbaud); Zuckmayer's Far West was dependent to a considerable extent on James Fenimore Cooper and Karl May.[22]

Not the choice of an American milieu *per se* relates the two authors and their plays to each other; rather, their concept of America as the embodiment of sensationalism and exoticism provides the common link. There is no need to go into detail; a few general remarks may suffice. In the *Erstfassung* Brecht gave instructions to shout certain lines from behind the curtain before the play was to begin. The imitation of newspaper sellers crying out glaring headlines was clearly designed to

---

[18] J.V. Jensen's *Hjulet* (*Das Rad*) was never translated into English according to Gerhard Nellhaus in CP, I, 435. Cf. also the extracts from the novel in D, 145-52. A very extensive discussion of Brecht's sources is to be found in Patty Lee Parmalee, "Brecht's America" (Diss. University of California, Irvine, 1970). Michael Morley, "Brecht and the Strange Case of Mr. L.," GQ, 46 (1973), 540-47, presents a new source for *In the Jungle*.

[19] "In the Quarry" (D, 23-24); "Woods" (D, 69-72); "In the Jungle" (D, 91-94); "Bar in the Jungle" (D, 94-96); "Hut in the Jungle" (D, 96-103). Cf. also CP, I, 426-32.

[20] "This is a city, one lives in such holes. My brother ran around in the jungle, the deserter" (D, 34).

[21] Cf. Bahr, "Im Dickicht," p. 21.

[22] Cf. Siegfried Mews, "From Karl May to Horace A.W. Tabor: Carl Zuckmayer's View of America." *Mosaic* 6/2 (Winter, 1973), especially 125-29.

titillate the curiosity of the spectators (cf. D, 9). Murder, the ruin of a family, lynching are, indeed, heavy fare; but Zuckmayer's drama is hardly less conspicuous in the depiction of gruesome, sensational events and the mysterious, strangely unfathomable behavior of its characters. Despite the differences of the two plays in their presentation of spectacular happenings, ill-disposed critics could not be deceived concerning the literary relationship between Brecht and Zuckmayer. In his extremely negative review of *Pankraz Awakens* Felix Hollaender wrote: "Brecht engendered Zuckmayer—and God save us from the offspring which Zuckmayer will bring forth."[23] It is hardly surprising that in plays in which such spectacular happenings take place, one cannot expect an even remotely authentic description of America or the reflection of actual conditions. In both plays the characters, their language, and their actions exhibit decidedly atypical traits. Not without good reason does Eric Bentley speak of the "menagerie"[24] of strange characters which populate Brecht's shadowy, mythical, and grotesque Chicago. Neither Brecht's Malayan Shlink from the Japanese city of Yokohama, who lives in the Chinese quarter of Chicago, nor George Garga, who according to one of Brecht's early notes, "is like A. Rimbaud in appearance. He is essentially a German translation into American from the French" (D, 134), correspond to the average red-blooded American. The same can be said of most of the other individuals. The cast of characters in Zuckmayer's play includes a considerable number of German-Austrian immigrants, among them two outcasts, whose adventurous past is comparable to that of the ex-pirate Pankraz. The friendship between the Sioux Teton Osage and old scout Florymont provides a literary reminiscence; there are similar friendships between males of differing races in both Cooper and Karl May. Moreover, Kaimann, Pankraz's former name, is a direct borrowing from the title of one of Karl May's novels, *Kapitän Kaiman*.

If sensationalism, exoticism, and the presentation of an America that was largely inspired by literary sources were the only basis for a comparison of *In the Jungle* and *Pankraz Awakens*; if, in fact, these elements constituted the substance of the plays in question, then one might agree with Felix Hollaender. In his review of *Pankraz Awakens* he hardly felt it worth the trouble "to seriously express an opinion about this immature, bewildering stuff, this infantile mischief."[25] An incisive critical review is justified, however, if, as may be assumed with some degree of certainty, exoticism and sensationalism are only surface phenomena which need to be penetrated to reach the substance of both plays.

[23] Felix Hollaender, *Lebendiges Theater* (Berlin, 1932), p. 46.
[24] Eric Bentley, "On Brecht's *In the Swamp, A Man's a Man*, and *Saint Joan of the Stockyards*," *Brecht* (D), p. 52.
[25] Hollaender, *Lebendiges Theater*, p. 44.

III

Interestingly, both Zuckmayer and Brecht later realized that the artistic shortcomings of their respective plays were related to the common choice of an American milieu. Zuckmayer was slightly apologetic about the American setting of *Pankraz Awakens* and had only few positive things to say about the play as a whole.[26] Characteristically, Brecht in 1928, when *In the Jungle* had become the more "Americanized" *In the Jungle of Cities,* attempted to defend his "choice of an American milieu" by rejecting the notion of his "bent for romanticism"—despite his earlier admission of *"romantic embroidery"* (D, 10). Rather, he now explained the American setting in terms of his dramatic theories and asserted:

> By means of a background (the American one), which by nature corresponded to my characters, so that it did not expose, but rather cover them, I felt I could most easily draw attention to the peculiar behavior of important, contemporary human types. In a German milieu these same types would have been romantic. They would have found themselves in opposition to their surroundings, rather than to a romantic audience. (GW, XVII, 972)

There is no need to take issue with the far-fetched claim that Brecht's types would blend naturally into an American environment; more to the point is Herbert Ihering's assessment of the real significance of America for younger playwrights:

> For Germany the spiritual experience of America seems to have attained an importance similar to the experience of Shakespeare a century and a half ago. Not personal knowledge, but the distant effect of America is important. Just as the apparent unbridled element in Shakespeare first burst forth during the Storm and Stress period as a fascination for the he-man [*Kraftmeierei*], it is only natural that its brutality is the first element transmitted from America. The vision of Chicago has already turned into a fascinating event in Brecht's *Jungle.* Not civilization, but rather barbarism can become fruitful for literature. Only through the artistic experience of America can America be overcome. Only in that way can the European drama once again become European and spiritual—in a regenerated sense.[27]

Herbert Ihering saw in the young dramatist's vision of America a factor which would lead to the rejuvenation of German drama. According

[26] "[The play] was set in a romanticized [*balladesk*] pioneer America. . . . The piece was uneven and murky, sketchy in plot, badly organized" (AweSvm, 327, 334). Further, Zuckmayer's use of the term *balladesk* suggests *sagenhaft* (legendary). In his unpublished letter to Mr. Korte (13 December 1972), Zuckmayer called the play "a wild spectacle" and referred to himself, Brecht, and Cas[par] Neher as "obsessed with Elizabethan extravagance."

[27] Ihering, *Von Reinhardt bis Brecht,* II, 74-75.

to Ihering, in many plays there was hidden under the guise of exoticism the attempt to come to grips with profound issues confronting modern man. Without doubt, in Brecht's case it is the dramatic presentation of man's alienation (*Entfremdung*), the all-pervasive theme of *In the Jungle,* which constitutes such a weighty issue. The phenomenon of alienation is most pronounced in Shlink's endeavors to overcome his isolation, his inability to establish genuine communications, which he experiences as inherent in the human condition. Shlink's goals lend meaning or metaphysical import to his fight and his love-hate relationship with Garga. Both men are changed during their struggle, which is waged with fierceness and ruthlessness—particularly on Garga's part. Garga sacrifices his mistress and his family in the process; nature provides an analogy for the struggle in the human realm.

All the important ingredients of *In the Jungle,* including its baffling obscurity and complexity which are, in part, due to the aphoristic quality of its dialogue, are also to be found in *Pankraz Awakens*—modified, to be sure, but still recognizable.

The correspondences between *In the Jungle* and *Pankraz Awakens* begin in the respective first scenes. In *In the Jungle* Shlink attempts to buy Garga's view (D, 14, 19) on books, although he ultimately considers it to be irrelevant (D, 13). Shlink wants to undermine Garga's position by attempting to convince him that he really cannot afford the luxury of an opinion: "I beg you, consider the ways of this planet and sell" (D, 21). For Garga's family lives in poverty and squalor, his dream of "Tahiti" is merely a romantic escape mechanism, and unfaithful Jane demonstrates the unreliability of human emotions. Shedding his clothes and with them his old existence Garga proclaims his freedom and asks for a ticket to the isles (D, 21, 22). At the end of the scene Shlink's creatures are certain that Garga will respond to Shlink's provocation: "We've really gotten to him. He'll toe the line . . ."; ". . . You've got to look life straight in the eye" (D, 22).

The very first words in *Pankraz Awakens* refer to a proposed sale, which, as in *In the Jungle,* does not take place.[28] Bembe, who like Shlink is a lumber-merchant and is likewise accompanied by a downtrodden and mistreated servant,[29] wants to buy the woods which afford Pankraz a refuge—though he cannot escape his troubled conscience. Pankraz resembles Garga in that his "inner self [is] dark, confused and

[28] Despite the similarity of the opening scenes, Carl Zuckmayer expressly denied any conscious borrowing from Brecht. Rather, he drew attention to James Fenimore Cooper's *The Deerslayer,* from which the basic situation is derived, i.e., that of the ex-pirate Tom Hutter who lives with his two daughters, weak-minded Hetty and attractive Judith [!], in an isolated cabin. The name of the woodsman Harry Hurry is also a borrowing from *The Deerslayer.*

[29] Cf., e.g., Moti Gui's sudden dismissal from Shlink's employ after twenty years of faithful service (D, 27) and his humiliation by Garga (D, 46) with Bembe's treatment of his "nigger" Kongo (K, 5).

closed off from the outer world."[30] The selling of his woods would rob Pankraz of the basis for his isolated existence and force him to face the world just as Garga is actually forced to abandon his obscure but comparatively sheltered existence in the lending library. Bembe's argument that in buying the woods and exploiting them he would act as "pioneer of progress . . . battering-ram of civilization . . ." (K, 3) and his intention "to bring order" (K, 4) are reminiscent of Shlink's goal, i.e., to shake the foundations of Garga's imagined security, to make him aware of the true conditions of life.

In *In the Jungle* Garga achieves his new awareness by means of the fight initially forced upon him by Shlink; in Zuckmayer's play the direct confrontation between protagonist and antagonist, which begins in both plays with a sales proposal, is not further pursued after the first scene. The friends Teton Osage and Old Florymont do not qualify as a counterpart to Shlink and Garga as their relationship is completely devoid of homosexual overtones. Nevertheless, Zuckmayer was inspired by something closely related to the idea of the struggle; the vitality exhibited by the fighter, especially by Garga. In Brecht's early works Zuckmayer found expressed "the conception of the strong man, the best man as the survivor . . ." (AweSvm, 321). In this context, Zuckmayer quotes the line, "The strong man fights, but the sick man dies," which, interestingly, is the refrain of a poem from Kipling's *The Light that Failed*.[31] It is sung by John Garga and Mankyboddle in the scene "At the Gargas" (D, 67) and must have been one of Brecht's favorites because Zuckmayer reports having heard Brecht sing it often. To some extent, the line quoted foreshadows Garga's later affirmation of life devoid of romantic notions or intellectual aspirations: "Bare life is better than any other kind of life" (D, 99). And: "The important thing is not to be the stronger man before God, but to come off alive" (D, 100). Garga comprehends the laws of the *Prairie* (D, 19) only too well and emerges as the victor.

As it turns out, Garga's victory is a dubious one. He looks back at the past fight with something approaching nostalgia and begins to experience Shlink's loneliness: "It was the best time. The chaos is used up—it left me unblessed. Perhaps work will console me. Without doubt, it is very late. I feel lonely" (D, 105).

In contrast to Garga's recognition of man's universal alienation, Pankraz's isolation is less representative as it is related to personal guilt (the murder of his wife) for which he seeks to atone in the wilderness much in the fashion of a defiant romantic outcast: "I'll bear it alone. I sailed across the sea, alone; the planks moaned under my step and the

---

[30] Bahr, "*Im Dickicht*," p. 21.
[31] Cf. CP, I, 429, and James K. Lyon's essay, "Kipling's 'Soldiers Three' and Brecht's *A Man's a Man*," in this volume, pp. 99-113. Brecht also used the line in *The Exception and the Rule* (GW, II, 807).

masts broke apart in the sky. I went through the forests alone; the leaves rotted in my footprints" (K, 39). Shlink's compelling, if aphoristic comments on the human condition in the "Jungle" scenes do not have an equivalent in *Pankraz Awakens*. "Man's infinite isolation makes enmity an unattainable goal. The planets are unrecognizable. Their encounter gets lost in the blue" (D, 92), he states and continues: "Yet they unite in order to produce beings to stand by them in their hopeless isolation. And the generations look coldly into each others' eyes. If you cram a ship full to bursting with human bodies, they'll all freeze with loneliness" (D, 92). These utterances reveal a profound pessimism which is not to be encountered in Zuckmayer's play.

Shlink's words shed some light on the motives for his fight with Garga; but just as the two main characters are unable to establish true communication, the other characters likewise suffer from their inability to establish meaningful contacts with other human beings. This is particularly evident in the case of sexual unions:

> The entire course of *In the Jungle* works to deny the romantic idealization of sexual love. Just as the love of Marie for Shlink is answered in the commercial sale of her body in the dung-draped forest, the traditional *gamos* is ironically celebrated in the wedding feast of Garga and Jane . . .—the feast of a criminal and a whore; and the apex of sexual love in *In the Jungle* is homosexual.[32]

The theme of isolation in *Pankraz Awakens,* although far less persuasively developed than in *In the Jungle,* can be most easily grasped. Despite a certain coquettish playfulness on the part of Pankraz's older daughter Judith in her refusal to accede to Bembe's wishes—he portrays himself as "a lonely man, hardened by life" (K, 10)—there is at least an indication of the impossibility to achieve a true union. In response to Bembe's question "How do I appear to you?" Judith answers:

> Like something I sometimes dream. I've caught a fish and take him for a walk on a leash. Then I sit down on a table—like this—and take off my stockings. The fish wriggles on the floor and shoots up into the air, because he thinks my white legs are water. Then he jumps coolly against my ankles, like impotent ripples against a bank, all the while saying: Kiktahan! (K, 11)

We cannot but attribute some significance to the passage cited above because it contains the word "Kiktahan," i.e., the term which Zuckmayer used as the first title for his play. In this context, "Kiktahan" indicates Bembe's desire to establish a meaningful relationship. Bembe's wish remains unrequited; like the fish he is robbed of the vital element he needs for complete fulfilment.

---

[32] Charles R. Lyons, *Bertolt Brecht: The Despair and the Polemic* (Carbondale, 1968), p. 33.

Moreover, it is not unlikely that the image of the fish jumping impotently against Judith's legs may have been directly inspired by one of Brecht's lines in "On the Drowned Girl" (GW, VIII, 252)—a poem which Zuckmayer knew well (AweSvm, 317). The line reads: "The fish swam coolly on her leg." To be sure, quite in contrast to Zuckmayer the line signifies the impassibility of nature in the face of death. Still, it should be noted that there is a remarkable correspondence, which can hardly be coincidental, in the image used by both Brecht and Zuckmayer. We would not do justice to Zuckmayer's achievement were we to assume that he was merely a passive recipient of Brecht's ideas and suggestions. There is at least one piece of evidence for a collaborative effort, a fragmentary poem of ten lines "after Zuckmayer and Brecht ," entitled "liebestod" (BBA, 524/19).[33] Interestingly, this poem is an almost *verbatim* verse rendering of Alit's dream which she narrates during her love-encounter with the Indian Teton (K, 17). The "poetically" inspired diction of both prose narration in *Pankraz Awakens* and verse rendering in "liebestod" resembles that of Zuckmayer rather than that of Brecht; yet, the themes of death by drowning and inevitibility of dissolution as well as the imagery depicting a submarine realm relate "liebestod" to the world of Brecht's early poems. In fact, in stanzas 12-13 of Brecht's "The Ballad of the Love-Death" (GW, VIII, 255), there is a faint evocation of the lovers in "liebestod" who are submerged in a wrecked ship. On the whole, however, the "Ballad" rather reeks with the stench of death and decay. Brecht's ballad thus exhibits the "anti-lyrical" tendency which Zuckmayer noted on occasion of the rehearsals for *The Life of Edward the Second of England* (cf. AweSvm, 319-20) which premiered in Munich on 18 March 1924. In a sense, Brecht's and Zuckmayer's different views of "Love-Death" are symptomatic for their treatment of sexual relationships in *Pankraz Awakens* and *In the Jungle* respectively.

Whereas in *In the Jungle* homosexual love is the "apex" of intrapersonal relationships, in *Pankraz Awakens* it is Pankraz's incestuous desire for his daughter Alit. Potentially harmonious relations between man and woman tend to become perverted by powerful sexual desires which reduce partners to mere objects but still create "profound lust" (K, 29) during the moments of union. In *Pankraz Awakens* Judith tells

[33] The fragment is listed among the *Joe Fleischhacker* materials (BBA-B, I, 305) and was presumably to be spoken by a member of the Mitchel[l] family. Although primarily concerned with the economics of the Chicago wheat exchange, *Joe Fleischhacker* is thematically related to *In the Jungle*—a fact which would explain the presence of Zuckmayer's [?] fragmentary poem among the materials of an unfinished play which does reflect Brecht's preoccupation with economics. For a discussion of *Joe Fleischhacker*, cf. Parmalee, "Brecht's America," pp. 84-215, 413. In a letter of 21 April 1974 Carl Zuckmayer stated that "Alit's Dream" from *Pankraz Awakens* was adopted by Brecht (with Zuckmayer's permission) for a sequence of verses (*Versfolge*), presumably entitled "On the Sunken Ship"("Vom versunkenen Schiff"). This sequence of verses is not listed in BBA-B.

the Graf: "Who knows what a man can do. But a woman can lie about everything. Everything. Even her own pleasure. Even the shivering of her skin" (K, 28). In a similar vein Marie informs Shlink: "I lay in bed with a man who was an animal. My whole body was numb, but I gave myself to him, many times, and I couldn't get warm. He smoked stogies in between. I loved you every minute I spent between those papered walls, I was so obsessed that he thought it was love and wanted to stop me. I slept into the black darkness" (D, 69).

While the sexual relationships in *In the Jungle* do not bridge "in human life the estrangement made by . . . speech" (D, 92), as Shlink states, the "mercy" springing from "love, the warmth of bodies in contact . . . the union of the organs" (D, 92) in the realm of animals is occasionally experienced by human beings in *Pankraz Awakens*. The encounter between Alit and Teton, Alit's sacrificial death are acts based on something akin to genuine love. Ultimately, there is hope for man in the chaotic world of *Pankraz Awakens*. True, the desired union and understanding do not materialize between Judith and the count. Their passionate wish: "We'll force life to be kind. . . . We'll love it once again" (K, 30), remains unfulfilled because they are in the grip of forces which they cannot control. The count's parting remark smacks of Garga's disillusioned cynicism in his rejection of bourgeois values—though in the count's case it is the city which holds the promise of a different, if not better, life: "I have to get out of here. I smell the city. I've inherited enough to last for three days in the Palace Hotel. Son of a bitch. . . . I'm beginning to speak loudly when I'm alone—it's time to set out" (K, 48).

The final lines of the play once more emphasize man's isolation in terms of nature imagery which Zuckmayer employs consistently. Unlike Shlink's prediction of a hopeless and bleak future, "And there will never be an outcome to this fight, George Garga, never an understanding" (D, 99), Judith's last words imply hope: "Spring is arriving late here. The trees are growing slowly, a ring every year. There are many together, standing there alone. They don't love one another, but they are greening" (K, 52).

IV

Nature imagery occurs in both Brecht's and Zuckmayer's plays. Yet there is a distinct contrast. The very fact that Garga's existence at the beginning of the play is based on dealing with or lending of lifeless objects whereas Pankraz's life is associated with living organisms, the trees in his forest, is indicative of a different emphasis. In *In the Jungle* images of animals, the pale sky, water, the wind, and cold combine to create the impression of man's transitory existence.[34] Baal's vultures

---

[34] Cf. Hart Wegner, "Die dichterischen Bilder im Frühwerk Brechts" (Diss. Harvard University, 1970), pp. 245-324.

92

also hover over *In the Jungle* and vermin prosper in the watery swamp of decay and death in which the Gargas live. The cold wind is inimical to warmth in human relations. Above all, the metaphor of the jungle which is used by "the playwright and the characters themselves . . . to describe the action" rather than emerging from the action as a dramatized metaphor,[35] is used by Brecht to project man's alienation. A prelude to the theme of alienation, which is fully developed in the three "Jungle" scenes, is given by the desolate Marie's remark—which is very reminiscent of Büchner: "The trees look draped in human dung, the sky is close enough to touch, but what is it to me? I'm cold" (D, 69). Such an excremental view of nature which does not alleviate man's isolation is entirely foreign to Zuckmayer. Witness, e.g., Alit's following lines: "The air has turned to frosted glass. The evening hangs like crape from the trees. The night wants to roar now. You [Pankraz] should not be alone" (K, 26).

We must turn to the world of *Baal* or such early poems as "Birth in the Tree" (GW, VIII, 85-86) to find a correspondence to Zuckmayer's view of nature—in which trees play a predominant role. Zuckmayer himself drew attention to "the great heaven of *Baal*, the choral heaven which is by no means to be understood merely as a physical phenomenon. Rather, it is a contrapuntal countervoice to death and decay" (AweSvm, 322). The idea of new life springing from decaying corpses, in a "natural cycle of becoming and passing away,"[36] Zuckmayer found expressed in Brecht's "Grand Hymn of Thanksgiving" (GW, VIII, 215-16) from which he quoted verbatim:

> Praise the tree which grows on carrion,
>   grows jubilantly toward heaven!
> Praise the carrion,
> Praise the tree that devoured it,
> But praise heaven also. (AweSvm, 322)[37]

Pankraz's defiant admission of responsibility for the murder of Alit resounds with certainty that she will give birth to new life: "Now you know why I did it. Go, if you want, and throw it [the corpse] to the rats. But I know she is lying like a root sprouting under the wood" (K, 39).[38] The idea that death lacks finality and is merely a phase in the ever-continuing cycle of organic growth is also conveyed in Zuckmayer's

[35] Lyons, *Bertolt Brecht,* p. 27.

[36] Klaus Schuhmann, *Der Lyriker Bertolt Brecht 1913-1933* (Munich, 1971), p. 89.

[37] Zuckmayer, *A Part of Myself,* trans. R. and C. Winston, p. 268.

[38] Cf. also K, 29: "And that it [that which is better] does happen on earth; that it already rests in the furrows like seed for autumn sowing, that the fruit will ripen, even if it comes out of our bones." In the short story, "Ein paar Brocken Erde," in the collection *Ein Bauer aus dem Taunus und andere Geschichten,* p. 97, a human corpse provides nourishment, shelter, and a facility for the procreation of insects and other small animals.

"Cognac im Frühling,"[39] a poem which Brecht seemed to like (AweSvm, 318). In *Pankraz Awakens* even in an advanced state of decay trees exude the intoxicating fragrance inherent in life-giving organisms: "Tree trunks ten meters in diameter. When one steps on them, one crashes down up to one's shoulders into the decayed dust, everything sponge and tinder. The rosin smells like brandy, there's so much strength in it" (K, 3). The vegetative life of the trees is clearly a reflection of vital processes in the human sphere. In a simile Old Florymont likens women to the sap in trees which causes growth but is also potentially violent and destructive: "The women in us are like sap in the life of a tree. A thousand fibers absorb them. They push their way into the core and then drive upwards from inside until the outer surface tears apart. Have you seen how the young maple bleeds?" (K, 7).

Most importantly, in the central scene of *Pankraz Awakens* the motif of violent and partially self-destructive growth in nature is linked to Pankraz's awakening, i.e., his eventual redemption despite his heinous crimes. The chaplain observes that nature presents the spectacle of chaos: "Do you know that I now sense how trees struggle against the pulse of their sap. Everything gets wildly confused." But despite the self-destructive tendency of nature, growth occurs as the count states: "But something is born in the process" (K, 44). Self-devouring animals provide an analogy for Pankraz's annihilation of his own kind. In the last analysis, no definite answer is provided as to the meaning of the chaotic fighting in nature, in the realm of animals, and in the human sphere—although there is hope for a mysterious transformation:

> DER KAPLAN: Something is also born among us, even if we rage like scorpions against our own blood. Don't you believe that Pankraz awakens?
> DER GRAF: That Pankraz awakens?
> DER KAPLAN: Is it really so senseless when spiders kill themselves after mating? And in cocks, who were men and had women, there springs forth a germ of a cell and turns them, while still alive, into productive mothers. It also happens with lizards and other animals. I once knew all that.
> DER GRAF: All that raises more and more questions without an answer.
> DER KAPLAN: Really, I firmly believe that Pankraz awakens.
>
> (K, 44)

· The repeated affirmation of the belief in Pankraz's awakening on the part of the Kaplan suggests a religious interpretation: "Pankraz is the embodiment of a type of man who is determined by his drives and

---

[39] Carl Zuckmayer, *Gesammelte Werke* (Frankfurt, 1960), I, 15.

passions, who gives in to his creaturely nature and yet strives for salvation."[40]

Indeed, Pankraz exhibits the "religious trait—a pagan one, to be sure, with overtones of the nature myth" (AweSvm, 322) which Zuckmayer ascribed to Brecht's early work in general. The Kaplan, a remote relation of the Salvation Army preacher in *In the Jungle,*[41] atones for his sins and paves the way for Pankraz's survival and eventual salvation by assuming the guilt for Alit's murder.

Brecht also depicted the fight between Garga and Shlink—which corresponds largely to the struggle in Pankraz's soul—by means of nature and animal imagery. The fight, which Brecht later described in terms of the boxing or wrestling match,[42] is waged with fierceness. Shlink, who loses his lumber business and commits suicide, the Garga family who is "sacrificed" by George Garga (cf. D, 33-39)—this sacrifice corresponds roughly to Pankraz's sacrifice of Alit—Marie, who becomes a prostitute, and Jane, who is murdered, are the casualties. Garga's dedication to the fight and to survival recalls the law of the jungle:

> How good it is to fight with a knife! Until one locks his jaws in and becomes insane from biting, drunk as though from Tokay. You'll feel your arms down to the roots of your heart, brother ape. . . . The forest! That's where mankind comes from, isn't it? Everything was so easy. They simply tore each other apart. I see them clearly, with quivering flanks, staring into the whites of each other's eyes, sinking their teeth into each other's throats and rolling down. And the one who bled to death among the roots was the vanquished, and the one who had trampled down the most undergrowth was the victor! (D, 92, 93)

In contrast to *Pankraz Awakens,* there are "no idealistic escape routes whatever."[43] In Brecht's play man's alienated condition is unalterable: "In the Jungle man is on his own" (D, 66). No hope for eventual communion or salvation is held out. The mood of the play is nihilism "stripped to its pernicious essence."[44]

In the final analysis, both dramas present different views of man and nature. Whereas Brecht equates the existence of man with the fight for

---

[40] Arnold John Jacobius, *Motive und Dramaturgie im Schauspiel Carl Zuckmayers* (Frankfurt, 1971), p. 46.

[41] In D, 31-32, Shlink spits into the face of the preacher who suffers the humiliation because he is given a house for the Salvation Army. Later, he unsuccessfully attempts to commit suicide (D, 85-86). In K, 43, it is the chaplain who, in a last gesture of defiance, spits into the face of the count.

[42] Cf. the preface to *In the Jungle of Cities* (GW, I, 126): "You will witness an inexplicable wrestling match between two men." In "On Looking Through My First Plays" Brecht speaks of "boxing matches" which inspired him to portray a fight to decide who is 'the best man'" (GW, XVII, 948).

[43] Max Spalter, *Brecht's Tradition* (Baltimore, 1967), p. 166.

[44] Ibid.

mere survival in an inhospitable jungle without transcendence, Zuck-mayer presents man as capable of redemption in a chaotic world in which the antagonistic forces in nature symbolize the principle of life—the recurrence of the life-death cycle within a dimly perceived divine order. Indicative of the different emphases in both plays is that Zuckmayer employs the warm *Föhn* wind (K, 42)[45] which hastens the decomposition of organic matter and thus prepares the fertile soil for new life, while in Brecht's play the cold "black wind" (D, 45, 61) casts a chill on everything.

V

As has been shown, we must go beyond *In the Jungle* and take into ac-count Brecht's entire early work, but notably *Baal,* the poems, songs, and ballads to gain a full understanding as to the scope and nature of Brecht's influence upon *Pankraz Awakens.* One striking parallel remains to be discussed, however, in order to show that *In the Jungle* did, indeed, very profoundly affect Zuckmayer's play. Just as the two dramas begin similarly with the sales situation, they end in a com-parable vein when both protagonists contemplate their departure to un-spoiled, primitive regions which hold the promise of unfettered freedom and an uncomplicated, simple life:

> GARGA: I'll move to the South and till the soil. . . . Bring some fresh clouds, east wind. We'll take a boat along the south coast—that's dangerous. We'll wait awhile for the wind.
> (D, 104, 105)

> PANKRAZ: [I'll go] north. There are still forests there where no one is cutting timber. They roll like seas around the mountains. There's still room there. . . . Let's set out! Weigh the anchor!
> (K, 51, 52)

In *In the Jungle* Tahiti as seen by Gauguin (D, 20)[46] had occupied a prominent place in Garga's imagination. It provided an imaginary escape from the drudgery of his existence, an unattainable goal before the fight. During the fight, the fight itself had become more important, and after the fight the ideal had become tainted. Linked to the Tahiti motif are the images of departure by ship (D, 44, 56). Ships in turn are associated with the ideal of freedom. After having organized the lyn-ching mob against Shlink, Garga asks rhetorically: "Are you free? Come down into the dark arena, a knife in your hand, naked in the cold darkness. Are you free at all? The brigs are rocking on waters without names. Are you free? Your beloved, freedom, is sailing on the ships!"

[45] Cf. AweSvm, 327, where Zuckmayer reports that he wrote *Pankraz Awakens* "in a single night, to the accompaniment of a howling *Föhn* wind."

[46] Brecht's poem "Tahiti" (GW, VIII, 105-106) presents Tahiti in a manner similar to the place the island occupies in Garga's imagination. Cf. also n. 48.

(D, 96). The metaphorical use of ships is complemented by fleeting glimpses of the free life of sailors who indulge in drinking, smoking, and sex—as did the pirates of Brecht's earlier works. In particular, Mankyboddle appears "rum-sodden and nautical" (CP, I, 428) in a scene (D, 57-59) which was deleted in the *Druckfassung*. Further, the use of the raucous song from Robert Louis Stevenson's *Treasure Island,* "Fifteen men on the dead man's chest-/ yo-ho-ho, and a bottle of rum!/ Drink and the devil had done for the rest-/ yo-ho-ho, and a bottle of rum!" in the Munich premiere[47]; Kipling's song with the refrain "The strong man fights, but the sick man dies" (D, 67); and even the reference to sentimental, popular songs with lines like "Stormy the night and the sea runs high" (D, 35),[48] evoked the adventurous, non-bourgeois, unfettered life of soldiers, sailors, and pirates. Not surprisingly, in a discussion of his play, referred to above, Zuckmayer professed to have adopted Brecht's technique of including songs and ballads in *Pankraz Awakens.*

Like Brecht's adventurers in his collection of poetry, *Manual of Piety,* in general and in his "Ballad of the Pirates" (GW, VIII, 224-28), which Zuckmayer explicitly mentions (AweSvm, 317), in particular, Pankraz is a social outcast whose very existence is a "vital, anarchistic protest against life in bourgeois society."[49] His element was the sea which offered both refuge from the restrictions of a confining social order and the chance to indulge in combat with nature. In moments of emotional stress and adversity, Pankraz evokes his past in ringing phrases and proclaims his absolute autonomy and defiance of human and divine laws:

> Listen how the wind howls in the masts. The ship lies before the storm with reefed sails and flies through the spray like a diver-bird . . . Dead Kaimann does not go overboard—he traps the heavy sea with the nape of his neck—he stands—the storm hacks with knives at the bend of his knees. . . . Dead Kaimann does not surrender, neither to heaven nor to hell! Marauders are sewn into a sail and thrown overboard! (K, 38, 40)

Pankraz's rendition of a pirate song, although it expresses the same wholehearted dedication to a life on the seas which is central to Brecht's

---

[47] According to H.O. Münster (D, 121). Later, "The Ballad of the Soldier," essentially in L. Lindau's rendering of Kipling's verse (taken from the story "Love-o'-Women"), replaced the song from *Treasure Island.* Cf. James K. Lyon, "Brecht's Use of Kipling's Intellectual Property," MfdU, 61 (1969), 381-83.

[48] The song is identified by G. Nellhaus in CP, I, 437. The line quoted was obviously one of Brecht's favorites as he uses it with minor variations in "Tahiti" (cf. n. 46), *Drums in the Night* (GW, I, 93), *Rise and Fall of the City of Mahagonny* (GW, II, 543, 544).

[49] Schuhmann, *Der Lyriker Bertolt Brecht,* p. 79.

ballad, smacks, at least in the circulated manuscript version,[50] rather of cheap sexuality and trite romanticism:

> Das Meer ist unser Boardinghause [sic],
> Das Meer ist unser Weib,
> Es spreisst [sic] die weißen Schenkel aus
> Und rollt den grünen Leib. (K, 40)[51]

This raucous, boisterous, and hardly poetically inspired song foreshadows to a certain extent the unrestrained and non-spiritual zest for life with which *The Merry Vineyard* is imbued. To draw conclusions from such a short excerpt as to the poetic and dramatic quality of *Pankraz Awakens* in general would be gratuitous. As has been mentioned before, the author himself turned out to be the severest judge of his youthful work.

Suffice it to once more call attention to the noteworthy fact, which hitherto has been almost completely overlooked by literary historians, that the subsequently famous author of such non-Brechtian plays as *The Merry Vineyard, The Captain of Coepenick,* and *The Devil's General* fell temporarily under the young Brecht's spell. Although *Pankraz Awakens* cannot be entirely explicated in terms of Brecht's direct influence, the fact remains that Zuckmayer created a work which in milieu, motifs, theme, characters, situations, songs, and dialogue is largely indebted to Brecht's early work in general and to *In the Jungle* in particular. Ultimately, Zuckmayer did not succumb to the fascination exercised by Brecht but succeeded in finding his own style. Nevertheless, Zuckmayer never failed to acknowledge his indebtedness to Brecht; in a tribute to his dead friend, he fittingly quotes from *In the Jungle* to express his sentiments about his previous close association with Brecht: "The chaos is used up." With a nostalgic glance backwards Zuckmayer adds: "It *was* the best time."[52]

---

[50] In the Zuckmayer archives in Saas-Fee there are fragments of *Pankraz Awakens,* among them the deleted parts of Pankraz's pirate song. They are, in their *epater le bourgeois* tone, much closer to Brecht than the verse cited in the text.

[51] "The ocean is our boardinghouse,/ The ocean is our wife,/ It spreads out its white thighs/ And rolls its green body."

[52] Quoted from an unpublished MS. entitled "Brecht" (used in a radio broadcast), p. 7.

KIPLING'S "SOLDIERS THREE"
AND BRECHT'S *A MAN'S A MAN*

James K. Lyon

A Man's a Man, overtly the most "Kiplingesque" of all Brecht's dramas, presents a problem to anyone wishing to trace this work to a specific source. Normally Brecht made no secret of his models. *Baal* was a reaction to Johst's *Der Einsame; He Who Said Yes* derived from a Japanese Nōh play; *Herr Puntila and His Man Matti* was sparked by the Finnish tales of Hella Wuolijoki; and *Mother Courage* had a work by Johan Ludvig Runeberg as a basis, to mention a few obvious examples. With the exception of an episode from Alfred Döblin's novel *Die drei Sprünge des Wang-lun* (to be discussed later), it is generally assumed that Brecht modeled this play chiefly on material he drew from Rudyard Kipling. Yet here the problem begins, for despite an ambiance clearly associated with Kipling, a reader conversant with that writer would be hard pressed to name specific works which might have served Brecht as a model for themes or plot. In this sense the play has both more and less Kipling than a number of other dramas such as *The Threepenny Opera* and *Mother Courage.*

The origin and development of *A Man's a Man* are in part responsible for this paradox. As early as 1917 Brecht had discovered the idea that human identity is interchangeable. He distilled it in a poem entitled "That was Citizen Galgei" (GW, VIII, 84). In it the identity of the citizen Galgei is transformed by "wicked men" who claim he is someone else named "Pick." He dies without refuting them:

Er konnt es nicht beweisen
Es stand ihm keiner bei.
Steht nicht im Katechismus
Daß er der Galgei sei.

Der Name stand im Kirchbuch
Und am Begräbnisstein?
Der Bürger Galgei konnte
Gut auch ein andrer sein. [1]

He couldn't really prove it
No one upheld his claim.
No catechism has it
That Galgei was his name.

Though it was in the church books,
Did the gravestone make it plain?
Citizen Galgei might be
Someone else again.

Galgei, who would later be christened "Galy Gay," marked the beginning of a dramatic concept that underwent a shift almost as radical as the restructuring of Galy Gay into Jeraiah Jip. By 1918 Brecht had intended to use this concept in a drama called *Galgei or the Fat Man on the Swing.* [2] A note from 1919 expanded on the idea: "Galgei on a swing. A simple man is driven by a dubious type of practical jokers into playing the role of someone else." [3]

---

[1] Cited here are stanzas two and three of the poem found in GW, VIII, 84-85.
[2] Hans Otto Münsterer, *Bert Brecht. Erinnerungen aus den Jahren 1917-1922* (Zürich, 1963), pp. 93-94; BBA-B, I, 276.
[3] BBA-B, I, 276.

When he settled permanently in Berlin in 1924, Brecht was still carrying with him the germ seeds of this drama set in Augsburg with a petty-bourgeois German protagonist named Galgei. Between then and 1925, when he finally began work on what became the transformation of an Irish dock worker named Galy Gay in the military barracks of Kilkoa, the concept underwent a drastic change that might be called a "Kiplingization." Augsburg was dropped, and India under the rule of the British Colonial Army replaced it. The "wicked men" became ruffian soldiers in that army, and the exotic lore about the British army in India, which Kipling transmitted to the western world better than any other writer, replaced the banal atmosphere of Wilhelminian Germany. This removal from the familiar environs of Augsburg to the extremities of civilization as Europeans knew it was in one sense an attempt to "estrange" his material by taking a fantasy trip into an exotic realm that probably never. existed in that form.

While it is impossible to know exactly why the basic concept for this drama changed, Brecht's extensive readings in Kipling's works after approximately 1916 doubtless had something to do with the change. Brecht was familiar with all the translations of the British writer's ballads circulating in Germany during his youth: a 1910 edition by Hanns Sachs, entitled *Soldaten-Lieder und andere Gedichte von Rudyard Kipling;* a 1911 rendering of the complete "Barrack-Room Ballads" by Marx Möller called *Balladen aus dem Biwak;* and a 1917 version by Otto Hauser known as *Rudyard Kipling. Indische Balladen.* [4] More important, he read a number of Kipling's prose works (all in German translation). It can be documented that he was well-acquainted with *The Jungle Books; Kim; The Light that Failed; Just So Stories,* and a large number of the short stories, including a complete edition of *Life's Handicaps* translated by Leopold Lindau under the title *Mylord der Elefant; Mancherlei neue Geschichten von Rudyard Kipling;* he also knew the story "Moti Guj-Mutineer" as well as a number of others dealing with Kipling's notorious "Soldiers Three," such as "The Incarnation of Krishna Mulvaney"; "Private Learoyd's Story"; "The Big Drunk Draf'"; and "The God from the Machine."

All this reading of Kipling produced an imaginative ferment that began to have its effect when Brecht again turned to the "Galgei" material in Berlin. It first manifested itself around 1923-1924 in a fragmentary (unpublished) poem that stands as one of the precursors of the final, "Kiplingized" version of *A Man's a Man.* Seven completed stanzas of "The Dead Colonial Soldier" (BBA, 451/29) describe what is obviously the death of a British soldier in India, though no place name is given. It relates how he is buried, and specifically how his face is

---

[4] Information documenting Brecht's acquaintance with specific works by Kipling mentioned both here and in subsequent passages, along with examples of verbatim borrowings from these writings, can be found in this author's forthcoming book *Bertolt Brecht and Rudyard Kipling: A Marxist's Imperialist Mentor* (The Hague, 1974).

covered, an aspect which seems to adumbrate the loss of identity central to the later play. A telling note on its connection with Kipling's India appears opposite stanzas three and four. The poet inserted the words "ref[rain]: soldaten wohnen, auf den kanonen" ("soldiers live on the cannons"), which is the opening line of the chorus in the famous "The Song of the Heavy Cannon" that launched *The Threepenny Opera* on its way to international success. There, two veterans of the British Indian Army join in a musical recapitulation of their military adventures from "Cape to Cutch Behar" and recall with gusto how they slaughtered the natives in battle. The poem about "The Dead Colonial Soldier" deals with similar adventures.

In another fragmentary warm-up exercise for *A Man's a Man* that probably originated around 1924, Brecht seemed about to use Kipling's ballad "Cholera Camp" in his text. An unpublished note entitled *Story of Yellow Jack* (BBA, 459/28-30) has a character named "Cake" who recounts how British soldiers fighting against the Sikhs in India once went several weeks without finding water. Cake, who becomes the soldier Jesse in the stage version (in the earliest written draft he is known alternately as "Cake" and "Jesse Cakewater"; BBA, 150/48-51), relates how they marched around the Punjal [sic] delta for several weeks: "Then the cholera came, and they called it 'yellow jack.' The song went something like this: xx and they sang it during the day, for entertainment. . . ." The text of the song the men sang at this point does not appear, but the one Brecht has in mind was probably Kipling's ballad "Cholera Camp," since he uses it again in another context with identical factors: yellow jack, a song, "Cholera Camp." The outline for the film script called *The Fly* (1938) reconstructs a similar situation where soldiers suffering from "Yellow Jack" sing a chorus of Kipling's ballad "Cholera Camp."[5] Brecht, who attended the University of Munich with plans to study medicine, knew that cholera was not the same as yellow fever. He was no doubt acting consciously. Kipling's ballad dealt with utter helplessness in the face of "ten deaths a day," and this attitude was more important than accuracy. In a fashion typical of a hedonistic young cynic, Brecht has Cake relate how the men divided into those who swore to abstain from women, whiskey, and smoking, and those who mocked the cholera. The idea for the former may have come from the ballad's observations that "There ain't no fun in women nor there ain't no bite to drink;/ It's much too wet for shootin', we can only march and think." But the result is the same for both abstainers and mockers—they all die. Nothing of this Brechtian vignette of British army life enters the completed *A Man's a Man* except the character "Cake" alias Jesse. But it represents another symptom of the creative fermentation going on in Brecht's mind as he prepared to recast the

[5] Reproduced in Bertolt Brecht, *Texte für Filme,* ed. Werner Hecht and Wolfgang Gersch (Frankfurt, 1969), II, 422.

world of Kipling and create his own mythological British India.

At the same time Brecht was writing *A Man's a Man*, Kipling's influence erupted in yet another of his creative activities. In the fall of 1925 and the winter of 1926, he assisted in a revision of Lion Feuchtwanger's play *Warren Hastings,* which was originally written in 1916. Perhaps "insisted on" would be more accurate than "assisted in," for Feuchtwanger's widow claims that Brecht was the prime mover in undertaking the revision at a time when her husband was turning away from the drama to the novel.[6] Brecht's hand is evident throughout in such matters as diction, lore about India, and dramatic structuring.

Among other changes, Brecht added the text of his own "Surabaya-Johnny" song to the performance, Anglicized proper names ("Marianne Baronin Imhoff" in the 1916 version became "Lady Marjorie Hike"), invented a newly constructed "Punjab highway" (*Pandschabstraße*) to describe one of Hasting's activities as a colonial governor, dropped some of the references to Hasting's pragmatic humanitarianism in feeding the starving masses, added statements on the corruption of the Indian court system and how Englishmen claimed they could not get a fair trial—in short, he "imperialized" the play. Judging by the diction, Brecht also must have been responsible for writing a passage that had been added near the end. It described how the East India Co. came to India, became a prostitute, and did business under the pretext of the Bible, Law and Order, etc.:

> You see, this talented girl always understood how to have morality behind her just as a ship has the wind. With the wind she was able to go everywhere. Out in front she opened a little shop with Bibles, law books, and *Weltanschauung,* but in the rear was the big Operation for special enterprises which had little to do with Bibles and law books. Both out front and in back they lived from the rice of the country. Several dignified gentlemen dressed in frock coats were working out in the front part which faced the beach. Because the articles they sold weren't moving fast, they had ample time to think up impeccable labels and to pack the money being made out back into boxes and send it to London. Periodically, when they wasted time and mistakenly stuck their noses into the behind-the-scenes Operation, they had to be punched in same.[7]

Based on these and other revisions, Brecht was very much aware of English colonialism and imperialism while he was writing *A Man's a Man* during 1925-1926. Much of his understanding had come through Kipling's prose. The prose he knew best included a number of stories that treated the exploits of three inseparable reprobates whose life style and adventures went farther than any single factor in shaping the world of *A Man's a Man*—Kipling's Soldiers Three.

---

[6] Letter from Marta Feuchtwanger dated 14 September 1969.
[7] Lion Feuchtwanger, *Gesammelte Werke.* XI: *Stücke in Prosa* (Amsterdam, 1936), 72.

Elisabeth Hauptmann remembers that Brecht was already well-acquainted with the Soldiers Three when she met him in 1924.[8] He had used an epigraph from Kipling about "three friends that buried the fourth" as early as 1921 in the first version of *In the Jungle of Cities*. Originally it preceded chapter twelve of *The Light that Failed* in a translation by one Leopold Rosenzweig. Brecht, who intended to use it as a song in that play, appropriated it almost verbatim, as a comparison of texts illustrates:

(*Kipling*): There were three friends that buried the fourth
    The mould in his mouth and the dust in his eyes;
And they went south, and east, and north,—
    The strong man fights, but the sick man dies.
There were three friends that spoke of the dead,—
    The strong man fights, but the sick man dies.—
'And would he were here with us now,' they said,
'The sun in our face and the wind in our eyes.'[9]

(*Rosenzweig*): Drei Freunde, die legten den vierten ins Grab—
Den Moder im Mund und die Erd' im Gesicht;
Zogen 'nauf nach dem Norden, nach dem Süden hinab—
Der kranke Mann stirbt und der starke Mann ficht.

Drei Freunde, die sprachen vom toten Freund—
Der kranke Mann stirbt und der starke Mann ficht—
Und sagten: "Wär er doch mit uns hier vereint,
Den Wind in den Augen und die Sonn' im Gesicht."[10]

(*Brecht*); (John und Mankyboddle singen):
Drei Freunde, die legten den vierten ins Grab,
den Moder im Mund und die Erd im Gesicht.
Zogen 'nauf nach dem Norden, nach dem Süden hinab,
Der kranke Mann stirbt und der starke Mann ficht.

Drei Freunde, die sprachen vom toten Freund,
der kranke Mann stirbt und der starke Mann ficht.
Sie sagten: Wär er nur mit uns hier vereint,
den Wind in den Augen und die Sonn im Gesicht.[11]

While the young dramatist had encountered these three soldiers earlier than 1921, and in other contexts, this passage comes closer to qualifying as the source for the major plot outline in *A Man's a Man* than any

---

[8] This and other information here attributed to Miss Hauptmann is derived from interviews held on 15 April 1969 and 29 October 1970.

[9] Rudyard Kipling, "The Light that Failed," *The Collected Works of Rudyard Kipling*, Burwash edition (New York, 1941), XV, 163.

[10] Rudyard Kipling, *Das Licht erlosch*, trans. Leopold Rosenzweig (Stuttgart, 1899), p. 210.

[11] Bertolt Brecht, *Im Dickicht der Städte: Erstfassung und Materialien*, ed. Gisela E. Bahr (Frankfurt, 1968), p. 67.

known work. The loss of the fourth friend and their wish: "And would that he were here with us now" reproduce the basic conflict that leads to Galy Gay's transformation—three inseparable comrades have lost their fourth man, though not by death, and they desperately need him back. While the idea of transformability of human identity probably was Brecht's invention, the three soldier friends unquestionably derive from Kipling.

The most persuasive and perhaps only conclusive evidence of direct borrowing from Kipling in this play centers around the famous "temple episode" where Uria, Jesse, and Polly try to rescue Jeraiah Jip, who was trapped inside when they tried to steal copper out of the pagoda. Their motivation, i.e., to get money for beer, has many counterparts in Kipling's tales. Schumacher asserts that Brecht used an episode from his friend Alfred Döblin's novel *Die drei Sprünge des Wang-lun* as the basis for the temple scene.[12] In this novel, the title character's pigtail becomes entangled in tar on the roof when he breaks into a temple, and he must pull out the hair to free himself, thereby leaving a tell-tale bald spot.[13] But a story by Kipling, specifically the first one from *Life's Handicaps* known as "The Incarnation of Krishna Mulvaney," is responsible for the main plot elements of the play after the three return to the temple and try to rescue Jip. To understand how much of Kipling Brecht retained, a brief recapitulation of "Krishna Mulvaney" is necessary.

As is often the case, Learoyd, Ortheris, and Mulvaney are thirsty but penniless. Mulvaney comes upon one Dearsley, a railroad construction superintendent in charge of a gang of coolies who raffles off a magnificent palanquin (Mulvaney refers to it as a "sedan chair") to the workers each week, only to force the winner to return it or lose his job. Mulvaney, acting in the name of "justice," agrees to fight him for it. He takes his two friends with him, and Dearsley chooses Learoyd as his opponent. Learoyd trounces the man soundly. Now it devolves upon Mulvaney to sell the palanquin in order to get money for more beer. On pay day he loads it full of beer bottles, hires native bearers to carry him, and sets out to do so. On the way he calls on Dearsley with the express purpose of mocking him. By being maliciously hospitable, Dearsley gets Mulvaney drunk and puts him and the palanquin on a train for Benares. From this point on, events begin to parallel those in *A Man's a Man.* Mulvaney sobers up enough to realize he has been duped, but when priests recognized the palanquin as one that belongs to a certain prestigious maharanee, they carry it into the temple with Mulvaney inside before he can escape. After witnessing a "Queen's Praying," he wraps himself in the silk lining of the palanquin, impersonates the god Krishna before the assembled royal beauties, and departs. On the way

[12] Ernst Schumacher, *Die dramatischen Versuche Bertolt Brechts 1918-1933* (Berlin, 1955), p. 517.
[13] A detailed comparison of similarities in the two episodes is found in *Brecht* (Ew) p. 139.

he relieves a priest of 434 rupees and a gold necklace in return for having bequeathed to the temple a "miraculous reputashin" for the next fifty years.

It is not known with certainty what German translation of this story Brecht read; that he read and remembered it can hardly be doubted.[14] The palanquin in which both the drunken Mulvaney and Jip are carried into a temple is the most obvious point of contact, though both also assume the roles of gods when they become sober. A recondite but unmistakable allusion to "Krishna Mulvaney" offers persuasive evidence of this filial relationship. After Jip begins to come to his senses (he has been removed from the palanquin and placed in a prayer box), his first impression is that he is riding on a train. The priest assures him, however, that it is only an after-effect of the beer in his head:

> JIP: Are we getting out soon, Jesse? This carriage is rocking something awful, and it's as narrow as a latrine.
> WANG: Mister Soldier, you mustn't imagine you're in a railroad carriage. It's just the beer in your honorable head that keeps rocking. (GW, I, 324)

These are more than the phantasies of a drunkard; this is obscured Kipling. The reference to being on a train seems almost gratuitous unless one recalls that Mulvaney did in fact ride on a train in the palanquin while he was drunk. Sleeping during most of the ten hour trip to Benares, he remembers half waking at one point: "Einmal bin ich halb wach geworden, und in meinem Kopf hat es schrecklich rumort—ein Klappern und Rollen und Rasseln, wie ich's noch nie erlebt habe . . . Jungens, der Lärm war nicht vom Bier, er war von einem Zug."[15] Unless one knows the incident behind this passage, it has virtually no meaning as Brecht uses it. In the context of Kipling's story, however, it becomes evident that both have been "railroaded," one in a figurative, the other in a literal sense.

In "Krishna Mulvaney" priests dragged the palanquin into the temple; in Brecht one priest and his assistant pull the palanquin, in which the

---

[14] A readily accessible German translation that this author thinks Brecht probably knew was *Soldaten-Geschichten,* trans, General von Sickart (Berlin, 1900). As so often happened, the translator made a selection of thematically related Kipling stories from disparate works. In this collection, all dealt with the Soldiers Three. "Krishna Mulvaney" appeared as the first one; the others were "The God from the Machine"; "Private Learoyd's Story"; "The Big Drunk Draf "; "With the Main Guard"; and "In the Matter of a Private."

[15] Since Brecht read all such passages in translation and since this was the most popular and readily obtainable version of stories about "The Soldiers Three" in German translation, von Sickart's translation is used here and in subsequent passages to show the similarity in textual material between Brecht's writings and some Kipling material he might have had before him. (Kipling original from *The Collected Works of Rudyard Kipling,* IV, 24-25: "Wanst I half-roused, an', begad, the noise in me head was tremenjus'—roarin' an' rattlin' an' poundin', such as was quite new to me. . . . Bhoys, that noise was not dhrink, 'twas the rattle av a thrain!")

drunken Jip is hiding, out of the rain and into the temple. In contrast to Kipling, Brecht's priest removes Jip from the palanquin and stuffs him into a prayer box. But his reason for doing so corresponds to Mulvaney's awareness that his presence as a god had economic value for the temple. In *A Man's a Man* the priest recognizes this, too, and decides to transform him into a god and attract more paying devotees to the temple: At the very most, we can make a god out of him" (GW, I, 321). Now the rapacious priest, not the soldier, has the bright idea that the only thing to do is to exploit the situation for pecuniary gain. He instructs his assistant to hang banners on the pagoda and publicize the god's arrival, for a god is no good if word does not get around: "What good is a god if word doesn't get around?" (GW, I, 321). When it does, Jip's poundings on the sides of the prayer box are construed as divine thunderings to signal the worshipers that they must contribute according to the number of knocks they hear.

After Jip has become sober, the priest keeps up the fiction by replying to his query of how he came there by addressing him half as a soldier and half as a god:

> JIP: How did I get here?
> WANG: Through the air, Mister General, you came through the air.
> JIP: Where was I when you found me?
> WANG: Deigning to rest in an old palanquin, sublime one. (GW, I, 326)

When Jip hears that his regiment and his companions have left for the Punjab mountains, he asks what he was doing when they departed. The reply supports the assumption that Mulvaney with his legendary thirst served as the model for Jip: "Beer, much beer, a thousand bottles" (GW, I, 326). Jip, like Mulvaney, had instigated the original action to get money for beer. Mulvaney filled his palanquin with beer bottles, while Jip filled his with vomit from his heavy drinking.

In Brecht, the priest Wang has the voice of "a fat rat" (GW, I, 325). In Kipling, Mulvaney talks of "a fat priest" who knocks on the palanquin while trying to awaken the sleeping inhabitant. This priest recognizes the palanquin as that of the prominent Maharanee of Gokral-Seetarun. When he fails to awaken Mulvaney, he uses a line that Brecht later reproduced with considerable fidelity if he did not consciously imitate it: "Ein fetter Priester klopft an meiner Tür. Ich . . . rühre mich nicht. 'Die alte Kuh schläft,' sagt er zu einem andern. 'Laß sie schlafen,' sagt der." [16]

In Brecht, the three soldiers enter the temple and hear groans emanating from the prayer box:

> POLLY: What's that, sir?
> WANG: That's my milch cow. It's asleep. (GW, I, 322)

[16] von Sickart, p. 45. (Kipling original from *The Collected Works of Rudyard Kipling* IV, 28: "A fat priest knocked at my door . . . I lay still. 'The old cow's asleep,' sez he to another. 'Let her be,' sez that.")

The appellation "cow" that both use to describe the woman allegedly sleeping inside is surely more than coincidence. It is difficult to believe that Brecht did not have Kipling's temple incident in mind. Other circumstantial evidence could also be added: the similarity in the temple ceremonies (Kipling describes the burning of butter, the strange music, the singing; Brecht depicts the burning of camel dung balls, a drum beating, strange music being played by a grammaphone); or the unwavering assurance the soldiers feel that their missing comrade will return in time (if Mulvaney does not return before the end of three days, he will be jailed when he does; if Jip does not return before sunrise, his machine-gun squad will be arrested as thieves). None of the correspondences cited above offers absolute proof of borrowing. Taken *in toto,* they make a persuasive argument that "Krishna Mulvaney" almost certainly provided the raw material for this incident, an episode connected to the central plot only in as much as it disposes of Jip so that the transmogrification of Galy Gay can take place.

It was stated earlier that the restructuring of a human being's identity in this play was probably Brecht's original idea. While this is true, at least one tale by Kipling almost might have introduced him to the notion of obliterating a man's identity—the story of "The Man Who Was." Available in several translated German collections of Kipling's tales before 1920, it tells the frightening tale of a former officer in the British Army who was robbed of his identity and personality through imprisonment and maltreatment by the Russians after being captured at Sebastopol in 1854. Returning to his old regiment years later, the man does not even know his name until it is located in the regimental rolls. Within a few days he dies. While one is tempted to suspect Brecht of knowing this story, it is pure speculation. To be safe, it must be classified under the rubric of "near-Kipling" in *A Man's a Man*—those elements which have counterparts in the British writer's works, but where no proof of contact exists.

Brecht has made it particularly tantalizing for the reader in many instances where elements look suspiciously Kiplingesque, but where a known tie-in is missing. Just how many of the Anglicisms and how much Anglo-Saxon lore he drew from the English story-teller is almost impossible to say. An earlier draft of the play (BBA, 150) contains considerably more English words than the 1926 and 1931 versions-- "camp," "queen," "Sergeant," "Tommies," "Worchesterregiment," "London Times," "Daily Telegraph," "Cholera," "three cheers," and many others. These terms and certain general information on the British Army could have come through the inevitable lore about the enemy army that was current in Germany during World War I, such as the designation "Tommy" or the song "It's a Long Way to Tipperary," both of which recur with great frequency in this early version (in almost every scene Brecht has one character or the other strike up a chorus of "Tipperary," a practice he excludes from the final rendering). But most of his specialized knowledge about the British Indian Army must have come through this literary spokesman of the Empire, though specific sources are elusive because Brecht uses precisely those elements which recur in many of Kipling's short stories. One thinks, for example, of the army elephants that play such an important role in the stories of India (e.g., "Her Majesty's Servants"). The three comrades employ a ruse connected with Galy Gay's alleged sale of the army elephant Billy Humph to gain control over him. The use of the term "nigger" as an appellation for the indigenous population of India is also something Brecht encountered frequently in Marx Möller's translation of the "Barrack-Room Ballads." In a German rendering of the short stories by von Sickart that Brecht might have read, a footnote in the story of "Krishna Mulvaney" even explains: "For the uneducated Englishman every colored person is a 'nigger'"[17]

In *A Man's a Man* Brecht seizes on this bit of lore in the "Song of Widow Begbick's Canteen" where the soldiers sing of fighting against "niggers" (GW, I, 310):

Und brüllt die Schlacht im Pand- schabvale	If the battle roars in the Punjab Vale
Fahr'n wir in Witwe Begbicks Tank	In Begbick's Bar we join the hunt
Mit Rauchen und mit schwarzem Ale	We smoke and drink her darkest ale
Erst mal die Niggerfront entlang.	In full view of the nigger front.

Repeated references in *A Man's a Man* to the staggering quantities of beer consumed by the troops have dozens of models in Kipling. Brecht's anachronistic designation of the British soldiers of 1925 as *Rotröcke* ("red coats") in early versions of this play probably harkens back to the Sachs or Müller translations of the ballads that use this term. From Kipling's short stories Brecht would have gained the impression that the majority of the military actions by the British Colonial Army were fought along the northern border. Consequently he creates an army whose duty in this play it is "to establish order on the northern border" (GW, I, 300) and whose troops are ordered to action in a Tibetan mountain pass midway through the play. Kipling's place names also constituted a treasure-trove for the exotic-sounding names he was fond of using. He drew on them freely in this play and elsewhere, from "Punjab" and "Peschawur" to "Rankerdan" and "Calcutta." These are but a few of many "Kiplingisms" that testify of a debt without revealing where it was incurred.

Brecht's genius in taking another's creative raw material and reshaping it almost beyond recognition accounts for the problem a reader has when he clearly perceives something Kiplingesque here but fails to recognize a specific source. Several examples will further illustrate this phenomenon of "submerged Kiplingisms." The text of the poem "Loot," for example, which he knew from the "Barrack-Room

[17] von Sickart, p. 15.

Ballads," would have furnished ideal background effects for the temple break-in episode: "Now remember when you're 'acking round a gilded Burma god/ That 'is eyes is often very precious stones." The ballad singer's attitude coincides with the views of Brecht's fighting men: "So, if my song you'll 'ear, I will learn you plain an' clear/ 'Ow to pay yourself for fightin' overtime."

Brecht also outfits his soldiers with a reputation for stealing. Galy Gay's wife tells him to avoid soldiers because they are "the worst men in the world . . . we can consider ourselves lucky if they don't commit burglary and murder" (GW, I, 299). This, too, could have originated in any number of Kipling stories which recount the thievery that the lower ranks engaged in to supplement their meager pay. Brecht absorbed it all, but he looted more skillfully than Kipling's soldiers and left fewer clues—only suspicions.

The opening scene of the play is in all likelihood a passage where he looted carefully. As he leaves the house, Galy Gay's wife observes: "You're like an elephant, the most cumbersome beast in the animal world, but when it starts running, it runs like a freight train" (GW, I, 299). Later Galy Gay himself tells the soldiers: "But I am like a passenger train when I start running" (GW, I, 307). In a German translation of "Moti Guj—Mutineer," Brecht had read a similar bit of elephant exotica: "Elefanten laufen nicht im Galopp. Sie bewegen sich mit wechselnder Geschwindigkeit. Wenn ein Elefant einen Expresszug einholen wollte, würde er nicht galoppieren, aber den Expresszug würde er einholen."[18] The words *Güterzug, Personenzug, Expresszug,* when added to the identical claim that an elephant can run with the speed of a train in spite of its cumbersome gait, constitute an unexpected bit of Kipling hidden in the opening lines. Here Brecht probably borrowed consciously and varied freely without altering the substance.

The transmogrification of Sergeant Fairchild from "Bloody Five" into a weak-kneed coward testifies that here, too, Brecht was using specialized army lore drawn from Kipling's stories. To ward off "attacks of sensuality" that accompanied heavy rains, he asks the widow Begbick for help. She demands that he change into civilian clothes before she will help him. He consents, and the result is a loss of respect in the eyes of his men. For them, the act of donning civilian clothes betokens a loss of virility. Because the army is about to depart for the north, this change of status is also tantamount to desertion.

When he first appears in this attire and gives an order, Uria responds by knocking off his hat (GW, I, 354). There follows the humorous sharpshooting event in which he becomes the laughing stock of the troops when he fails to hit an egg with his army revolver. Knowing

---

[18] (Kipling original from *The Collected Works of Rudyard Kipling* IV, 362: "Elephants do not gallop. They move from spots at varying rates of speed. If an elephant wished to catch an express train he could not gallop, but he could catch the train.")

something of Kipling makes this loss of prowess assume different dimensions. Repeatedly one hears of the contempt his soldiers feel for British civilian employees in India, especially civil servants. This is an essential element, for example, in the "Krishna Mulvaney" story. But their ultimate scorn is reserved for former soldiers who take civilian positions in India. Precisely this had happened to Mulvaney in the story of "The Big Drunk Draf'" which was one of those tales Brecht knew from collections dealing with the Soldiers Three. Mulvaney, retired from the service, returned to India because of his wife. He then experienced that "great and terrible fall" into semi-disgrace in the eyes of his old comrades. This explains Fairchild's sensitivity about civilian clothes as a badge of ignominy at several points in the play: "Yes, go ahead and mutiny, you sons of a cannon! Look at my suit and laugh" (GW, I, 354); "Where is my name? Even my coat is gone, the coat I wore! . . . What kind of clothes do I have on? Are these suitable for me?" (GW, I, 368).

Mulvaney's wife tried to coax him into letting his beard grow, for "Twas so civilian-like." Mulvaney, who yearned for the old life, resisted this attempt to brand him with the one badge that distinguished civilians from the military more than any other one—a beard. Again Brecht unobtrusively inserts this bit of exotica from Kipling into the play at a strategic point which marks the beginning of the final stage in Galy Gay's transformation. At the close of the trial, the third of four steps in this process, Galy Gay concludes the scene by saying:

> GALY GAY: Widow Begbick, I'd like you to get a pair
> of scissors to cut off my beard.
> BEGBICK: Why?
> GALY GAY: I know why. (GW, I, 349)

Brecht knew why, too—from Kipling.

Most interpreters have subscribed to the view that *A Man's a Man* depicts the world of Kipling's "Barrack-Room Ballads."[19] Steffensen, for example, considers the "Song of Widow Begbick's Canteen" to be a parody based on one of these ballads, though he does not specify which one.[20] Willett has called attention to similarities in tone between the lines "Mach das Maul zu, Tommy, halt den Hut fest, Tommy" in this song and lines like "For it's Tommy this, an' Tommy that, an' Tommy wait outside" from the ballad "Tommy."[21] And echoes of the ballad "Loot" do reverberate through the temple pilfering scene. But the extent of Kipling's presence in this play far exceeds what Brecht could have gleaned from the "Barrack-Room Ballads" alone. The short stories constituted his primary source of lore for *A Man's a Man.* They, more than the "Barrack-Room Ballads," led to the creation of the

---

[19] For a representative view, see *Brecht* (E/2), p. 286.
[20] Steffen Steffensen, *Bertolt Brechts Gedichte* (Copenhagen, 1972), p. 35.
[21] *Brecht* (W), p. 90.

Kiplingesque atmosphere one commonly associates with it.

A cursory examination of what Brecht did with material from the tales and the ballads seems to confirm such an assumption. With the exception of part of a single line borrowed from "The Widow at Windsor" that he used twice in his career,[22] his works contain no further allusions to or images, paraphrases, or other material from the original "Barrack-Room Ballads." Given his admitted propensity for re-using what he liked, and given the large chunks of Kipling he borrowed from other sources, their impact was obviously limited. But he returned several times during his career to the Soldiers Three from the stories. True, by the time he was finished they had become independent creations only faintly similar to the originals; but the frequency of their recurrence reflects how well he knew them and what an impact they must have made.

The stanza about "three friends that buried the fourth" first recorded in 1921 marks the chronological debut of these mythical three in Brecht's œuvre. The fragmentary poem "The Dead Colonial Soldier" of 1923-1924 also alludes to them in its reference to the "Song of the Heavy Cannon"—which in its nascent form was in fact called "Song of the Soldiers Three" (GW, VIII, 127), and originally three British soldiers were to have sung it. Miss Hauptmann confirms that the Soldiers Three were the inspiration for it.[23] But as so often happened, Brecht liberated them from their original source and ended up with a Kipling-inspired but highly original creation. The next step in their evolution is possibly subject to dispute—the long lyric cycle known as "The Soldiers Three: A Children's Book" (GW, VIII, 340-63) of 1932. One might well argue that it has nothing to do with Kipling's Soldiers Three, and that Brecht's admitted fascination with the numeral three makes its application to soldiers who personify Hunger, Accident, and Coughing (presumably tuberculosis) purely coincidental. No doubt, such an assumption should not be disregarded. Furthermore, they have just fought in World War I (on whose side one does not learn), which removes them even further from Kipling. But like Kipling's Soldiers Three, they, too, are half-civilized anarchists who live outside conventional law and create, as it were, their own laws and social order. Willett is right in seeing Kipling as the ancestor of all of Brecht's bloated and caricatured soldiers in this and later works.[24] One wonders how a highly self-conscious writer like Brecht who knew the Soldiers

---

[22] The line in question was borrowed from Marx Möller's rendering of "The Widow at Windsor." It began: "The widow at Windsor in widow's weeds/ Has many millions in her coffers." According to Miss Hauptmann, this was the source of Brecht's opening line in a song for his adaptation of Marlowe's *Edward the Second*. He varied Marlowe's original to read: "The Maidens of England in Widow's Weeds."Later he used Möller's line verbatim in his poem "The Caledonian Market" (GW, IX, 534).

[23] Interview of 29 October 1970.

[24] *Brecht* (W), p. 91.

Three so well could have used the same designation without hearing overtones of Kipling's three. Consciously or not, he linked them loosely to a line that goes back to British Colonial India.

The final evolutionary stage is reached in "Song of the Three Metaphysical Soldiers" (GW, VIII, 395) written shortly after the previous one. In both title and content it extends the idea of three soldiers as metaphoric figures. The editors of GW point out the connection between it and Brecht's lyric cycle "The Soldiers Three: A Children's Book."[25] Without being too bold, one might also assert that Kipling's Soldiers Three are legitimate, albeit distant ancestors of this poem, too.

Brecht's fascination with Kipling's the Soldiers Three and their exploits can be explained without difficulty. They fit into the rubric of the adventurers, freebooters, outsiders, and anarchists he used to populate the landscape of his early poems and stories. In another sense, they are only one step removed from the gangster types he turned to in later works. He himself forged this link between gangsters in uniform and gangsters generally in *The Threepenny Opera,* for Macheath was a veteran of the British Colonial Army in India. His progenitors can be found in the Soldiers Three.

Without doubt one could mine *A Man's a Man* for a good deal more hidden material that has counterparts in tales of the Soldiers Three and others by Kipling. Jesse, Uria, and Polly take turns reminding one of Mulvaney, and Galy Gay is typical of the civilian innocent who falls into their hands and gets "fleeced." Willett is certainly correct in seeing a relationship between Kipling's soldiers, the three protagonists in this play, and the Good Soldier Schwejk.[26] His observation that "Galy Gay is really a Schwejk fallen among Mulvaneys" rings true, though it is uncertain whether Brecht was aware of Schwejk while writing *A Man's a Man.*[27]

The mock execution of Galy Gay has faint similarities with the ballad "Danny Deever"; the "Oh dear, what fun we had in old Uganda" song from *The Elephant Calf,* which contains reminiscences of soldiers who fought against Papa Krüger in the Boer War, also stands in the tradition of "Fuzzy-Wuzzy"; it might have come from any one of a number of ballads about the Boer War. Peter Horst Neumann sees the eleventh scene as a variation of the situation in "My Lord the Elephant," where one elephant blocks the movement of an entire British Army unit through a mountain pass in the north when it refuses to cross a bridge.[28]

---

[25] GW, X, 11*.

[26] *Brecht* (W), p. 91.

[27] John Willett, letter dated 26 August 1968. The first exposure to Hašek's character that can be dated with certainty came when Brecht helped adapt the novel for Erwin Piscator's stage in 1927.

[28] Peter Horst Neumann, *Der Weise und der Elefant. Zwei Brecht Studien* (Munich, 1970), pp. 85-86.

Mulvaney finally persuades the beast to move on, thus clearing the pass. By analogy, Galy Gay, who is "unstoppable, like a battle elephant" clears a pass in the mountains for troops delayed in their march to Tibet. This analogy sounds plausible, but proving it is an exercise in futility. Like each example mentioned above, Kipling's presence is both indisputable and obscured.

Because of his political and artistic development, Brecht turned to Kipling less frequently and more selectively after 1926. This is not to say that he forgot or abandoned the British writer. But from this point on, there is no other work where the world of Kipling dominates as it does here. In this sense, *A Man's a Man* represents a watershed in the relationship of the two writers. Kipling had played his part well, and Brecht was ready for a new kind of theater.

SAINT JOAN OF THE SLAUGHTERHOUSES[1]:
STRUCTURES OF A SLAUGHTERHOUSE WORLD

Darko Suvin

I. Cosmology and Diegetics:
The Ups and Downs of Salvation

The universe of Brecht's play *Saint Joan of the Slaughterhouses* is divided into what one might call (with a retrospective use of his *Schweyk in World War II*) upper spheres, lower spheres, and a limbo or no man's land in between. The upper spheres are those of politicoeconomic power and decision making. They are constituted by the meat packers at the Chicago stock exchange, culminating in Mauler. However, Mauler becomes the head of the vertical cartel only because he is connected to a larger mysterious universe of high finance and presumably ultimate, unquestioned capitalist power in New York. The lower spheres are composed of the stockyard workers, marked by powerlessness against a destiny that comes from above "like the rain" (674, 720).[2] That destiny, their "misfortune," is composed both of inclement nature ("the terrors of cold Chicago," 669), and of the politicoeconomic climate created by the capitalists in their Hobbesian system of mutual preying. Marginally, perhaps, the lower spheres involve also the cattle-raising ranchers from the "Missouri" prairies and,

[1] Both "stockyards" and "slaughterhouses" are valid translations of different aspects of *Schlachthöfe;* for my purposes I prefer to use the latter term. This essay was written after the experience of an experimental drama project at McGill University, whose result was a production of *Saint Joan* in March 1973. Cf. program *Saint Joan of the Slaughterhouses,* ed. D. Suvin, and a collection of the collaborators' articles and discussions in *A Production Notebook to "St. Joan of the Stockyards,"* ed. M. Bristol and D. Suvin (Montréal: McGill University, 1973). I have learned very much from my students who were also the cast of the performance, and from my colleague Michael Bristol, the director of the performance. My thanks also go to Donald F. Theall, without whom this Drama Module would not have come about, to Bernard Dort and Werner Hecht for indicating and supplying some materials difficult to find, to the late Elisabeth Hauptmann for a stimulating discussion, and to the BBA. I have avoided providing notes except where absolutely necessary, but I am very conscious how much I owe to the secondary literature on this play, on which I hope to provide a commentary in the near future. For the criticism on *Saint Joan* to which I am indebted, I refer to *Brecht* (G). Further I should like to mention Giorgio Strehler, Interview with Renato Palazzi, *Cahiers Théâtre Louvain,* 12/13 (1971); Manfred Wekwerth and the Berliner Ensemble staff (for notes assembled in *Die Heilige Johanna: Schauspielermaterial,* dittoes); Gisela E. Bahr, *Die heilige Johanna der Schlachthöfe. Bühnenfassung, Fragmente, Varianten* (Frankfurt, 1971); Patty Lee Parmalee, "Brecht's America" (Diss. University of California at Irvine, 1970).

[2] Since the translation by Frank Jones, *Saint Joan of the Stockyards* (Bloomington, 1971), was usable neither for the stage nor for philological purposes, a new translation of Brecht's play was made at McGill University by Richard H. Howe. It was then revised for the stage by some cast members and myself and later retouched by the translator. I am using this unpublished translation, but the responsibility for the final formulations is mine. All page references in the text are to GW, II.

at the lowest end of the ladder, the cattle led to slaughter.

The topology of the play is a fusion of the robust oppositions of German Leninism with a simplified version of the medieval, Dantean salvational vertical. The basic opposition between two classes, taken from European sociopolitical reality as interpreted through *The Communist Manifesto* via the Leninist storm and stress of the twenties, is expressed through the image of huge masses standing against each other like armies with front lines. The Black Straw Hats' marching with drums and flags as "Soldiers of the Lord" (684) "everywhere where unrest prevails" (674) is only a particularly explicit case of the general militarization of life under imperialism (as was their prototype, the Salvation Army, which Brecht studied attentively), an example of the front line dividing society:

> . . . built up
> In giant squadrons facing each other
> Employers and employees
> Battling fronts: irreconcilable.
> Run round between them, reconciler and mediator
> Of use to neither, and perish completely. (725)

In classical urban insurrectionary language, the front line in a civil war is at the barricades:

> SLIFT: The main thing, where do you stand, man? This side or that side of the barricades?
> SNYDER: The Black Straw Hats stand above the battle, Mr. Slift. Therefore, this side. (721)

Such a front line is permanent, since economic warfare never ceases. The "border of poverty" (756) exists not only as a financial statistic but in the actual topography of the city's Packingtown slums, which recall Sinclair's *The Jungle*. In classical American idiom, which Brecht did not use here, it is the line that separates the right side from the wrong side of the railway tracks. In moments of acute conflict approaching civil war, such as the attempted general strike, it is the front on which an actual army actually employs machine guns and tanks (752, 753).

At this front line, the workers' only weapon is their number, organization, and solidarity (741, 749, 758). That is an indispensable condition for counterviolence, for a counterarmy in process of formation (741, 749, 751, 758, and especially 753). The imperative of organization into a tight "net" (742, 759) is also decisive for Joan's final role and failure, of which more hereafter.

In this basic Leninist opposition, a sociological stratification of upper (oppressor) and lower (oppressed) class (718, 723) is on the verge of being collapsed and resolved into a *secessio plebis,* into a strategic horizontal of two opposed enemy formations. However, in Brecht's play, this collapse (prophetically, for German reality) does not come about, and the momentarily threatened static vertical remains dominant, powerfully reinforced by a Dantean moral topology. Grim Chicago with its "omnipotent cold" (679), its rains, its snowstorms attacking the huddled poor (722 and later), its "wind in the depths" (778), is not too far from the nethermost circle of Hell congealed by Lucifer's fanning. The correlation of the physical depths of hunger and cold (711, 732) with the moral depths of the "cold skinning" of man by man (710) can be compared to *Inferno* episodes such as the Ugolino one. However, Brecht's vertical cosmology of "Heaven and Hell, up and down" (762), differs strongly from Dante's not only because it is dramatically foreshortened but, more significantly, because its upper spheres of socioeconomic power are throughout the play a sardonic anti-paradise of preestablished disharmony. They are characterized in great detail right up to Joan's final prophetic maledictions which sum up the pertinent oppositions:

> THE PACKERS AND RANCHERS *(very loud, so that Joan is drowned out)*: If the building shall rise high
> Top and bottom must apply.
> Therefore keep each in that place
> God has given him in this race.
> Pace by pace
> Have him work his proper measure:
> Should he rather take his pleasure
> 'Twould our harmony displace.
> Down below the low are right,
> The mighty are throned on heights. . . .
> JOAN: But those who are down are kept down
> So those on high can stay high,
> And the baseness of those up high is beyond all measure.
> And even if they got better, that would
> Not help, for unmatched is
> The system they made:
> Exploitation and disorder, bestial and so
> Incomprehensible. (780-81)

The earlier quotation about Joan as "reconciler and mediator" (725) indicated that between the two fronts there is—as befits this slaughterhouse world—a category of "middlemen," ideological rather than commercial. They are identified openly as such in that passage because both Joan and the Black Straw Hats are such ideological middlemen, who are at that point splitting apart. With the intensification of the gulf between high and low, the Black Straw Hats are openly aligning themselves with one "side of the barricades" and Joan with the other. This no man's land between the front lines is also somewhat like the Dantean limbo where dwell souls that have not had sufficient fortitude even to commit their own sins, and therefore bear the brunt of Dante's deepest contempt. It is characteristic of this play, however, that such "men in the middle"—an artistic transformation of the middle classes between the capitalists and the workers—are in the focus of interest. In a strange way, Mauler with his lofty and base souls, and the close links to Joan, can also function as a mediator between up high and down below, but only in the interests of up high. More will be said of such communications in Part III of this essay.

Thus, the basic oppositions in the universe of *Saint Joan* are vertical (upper, in between, lower), with secondary oppositions in each of the three horizontal layers: the war of packer against packer, the alternative orientations of the middlemen, the different degrees of consciousness between workers, strike leaders, and ranchers. An understanding of the diegetic unfolding of such oppositions seems indispensable for all subsequent discussions. It can be briefly summarized in Tables 1 and 2. The play is clearly divided into two parts plus the ending. Up to and including scene viii the figures, as well as the action, shift between the various spheres: Mauler goes to open a hospital, the poor workers and ranchers are taken to the stock market and to Slift's house, the packers visit the Black Straw Hats, while Joan circulates freely through the whole system. Between scenes viii and ix a good director will locate his single interval. In ix, the secession of the workers is existentially (though not ideologically) a *fait accompli:* the action shifts between the upper and lowest spheres; they are juxtaposed directly without intermediaries, but the figures can no longer cross the gap (except for the newsmen who function as camouflaged scouts in enemy territory, and for Mauler's "crossing the border" toward the end). The ending (x-xii) consists of Mauler's illumination. Scene xi is compositionally dubious; it would probably gain by being—as in the earlier versions— amalgamated with scene ix. In the grand finale (xii) all figures meet for the first and last time under the aegis of victorious Mauler in the "canonization" of Joan.

Within such a division, *Saint Joan* develops following several interlocking rhythms. In the upper, primary, politicoeconomic domain, it follows the *unfolding of the crisis cycle* or spiral marked by the letters from New York detailing the phases of the cycle in scenes i, vi (but vi is related to v), ixb, x.[3] The four phases of the "terrible cycle"(704-705), freely adapted from Marx, are its beginning (overproduction: scenes i-iv), rise (speculation: v-viii), culmination (crash: ix-x), and stabilization on a higher level of cartelization, with the workers bearing the costs both as laborers and as consumers (x).

---

[3] See Käthe Rülicke, "Die heilige Johanna der Schlachthöfe: Notizen zum Bau der Fabel," SF, 11 (1959), 429-44; Peter Demetz, "Vorwort," *Die heilige Johanna* (München-Wien, 1964), pp. 25-26; Bernard F. Dukore, *Drama and Revolution* (New York, 1971), pp. 308-11.

Table 1. Vertical and horizontal oppositions: synchronic

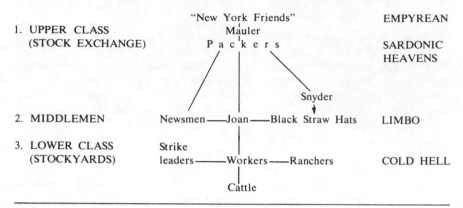

Table 2. Unfolding of oppositions: diachronic

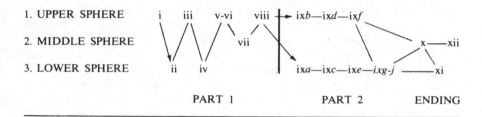

In the central, ideological domain (central both in the vertical scheme of Tables 1 and 2 and in the sense of holding the center of the spectators' attention), the three scenes in which the action shifts from the highest to the lowest sphere (ii, iv, and ix*a*) are also Joan's three "descents into the depths." This whole aspect of the play reposes on a metonymic system of vertical positions and tendencies. In her *first descent,* Joan recognizes the degradation of the workers. "The lowliest" (672) are "going under" (673), and it's no good preaching to them a spiritual uplift ("strive up, don't strive down," 674) and reprimanding their striving after "lowly pleasures"—"this little bit to eat and pretty apartments and movies" (675)—while they are starving and freezing:

> That rises no higher than the rim of a bowl. . . .
> Living from minute to minute uncertainly,
> They can lift themselves no longer
> From this lowest ground. . . . (677)

In her *second descent,* Joan recognizes that the ultimate cause of this degradation is not ethical but economical—the workers cannot afford a goodness or a just anger whose price would be starvation in cold Chicago: "Don't you see that it rains on their wickedness?" (696). After she has tried the appeal to the good capitalist's conscience (v and vi) and moral indignation against the bad capitalists (vii: "you up there doing such things," 707), Joan realizes in her *third descent* that the workers have to help themselves against the upper class and the religious middlemen. However, she is deterred from becoming a consistent participant in such self-help by cold, credulity, and pacifism—basically, by not having shared the existence of a worker, which leads to a failure of imaginative sympathy and thus to her downfall:

> [A violent person] is surely
> Full of deceit against his fellow-men
> Outside of all bonds
> That are customary among men.
> No longer belonging, he would find
> Himself, in a world no longer familiar
> No longer at home. Above his head
> The planets would run no longer
> By the old rule. Words would
> Change their meaning for him. . . .
> Three days in Packingtown in the morass of the slaughterhouses
> Joan was seen
> Stepping downward step by step
> To clear the mud, to appear to
> The lowest. Three days downwards
> Striding, weakening on the third and
> Swallowed by the morass in the end. Tell them:
> It was too cold. (754-55)

Finally, Joan's death (xii) is a *last descent* into the depths. Her downfall is inexcusable and unredeemable: "The stone does not excuse the fallen" (758-59). It is therefore only very ambiguously negated within the play, which has no happy end. Not only is the canonization by the massed choirs of capitalist consensus a consciously false uplift—

> SNYDER: Arise, Joan of the Slaughterhouses,
>   Intercessor for the poor,
>   Comforter of the lowest depths! (778) . . .
> THE BUTCHERS: Climbing means: on others climbing,
>   And this heavenly upwards-striving
>   Also must be downwards-trampling (781)—

but even Joan's own belated uplift is still theoretical and reactive, couched in and imaginatively tied to the dominant class terminology of socioethical up and down, and therefore perceivable as despairing and somewhat hysterical: "And those who tell them they can rise in spirit/ while stuck in mud, their head should also be/ smashed on the pavement" (782-83). This should prevent the careful spectator from investing her, even at the end, with the saintly and therefore infallible

119

character of Shaw's Saint Joan—from staging his own sentimental, middle-class canonization. But it does not at all lessen the validity of most of her insights—certainly not of those supported by the general drift of the play. Her final realization in scenes xi-xii is that it is necessary and possible to change the world radically, and that this will inescapably have to be done by solidarity and force:

> I for example have done nothing.
> For let nothing be counted good, no matter how it looks, but what
> Really helps, and let nothing be held honorable but what
> Changes this world finally: it needs it! (780)

Joan's descents into the depths are thus harrowing, but they do not lead to any radical, salvational Harrowing of Hell, only to an understanding of how desperately that is needed:

> Fast disappearing from this world fearlessly
> I tell you:
> Take care that when you leave this world
> You were not only good but left
> A good world! (780)

The Workers are subject to iron laws of political economy; Joan wanders around trying to understand them and the laws they are subject to. Oscillating between the upper, central, and finally also the lower level, *Mauler's line* is the third and final rhythmic determinant of *Saint Joan*. As mentioned, Mauler is also an intermediary. As "the contemporary stage of the Faustian Man" (4*) he has two souls: the base, business soul, striving toward *Fleisch* (the untranslatable pun on "flesh" and "meat" on which so much of this play reposes), belongs to the politicoeconomic domain, but the lofty, sentimental soul striving toward *Geist,* belongs to the ideological domain and makes of him the *animus* of Joan's *anima*.

Mauler is physically present in the whole first half of the play, except for scenes iv and vii, which, however, show the result of his actions. In the second half, after being in the center of action in the upper-sphere scenes, he—most interestingly—in scene ix*h* "crosses the border of poverty" (755) into the lower spheres, symbolically shedding his riches, wiped out in the crash, by letting go his detectives (who protected him in those spheres in the prefigurative scene ii*b*). His experiences in that theologico-political hell or purgatory, his "humbling" (x), lead to his final ascent or "exaltation" (765). That ascent and enthronement, which is Mauler's real Assumption into the Heavens of full power as opposed to the window dressing of Joan's canonization, is due to a double illumination of his. In the ideological domain, he has recognized (in scene x, at the Black Straw Hats', where he realizes that the drowning have to clutch at straws), that salvational beliefs too are manipulable, with an effect even greater than the manipulation of politicoeconomic information he has been so adept at. After this, he was able to recognize in the politicoeconomic domain that the ideologically subjugated workers are potential consumers, not just producers. His realization comes as a consequence of Joan's urge to raise their moral and economic "purchasing power" (705). Thus, Mauler's journey into the dark and cold nether regions is the obverse of Joan's; ready to lose all, he gained all. Where Joan's single-minded search high and low for good availed her nothing, Mauler's double soul proved able to valorize all twists and turns that happened: "Misfortune downs the down and out/ It lifts me up, by spirit's route" (757). Therefore, in the ending of *Saint Joan of the Slaughterhouses,* Mauler fuses his function as protagonist with that of undisputed arbiter, indeed the *metteur-en-scène* of this world play. He, the perfect capitalist, can keep both souls—the spiritual (lofty) one serving the business (base) one, of course. "At the end of *Saint Joan,* those up high ascend one more step, whereas those down below descend to the same degree."[4]

Such an insistent use of a medieval or baroque cosmogony, with its moralized vertical, as well as the innumerable biblical structural elements, testifies to the salvational character of *Saint Joan.* One of the recurrent biblical references is that to the seven days of malevolent creation (722, 733, 761, 763)—even though the seven days are inaccurate in the context of the play's chronology; another is the various temptations of both Joan and Mauler on their different *viae crucis.* *Saint Joan's* black or atheist variant of Dantean cosmology, straining but failing to turn into a Leninist horizontal Armageddon, is rather similar to medieval Mysteries through its vertical dimension and to Shakespearean histories and problem plays through its horizontal dimension. Like a (left or Feuerbachian) mystery play, it alternates between various moral and/or power statuses; like, e.g., *Troilus and Cressida* or *The Merchant of Venice,* but translated into class warfare it alternates between opposed camps, with some go-betweens and renegades. This cosmology and composition are eminently supple, suited to showing matters of both global and indeed cosmic import (as in the Middle Ages) and intense figures, representative of clashes between opposed camps (which are sometimes internalized within the same figure, as in the Renaissance). Of course, the ideology and world view would be diametrically opposed to that of the great dramaturgies of European class civilization. One could think of Brecht as a writer of medieval mystery plays who was (as Blake said of Milton) of Satan's party, or as Thersites writing *Troilus and Cressida: die Dramaturgie wird durchforscht werden* (the dramaturgy will be researched into), to coin a Brechtian slogan. The destiny of Man is Man, and salvation will not come from above, but through political economics and ideology: "Only force helps where force rules, and/ Only men help where there are men" (783).

[4] Bernard Dort, *Lecture de Brecht* (Paris, 1967), p. 104.

121

II. Anthropology: The Political Economics of Fleshly
(Slaughterhouse) Existence

The basic vertical configuration of the universe of *Saint Joan of the Slaughterhouses* allows for several lines of communicating things and ideas between its constituent classes: from up downward, from down upward (both can be established directly or by means of middlemen), and horizontally within each class. Those power lines are, as indicated in Part I, of two main kinds—*politicoeconomic* (material power) and *informational* (ideological power). This section will discuss the politicoeconomic interactions.

There are further exchanges transacted in this play than just those of the stock exchange where cattle are turned into profit and speculation. This is in effect also a labor exchange, where the labor power and, indeed, the brute existence of laborers (workers and ranchers) are also bartered for. The axiological backbone of this play is Marx's labor theory of value, i.e., that all values created by the production of goods flow exclusively from the action of labor on natural raw materials—so that all other autonomous functions in the process of production, primarily that of the capitalists, could be dispensed with. In that light, it is not only Mauler who is a modern Faust, with Slift as his Mephistopheles; in a way, Humanity as a whole—represented by the Workers—has also entered upon a losing pact with the devil of Capitalism. It is thereby animalized and reduced to the position of cattle slaughtered by the jungle predators and bloodthirsty devourers of raw meat. A second strain of imagery, fleshing out the skeletal topology of vertical and horizontal, is a turning of *cattle and men* into *flesh*, bloodied, bought and sold, renewed (through food: meat for the rich or soup for the poor), or lacking such renewal (in hunger). This second pattern will serve to discuss the political economics of raw existence, the "reproduction of immediate life,"[5] in *Saint Joan*.

The topography of this play is, of course, based on the opposition of *stock market* and *stockyards*. The stock market subsists on the exploitation of workers to the point of freezing and starvation; the stockyards subsist on the slaughtering of cattle. One basic relationship of the figures in this play (let us remember that in an earlier version Brecht had choruses of oxen, swine, and workers in the finale) can, with due prudence and confirmation by the subsequent discussion, be formulated as *Packers : Workers = Men : Cattle*. The power wielders deal with the lower, powerless class in analogous ways: the lockout and subsequent actions of the Packers against the workers cancel their "human face"; it is a kind of bloodless, "cold" slaughtering. It can, however, in a

---

[5] Frederick Engels, "The Origin of the Family, Private Property and the State," Karl Marx and Frederick Engels, *Selected Works* (London, 1968), p. 455.

crunch turn to actual bloodshed, a "hot" slaughtering, by the army and police who are "bashing [their] heads in" (745):

> MAULER: I want to tell you my true opinion
> Of our business:
> So naked, only buying and selling,
> Each man coldly skinning the other man.
> It can't go on; there are too many that
> Howl in misery, and there'll be more
> [That fall] into our bloody cellars. . . . (710-11)

The "many," the deliberate ambiguity of "*Was da* in unsere blutigen Keller fällt," equates the workers and cattle. Complementarily, Joan's weighty passage from the finale identifies the disjunction between the upper and lower human spheres as an almost biological or geographical one, with not only different knowledge and value measures but even different languages, and concludes with the same reified pronoun ("Und *was* Menschengesicht trägt/ Kennt sich nicht mehr"):

For there is a gulf between those up high and those down below, bigger than
Between the Mount Himalaya and the sea,
And what goes on up high
Is unheard of down below,
And unheard of up high what goes on below.
And there are two languages high and low,
And two measures for measure,
And whatever wears a human face
Can know itself no more. (780)

Brecht's primal vision of "a jungle of cities" (not a lush, but a cold jungle, a tangled thicket frozen by the winds of exploitation and alienation that blow across the Luciferic wastes of Lake Michigan), his constant preoccupation with a Social-Darwinist bestiary, expands in *Saint Joan* into a complex set of references to the bestial, carnivorous Slaughterhouse World. There, the lower class is butchered by the upper-class predators, whose internecine struggles are thereby reduced to a fight over the spoils. The function of the strike leaders and stockyards activists—the rabble-rousers—is, in fact, rousing the rest of the workers from a cattle-like stupor to an active and human, if violent, intervention into their own crassly alienated destiny (cf. 783).

Especially striking in this "world like unto a slaughterhouse" (672) is the *parallel between oxen and men*. "Cattle" (*Vieh*) in the collective form is used in *Saint Joan* only in connection with the buying and selling, marketing and pricing, of stock-market (*Vieh-börse*) operations (678, 699, 700, 708, 726-27, etc.). But oxen are often almost persons, pathetically equipped with feelings, although not with articulated speech: The play opens with Mauler's lament for the "blond ox," "looking dumb to heaven," and being slaughtered, and with his resulting aversion for this "bloody business." Explicitly, Mauler associates the ox and himself: "'twas as if it [the blow] was meant for me" (667); "such oxen's achings/ Shut up no more within this breast" (668). Later, this sentimental identification is doubted by his competitors. They know his "business soul," buying "anything and everything that even looks like a hog or an ox" (716), better. As Slift puts it, "He saw the poor ox die and decided/ Instead of this poor ox/ He'd slaughter rich man Cridle" (686; see also 682). But Mauler, strengthening the identification of oxen with innocence, gives them even precedence to the workers Joan pleads for—

> Oxen I pity, Man is bad.
> For your plan, men are not ready.
> First, before the world can change,
> Man must change (688)—

as well as against the packers:

> You brazen butchers, howl in your mothers' laps
> When the tormented creature ceases screaming!
> Go home and say, one amongst you
> Could hear no more the oxen screaming
> And chose your screaming over theirs!
> I want my money and peace for my conscience! . . . (699)
> THE PACKERS: . . . You filthy butcher! Here, take *our* flesh, cut your
> part out from it!
> MAULER: He who is an ox may not wonder that one gets hungry looking
> at him. . . .
> So, Graham, now I demand to have your cans!
> You can stuff yourself into them.
> I'll teach you the meat business [*Fleischgeschäft*]. (740)

Mauler is also at his most Shakespearean, one of the wholesale butcher barons bearing "the yoke of responsibility" (769), when speaking about oxen and *Fleisch*. The above parallel to Shylock's pound of flesh can also be found in this Merchant of Chicago's earlier "Would you have the nerve/ To carve your meat from such misery?" (698). In keeping with Brecht's double-soul theory of Hamlet,[6] echoes of his vacillation can also be heard in a moment of lucidity:

> But this is a business in which it is
> To be or not to be, that is: am I
> The best man in my class or shall myself
> The dark road to the slaughterhouses take. (730)

Mauler and the Packers are not alone in insisting upon such a metaphoric fusion. In the first chorus, the Workers do protest too much:

[6] Cf. *A Short Organum for the Theatre*, GW, XVI, 696.

> Who do they take us for? Do they think
> We'd stand here like oxen, ready
> For anything? . . .
> Why aren't you open already, you skinners. Here
> Stand your oxen, you butchers, ready! Open up! (669-70)

Luckerniddle, who fell into the bacon boiler, is referred to by the young worker as "Uncle Bacon all dressed up in his tin can" (690), and his bosses as "butchers" by Mrs. Luckerniddle (691). The frequent use of this appellation is in the Slaughterhouse World context to be taken as something more than a dead metaphor. Mrs. Luckerniddle, having gone hungry for two days, begins to "devour" the hush-money food "like a beast" (695). Brecht uses here, as often in the play, *fressen,* another word play on brutalized human but also properly bestial eating: e.g., *gefrässig* (678) and *Fressgier* (706) for the workers, and *die Fresse,* "the bloody snout" (701), for the speculators. It is made quite clear that Mrs. Luckerniddle has been reduced to such subhuman status by the political economics of the stockyards and the existential pressures of the Slaughterhouse World upon human as well as bovine flesh.

Therefore, when in the development of the play, in scenes v-vi, and then especially in the stock-market dealings in ix and x, oxen begin to be used alongside cattle for business-deal purposes, they have already been associated with suffering humanity in and of the stockyards and slaughterhouses. Obversely, those in power are not only butchers, skinners, knackers, or grinders; they are also—as Joan, the conscience of this play, realizes—wild beasts:

> Have you no respect at all for the human face? Then it could be that
> they [the poor down below] don't look at you as men either any
> more, but as wild beasts that simply must be slain in the interests of
> public order and safety! . . . Yes, don't look so dumb, one shouldn't
> treat men like oxen, but you're not men, get out and be quick about
> it. . . . (723)

It is for this specific reason of inhumanity and bestiality that Joan proceeds to drive the money-changers from the temple. There is another biblical association with oxen, the reference to "muzzling the kine that tread the corn" (707-708). Further, in her parable of God calling on Adam in the garden of Paradise, the hind is an Edenic cow, from a time when animals had not differentiated into domestic and wild. This is even clearer in the German term *Hirschkuh,* literally "hart-cow": "Adam . . . has his hands so to say up to the elbows in a hind again, and so he hears the voice of God all bloody . . . " (728). The parable applies not only to Mauler's sensibility about oxen but also to Joan, who will die, as well as to the workers whose alienation from humanity will continue and grow as a result of Mauler's actions. Finally, when Joan comes to the cattle market with the poor, she chides the Packers for "making meat more and more expensive" and recounts an *exemplum* about Judgment Day:

> . . . how will you look then, when our Lord and Savior lines you up
> and asks with his great eyes: Where are my oxen now? What have
> you done with them? Did you make them available to the public at
> accessible prices? . . . then the oxen behind you will scream in all
> the barns where you've hidden them so that their prices should rise
> into the wild blue yonder, and with their screaming they will bear
> witness against you before the Almighty Lord. (703-704)

Here it is Christ's mute question and great eyes that identify him as the
Lord of the Oxen. The ox can therefore appeal to Christ "blond and
huge and looking dumb to Heaven" (667). Such an identification is well
prepared by the traditional association of Christ with meekness, suffering, the ox present at his birth, etc.

Slaughtered, skinned, and gutted oxen are transformed into flesh
(meat) and blood. This applies to all cattle—as can be seen from the
graphic account of new "self-service" swine slaughtering (681). I have
already commented on how much of the force of the constant punning
on "flesh" and "meat"—which not only identifies dead cattle with living
humans but can bring in many other allusions, from Shylock to sex—is
blunted in English. Nonetheless, the constant references to it (there are
about fifty in Saint Joan), together with the perpetual mention of
slaughtering, butchers, the bloodiness of the business in general and of
Mauler in particular (670, 678, 685, 686) analogous to bloody warfare
(714, 765-67, etc.), establish a powerful, dense atmosphere reeking of
the stock pens and slaughterhouses. The play's events are causally connected to and coterminous with a constipated meat-market (*Fleisch-
markt*; 667, 770); the strike leaders call the packers "meat people"
(*Fleischleute*; 741); the *Fleischgeschäft* is *meat* business in relation to
packers (the *Fleischring*) who sell the canned meat and in relation to the
cattle within the meat cans (668, 697, 719, etc.), but in relation to the
workers who cook the "filthy soiled meat" in their "shit-holes and slop-
kitchens" (670), yet cannot buy it because of low purchasing power
(705), the *Fleischgeschäft* it is a *flesh* business, cannibalistic in implication: "Of course, if everyone has to hack up his neighbor with an ax
just to have a piece of ham on his bread . . . how could then any sense
for higher things not choke within the human breast?!" (705). It is from
the workers as producers, consumers, tenants (see 676), and so on, that
Mauler, the Shylock-like meat and flesh king (*Fleischkönig*; 670, 671,
719), draws the stuff for his black transmutation: "From ruined houses
he draws rent, from rotten/ Meat gold . . . " (680). He himself has the
"weakness" of boggling at the slaughter but profiting from its results,
graphically materialized in his consuming the raw meat, the bloody
steak (711) which immediately and magically restores him to his senses.
This striking stage metaphor reposes to a significant degree on the
notion of an unholy communion with the flesh of the sacrificial oxen
that he has recognized as not only man-like in their suffering but higher
than man in their innocence. Its evil transsubstantiation enables Mauler

126

to grow into an Atlas, who bears on his shoulders a whole world of *Fleisch* (713). This personification is then cosmographically expanded—using Voltaire's proportion from *Micromégas*—to a stockyards porter of the larger planet and deity of Saturn, and the buyer of all the cattle from the still larger star of Sirius (716). Finally, in the ending of the play, the *Fleisch* is cut down, both by burning a third of all cattle (meat) and by locking out a third of the workers (flesh) whose wages are also lowered by a third (771). The result is that the "dark time of a bloody confusion" is replaced by "law and order" (771-72), which means a higher price for meat (776). The harmony of the meat market, the proportions of fleshly and bloody power and existential exploitation which form the body politic of this microcosm, are reestablished:

> Now take a breath! The market now gets well!
> The bottom point has once more lost its spell! . . .
> And once again the world whirls in the right course. (772)

III. Ideology: Communications, Informational Exchange

Thus, the Marxist political economics undoubtedly present in *Saint Joan*—the labor theory of value and the crisis theory—happens in the flesh and blood of the workers and packers, Mauler and Joan. Political economics determining the existential destiny of all strata of society represent a first, basic exchange system or code in this play. But there is a second code or system of interaction and exchange, composed of the *bits of information* passed or suppressed through various communicational networks.

The informational interaction works on three lines.[7] The first line is an extremely well-developed and manipulated network of communications *within the upper class.* Mauler is, if not at its fountainhead—that is in "New York," literally behind the scenes—at least at its first cataract or dam (see Joan's dam parable; 704); in the microcosm of the play he controls the flow of crucial items of information. Because he receives them just a short time before anybody else, he can bend events. Mauler withholds the economic information from New York from other packers while acting through Slift, but in the climactic fourth message, Mauler communicates it to them as his trump card for reorganizing the meat trade into a vertical cartel. *A fortiori,* all such in-

---

[7] The crucial pieces of information are communicated by way of letters. Of the letters from New York to Mauler, we learn only at the moment of their delivery. Of the letters from strike headquarters to a key group of strikers, we learn at the moment when they are sent out; the supposedly crucial one never arrives because of Joan's defection in the face of hunger, cold, and violence. This is a form at least as old as *Romeo and Juliet* and, of course, Schiller (where Brecht got it). Brecht uses it sometimes heretically and sometimes nonchalantly; he is interested more in the signified than in the signifier. However, in a contemporary performance, the director would do well to use, if not Telsat, then at least a post-Graham-Bell form of means of communication.

formation is withheld from the workers and the general public, misinformed through newspapers. This first line of informational interchange is one of *privileged information, the* classical weapon of all ruling groups. By means of it, Mauler manipulates the stock exchange (which, in itself, is a system of financial information, among other things). As was discussed in Part I, this also shapes the rhythm of *Saint Joan*.

The second line of informational flow is a truthful but extremely precarious informational system *within the working class* (there is no hint of a system which would link the "Chicago" workers with the "Missouri" ranchers or others). It is a "net" (742, 759) whose meshes are improvised and therefore liable to slippage. Joan becomes such a crucial mesh which gives way: the information does not circulate in a closed system, its truth seeps out and is lost. With it, the struggle for social justice is also lost. Parabolically, this functional failure and not the final scene is Joan's death.

There is a line of communication that is different from these two horizontal lines within the opposed spheres and classes of the stock market and the stockyards—the third and dramaturgically central line of information that flows vertically, *between the capitalists and the working class*. Its medium is all the middlemen in the play—the economic middlemen who appear very briefly in scenes v and ix and in the finale are the least important among them. The important bearers of the communicational vertical are the Black Straw Hats, Joan (who splits off from them), and Mauler, with his command of the press and his personal descent into the depths. The Black Straw Hats are the professional middlemen who deal in lifting up the souls of the workers and at the same time in counteracting any this-worldly uprising of the nethermost class, which would flatten the whole vertical structure. By Brecht's definition, they therefore function from above downward. As Mauler finds out, their pervasive metaphor of helping the sinking people from drowning in the morass or sea of troubles is predicated on their being the indispensable straw to be clutched at; no drowning, no need for straws—that is the basic vested interest and blind spot of clerical charity-mongering or political reformism:

> . . . Man is
> For you what helps you, so too for me
> Man was only what was prey. But even
> If man meant only that: who is helped
> 'Twould make no difference. Then you'd need drowning men.
> For then your business would be
> To be straws. So goes everything
> In the great circulation of commodities and planets. (764)

Superadded to the static vertical of up and down there is in the play a dynamic vertical of upward and downward which indicates these "mediating" relationships (cf. Part I above) as, e.g., in this early speech of the Black Straw Hats' Lieutenant Dark:

> But how do you expect to move upward, or what with your lack of understanding you call "upward"? Through brute force? As if force had ever turned out anything other than destruction. You think if you rear up on your hind legs then there will be Paradise on Earth. But I tell you: that way one makes no Paradise, that way one makes chaos. (675)

Other, quite effective forms of communication between the capitalists and the workers are the falling wages with which the play begins and ends (669, 771), the "rising misery" balancing the "rising profits" (748-49), and the "putting down" of the general strike (772) by the military. Further, the battle between the capitalists on the stock market is fought by means of the ups and downs of the foreign tariffs and various prices. Finally, personal destinies can also be described in those terms: Luckerniddle "falls into the bacon boiler" (689); "Lennox has fallen" (literally, "has been felled"; 682); "careless questioners" such as Joan, asking uncomfortable questions about earthly affairs, "From step to step / Groping downwards to the answer never given/ . . . . vanish into filth!" (679).

At the end of the play, the Black Straw Hats find that the "up" in whose service they operate means Mauler rather than God. They are thus identified as bearers of a specific long-range informational or ideological system, communicating values predicated upon the existence of an upper and a lower class in the scheme of things. Mauler's henchmen in the press are, complementarily, bearers of a specific short-range informational system, communicating primarily bits of "hard" news which turn out to be "soft," nonfactual—such as the news of the factories' opening, whose spreading breaks the strike. Through all of these helpers, Mauler operates in the same downward direction as the Black Straw Hats, only starting from a greater height and descending to a deeper humbling in and understanding of the depths. He and Joan are equal masters at communicating a public image, and the only non-lower figures who have an ear for and a certain insight into the basic fact about the lower spheres: their undeniable and persistent existence. Mauler can therefore take up Joan's idea of them as not only labor power but also purchasing power. Thus he combines a long-range or basic insight with short-range improvisations, old alienations with new. It is therefore logical—or better, congruent—that he can incorporate the Black Straw Hats into the overall scheme of his vertical and downward cartel as natural allies (Table 3).

Table 3. *Directions of interaction*

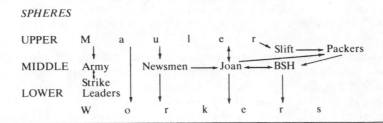

SPHERES

The only tries at communication and pressure going from below upward come from Joan and the strike leaders (Communists). The ideological failure of the one and the pragmatic failure of the others are complementary; the reasons for the complementarity are not explained in the universe of *Saint Joan* and would have to be inferred from the larger context of Brecht's opus. Beside the general Leninist doctrine of the allies necessary for a working-class revolution, one might speculate that the implications in Brecht's mind were very similar to those that, at the same time, led Antonio Gramsci to formulate the concept of a new "historical coalition" and a new type of class hegemony.[8] Joan might be characterologically a naive religious girl from the provinces who has just entered the large city. (To be sure, there are no clear indications as to that in *Saint Joan,* but the genesis of the play seems to point that way). However, her behavior and sociological function between the blocks of capitalists and workers are those of a petty-bourgeois intellectual. She is an intellectual because her basic motive—like that of Brecht's prototypical intellectual Galileo—is "I want to know" and "I must know it," a refrain she repeats half a dozen times (first in scene ii*d*, 679). Like Galileo, she formulates or at least implies in the course of the play a series of cognitions or discoveries. But she is also a petty-bourgeois idealist, failing at the crucial moment when it was necessary to abandon the mediating role and throw her lot totally in with the cold, starving, and lonely lower class. (In that respect, she might be thought of as a sympathetically drawn obverse of Mayakovsky's Menshevik or Reconciler in *Mystery Buffo.*) Therefore, her final cognitions about leaving a good world, about the bestial system which must and can be destroyed by the same means by which it is maintained—i.e., by men using force—are for Brecht as valid as Galileo's final self-accusations. But those of Joan's actions and utterances that retain the images of the intellectual as pivot and mediator should be taken more as charac-

[8] See Gramsci's prison notebooks, especially those published as *Il materialismo storico e la filosofia di Benedetto Croce* (Turin, 1948), and *Note sul Machiavelli, sulla politica e sullo stato moderno* (Turin, 1949), with explicit discussion of the relations between structure and superstructure. All of this was, of course, unknown to Brecht at the time.

terizing her debilitating ideology than as the upshot of the play's logic. One could mention here such masterly and quotable passages as Joan's vision of the columns marching through Chicago (734). Her vision clearly echoes the "Chicago Commune" chapter from Jack London's *The Iron Heel*. Joan's vision is also—as evidenced in the whole metaphysical imagery, the final confession ("What happens then, I don't know"), and the uncomprehending reaction of the workers—a direct prelude to her failure in that climactic scene ix. But to my mind the clearest example is the famous "seesaw parable" (749). Though it correctly identifies the capitalist system as the unity of an opposed "up" and a "down" and can therefore be taken as a step in Joan's development, it still postulates an unmoving fulcrum—which is homologous with her own vantage point in the social middle. A seesaw is defined by the *balance* between *opposing ends*. The vision of the opposing ends is thus a recognition of indestructible class contradictions: " . . . those who are up/ Only stay up because these stay down/ And only as long as these stay down." But it is at the same time the recognition of a fixed balance between mutually dependent ends; and the whole image is itself a static balance between a recognition of facts and value judgment. As Marx remarked, the recognition of class struggles is not an invention of his, but of a clear and conscious bourgeois historiosophy; one can very well recognize them and still draw value judgments diametrically or significantly opposed to those of the working-class movement. This is precisely what Joan does immediately after her seesaw speech: "Yes, it seems almost like a play to me, therefore/ Unworthy, if I stay here" (751). A seesaw is, after all, a plaything, a children's game, and Joan's position is here that of a spectator, exactly as a few moments earlier:

> JOAN: . . . I am for your cause, heart and soul.
> THE SECOND STRIKE-LEADER. Our cause? Well now, isn't that
>   your cause? (742-43)

Thus, Joan has found out that the Black Straw Hats' system of communications works only one way; and as a religious genius, she tried to become her own autonomous ideological middleman with a two-way system (just as the historical Joan of Arc had her own communications both with God and with the French people). Yet she never adopts the truly radical, revolutionary perspective of another, horizontal system of interactions which would abolish classes and render unnecessary any communication between upper and lower humanity—whether one-way or two-way. Therefore she functions—Mauler's Mephisto recognizes this—as an "ethical" reformist and can finally be used by an ideologically and organizationally updated but structurally unchanged vertical slaughterhouse system:

> SLIFT: That's our Joan. She's just in the nick of time. We want to
>   bring her out in a big way, for through her humanitarian effects
>   upon the slaughterhouses, her intercession for the poor, even

through her speeches against us, she's helped us to get through some trying weeks. She's to be our own Saint Joan of the Slaughterhouses. We want to set her up as a saint and spare her no respect. On the contrary, just that she's seen with us should prove that humanity holds a very high place in our esteem. (778)

It should be mentioned that there is a third code or exchange system conspicuous by its absence in *Saint Joan,* that of erotics. This absence is by itself a significant aspect of the play. The sparse hints, such as Slift's little speech about denying that Mauler slept with Joan (726-27), merely point out how totally the erotics are overwhelmed by economics, by the dire necessities of personal and class survival. Emblematic of that dehumanization, which turns flesh into meat and food, is the case of the Luckerniddles. There is no possibility of writing a play about erotics as long as survival economics and destruction (including brainwashing, destruction of true information) loom so large in the present world, Brecht concluded in the mid-twenties.[9] Much later, he tried to integrate erotics and existential politics: in *The Good Woman of Setzuan* he dodged around such a synthesis a bit, and only in *The Caucasian Chalk Circle* did he discreetly succeed. To my mind, the rather successful fusion of erotics and existential politics is another reason for thinking of *The Caucasian Chalk Circle* as Brecht's best play. But in *Saint Joan* Brecht deals basically with the *mutual relationships of the politicoeconomic and informational exchanges* or interaction systems between the figures.

These two systems or codes, so powerfully present in the play, relate to each other as basis and superstructure. However, though jobs, work, hunger, meat prices, and the like are clearly shown as basic, Brecht manipulates this well-worn and slippery metaphor much better than most Marxists. True, the information (and misinformation) is ideology. Yet ideology is extremely important; in fact, it turns out to be crucial for the outcome of the politicoeconomic interactions. Mauler's first reaction, when found by the Packers in the Black Straw Hats' mission and asked to save the market, is to inquire how many of "such Bible shops" are around (scene x). He knows that the stock market has crashed and that troops had to be called in; yet his first order of business is not police or credits, but consolidating the "Bible shops" in a proper and efficient spirit. This exemplifies Brecht's profound understanding of the relation between ideology and economics, so much more sophisticated and in advance of his age than one would have thought. In fact, on the strength of this play alone, it becomes clear that he was one of the great pioneers of the theory of communications and its sociopolitical function. Unfortunately, his theory is, for the most part, not explicit, but implicit in his plays, his interest in radio and film, and his other writings.

[9] See Brecht, "Dialog on Bert Brecht's *A Man's a Man,*" GW, XVII, 978-80, which seems to me an explicative document of first order.

IV. The Seesaw Structure: Time Horizons and Elective Affinities

Thus, through the whole play, there runs a counterpoint between the "existential" (politicoeconomic) and the "image-building" (ideological) domains or themes: How does one program the consciousness of people, especially the working classes, so that they will accept Mauler? Right at the beginning, there is again an exemplary situation, when the newsboys cry: "Chicago Tribune, noon edition! Meat king and philanthropist Pierpont Mauler attends the opening of the P. Mauler hospitals, world's largest and most expensive!" (671). Yet on the stage one sees that he is accompanied by two private detectives to keep him from being "knocked off" (scene ii*b*)—a classical estrangement effect arising out of the clash of infrastructure and superstructure. This kind of counterpoint of reality and image grows with the play and culminates in the canonization of Joan, which is a *locus classicus* of image building. It would deserve extensive study as such, in comparison with the finales of Schiller's *The Maiden of Orleans* and Goethe's *Faust,* which Brecht satirically inverted because they also deal in image building.

Homologous to this thematic counterpoint are the relationships on two deeper structural levels of *Saint Joan.* The first is the complementary use of politicoeconomic and salvational *time horizons.* The time indications are sometimes not so much complementary as simply alternative, since Brecht uses them with as high a disregard for linear causality or logic as Shakespeare shows in his anachronisms; e. g., it is impossible to establish a precise chronology of the events in *Saint Joan.* The second is the main dramaturgic peculiarity of this play, the Mauler-Joan relation, including the relation between Mauler's "two souls."

Politicoeconomic time is quantitative and equivalent to money[10]; it has to do with wages, prices, payments, and business deals. It is, of course, present in its pure form in the deals on the stock market, especially in scenes v, vi, and ix. It includes precise clock time tied to contractual deadlines, from Mauler's two minutes to decide about buying all the cattle in Illinois (716) through the five days' grace to Cridle (683) to the forty months' rent the packers offer the Black Straw Hats (724); here the equivalence of time and money is even semantic. It culminates in Graham's quasi-Homeric account of the stock-market crash (765-67). With a sudden widening of the play's horizons the various news items transmitted by loudspeaker indicate the collapse of this entire time horizon: "The Bank of England closes down for the first time in three hundred years! . . . The Five Year Plan in four years!" (783). The workers, directly dependent on the stock market, are also

[10] I have tried to deal with such reifications as pertinent to modern drama in "On Individualist World View in Drama," *Questions des Genres Littéraires,* 9/1 (1966), 5-24, and "Beckett's Purgatory of the Individual," DR, 11/4 (1967), 23-36. There is, of course, a huge literature on that problem of time/money equivalence, from Marx, Simmel, Lukács and von Martin to the present.

under the sway of the time horizon which works in meat and flesh; their time horizon is determined by wages and working time: "At least we demand/ The old wage, which is anyway too little, at least/ The ten-hour day, and at least . . . " (670). This dependence is paradigmatically shown in the *exemplum* of Mrs. Luckerniddle, who drops inquiries about her husband—in effect sells them—for twenty lunches: "I have, you know, not eaten for two days" (694). The zero level of human existence, including human time horizons, is marked in *Saint Joan,* by the locked-out workers' cold and hunger—a cluster mentioned with the same obsessive frequency as the oxen-meat-blood image cluster. As Joan concludes, surely Mrs. Luckerniddle would have "asked about him who gave her support/ For yet some time, as is proper/ But the price was too high that amounted to twenty meals" (696).

On the other end of the spectrum of social time,[11] the Black Straw Hats initially pretend to being exempt from politicoeconomic time, to being the bearers of a qualitative, *salvational* time horizon. They work for practically no money; they preach that earthly politicoeconomic uprising and wages are to be forsaken for the more sublime vertical of Heaven; and to combat hunger and cold they distribute some warm, fatless soup. Soup is indicative of the Black Straw Hats' relation to the workers; the former dispense it and the latter eat it. Conversely, Mauler eats steak; Joan as middleman eats some unidentified leftover food of Mauler's, and later, when she is with the workers, "snow", i.e., nothing. But soup, as well as rent, soon runs out without the money of the packers, and Paulus Snyder—the successful clerical *apparatchik*[12]—has to accept their politicoeconomic horizon, reducing the salvational pretense of the Black Straw Hats to a conscious "opium of the people" (scene vii). Joan, on the other hand, parts company with them because she is the other half of a famous but often truncated definition of Marx's—"the heart of a heartless world."[13] Beginning with a general and abstract though already exceedingly powerful sketch of the time correlative to the Slaughterhouse World—

> In a dark time of bloody confusion
> Ordered disorder
> Planned arbitrariness
> Dehumanized humanity. . . .
> We want again to introduce
> God (671-72)—

she insists throughout the play on the necessity of a salvation, of a new

[11] See, e.g., Georges Gurvitch, *The Spectrum of Social Time* (Dordrecht, 1964).
[12] I suspect that the opposition between the *apparatchik* named Paul and a religious genius with salvational pretensions goes back to Shaw's disquisitions on Christianity prefatory to *Major Barbara* and *Androcles and the Lion.*
[13] I owe this most appropriate association to a discussion with Raymond Williams, reproduced in *A Production Notebook to "St. Joan of the Stockyards,"* pp. 184-98.

creation. Her references to the seven days of snowfall (722) and her Martin-Luther-King-like dream of a protest march through Chicago, "Showing our misery's whole extent in public places/ Calling upon whatever looks like Man," which she dreamed, significantly, "Seven days ago" (734), are pertinent examples. Such a new creation is qualitative and equivalent to human lives. It would also be a Judgment Day upon the old creation, as is clearly shown by the parable discussed above about the abuse of oxen revealed on Judgment Day (703-704). But Joan comes to recognize that salvation must work through jobs, wages, and prices and tries to persuade the packers and then public opinion to adopt her views. Since the whole system is "Exploitation and disorder, bestial and so/ Incomprehensible" (781), and since she fears a world "no longer familiar" (754), she does not succeed in fusing the salvational and politicoeconomic time horizons. Nobody does, in this black play. But Pierpont Mauler succeeds in yoking them forcibly together.

In fact, Mauler's "two souls" can be defined as tending not only spatially up and down (or thematically, to sentiment and business), but also temporally to salvation and profit: "I want my money and peace for my conscience!" (699). He is a master at manipulating the two time horizons against each other. The play begins with his wish to end seven (biblical) years of servitude to political economics:

Ever since I went into this business, therefore seven
Years, I've avoided it [visiting the slaughterhouse], Cridle I can
No longer: e'en today I'll give it up, this bloody business.
You take it, I'll give you my share real cheap. . . .
          . . . So fast
Must now this Lennox fall, for I'm myself
Quite intent on becoming a good man. (668)

But his goodness is purely self-seeking; he is very willing to use political economics without allowing for, e.g., the change from "good times" to "bad times" when his contracts are questioned (682). His spiritual soul knows that the salvation of a human being is more important than ten million dollars (762), but also that "Seven days I held/ This city of Chicago by the throat" (763); yet his business soul tries to use money, the congealed form of politicoeconomic time, for a fake salvation: "So go and tell them that money is coming, it will be there on Saturday night. Mauler is getting it. Even now he goes to the cattle market to get it" (729). Though Joan sees through him in this particular instance (the fake Sabbath will be achieved at the expense of the locked-out workers in the snow), at the end Mauler succeeds in keeping both souls and both time horizons—the lofty, salvational one serving the base, politicoeconomic one—by staging a false salvation, a blasphemous canonization. Mauler refurbishes the falling building of capitalism, an image he develops in two remarkable speeches. The first one, "On the Necessity of Capitalism and Religion" (scene viii), scolds Joan for opposing money, the paramount means for holding together a stable social edifice in "the disfavor of the planet":

> For otherwise everything would have to be completely torn down
> And the plans changed from the ground up, according to a quite
> different
> Unheard of, new evaluation of man, which you don't want
> Nor do we, for this would happen without us and without God. (731)

At his nadir, after the crash, Mauler retracts:

> And about that thing made of sweat and money
> That we've built up in these cities:
> It's already as if one
> Made a building, the biggest in the world, and
> Most expensive and practical, but
> By oversight and because 'twas cheap used
> Dog shit for material, so that staying
> There would yet be difficult and in the end his fame
> Just that he'd made the biggest stink in the world. (757)

But that depression does not last, and in Mauler's triumphant finale the politicoeconomic building and time horizons are reaffirmed, having bent to their purposes Joan's initial, insufficiently precise need for salvation: "In a dark time of bloody confusion/ Dehumanized humanity/ . . . we want/ To make possible the order-promoting work of you Black Straw Hats/ Through generous outlays of money" (771-72). Money, which was earlier identified with excrement, has now transmuted Joan's concern with God into the Black Straw Hats' concern with keeping the excremental vertical building in "order." A Swiftian scatological image is fittingly applied to an axiologically empty world.

Finally, the characterological and textual centerpiece of *Saint Joan* is the tension between high and low incarnated in Mauler, in Joan, and in their mutual relationships as their personal strivings or "souls." Even without Brecht's explicit reference to "the Joan-Mauler type,"[14] it is clear there are deep elective affinities between the "double-souled" captain of industry and the salvationist girl. They are the only figures who partake of all levels of the play. Their wanderings through its topography are almost symmetrical and inverse: Mauler's curve of power descends to its lowest point in scenes ix and x and ascends again to its zenith at the end (if we forget the loudspeaker reports); the newsmen tell Joan at her high point in scene ix that she has had "great success, but now the affair is over" (754). In scene ix, Mauler falls too, but his insights and the backing of "New York" permit him to rise again. Joan's insights come too late, and she has no power base; an alliance with the strike leaders might have helped her achieve it—provided the leaders had had a better system of communications and the masses of

---

[14] GW, XVII, 1018.

workers a consciousness resembling that of their leaders. But such conditions do not obtain in this microcosm. The precarious state of the workers' "net" of communications, of their class consciousness, and of Joan's late maturing are all of a piece—they are dramaturgic correlatives of Brecht's basic diagnosis of Germany and the revolutionary movement of that time. True, as always his plays are open-ended and permit the spectator to imagine other outcomes should a sufficient number of conditions be changed: a diametrically opposed outcome will be explored by him in his next stage play, *The Mother*. My point is that the conditions to be changed would include the entire atmosphere of *Saint Joan of the Slaughterhouses*. That is why tinkering with Mrs. Luckerniddle to make her into a Communist Party adherent in later versions is not very convincing. Thus, Joan's death can counterbalance Mauler's victory only outside the play: by leading to an increment of understanding in the spectators and making them—with the help of changing economic and political conditions revealed at the end of the play by the loudspeakers—into Joan's continuators. As usual, the culmination of a Brechtian play lies outside, not inside it.[15]

Looking backward at Joan and Mauler from Shen Te and Shui Ta as well as—*a contrario*—from Grusha and Azdak, it becomes clear that they are in some crucial ways two halves of a hermaphroditic whole, who might be called the superior, idealistic, or farsighted bourgeois man of action (almost a Nietzschean superman). Mauler despises the run-of-the-mill capitalists, possibly more than Joan does, and he is delighted when she expels them from the "Temple." When Joan finally tries to do something for the workers against Mauler, she cannot accomplish it. Mauler readily takes over her initial idealistic diagnosis of "the dark world of dehumanized humanity" and finally uses her even in her death. Indeed, his double nature or "two souls" are by a whole system of correspondences (primarily, their upward and downward strivings) connected to his relationship with Joan, who is, as it were, his externalized sentimental soul—*Mauler : Joan = meat king : oxen pitier*. Just as Mauler is one rung above an orthodox meat king and has an almost godlike function for this world, so Joan is not the pitier of oxen but of workers (the "next rung" category in the vertical topology of suffering and powerlessness in his play).[16] Further, both the upward and the downward striving are perverted in comparison with the norm of a fully humanized union of reason and emotion. Mauler's reason is used only as a "scheming brain" (668) in politicoeconomic warfare; Joan's develops too late. Mauler's muddled, sentimentalized emotions serve his schemes; Joan's subjugate and fragment her understanding. In certain subtle but strong ways, the "two souls" and the Mauler-Joan relation-

[15] See my "The Mirror and the Dynamo: On Brecht's Aesthetic Point of View," *Brecht* (M), pp. 80-98.
[16] See also the passage referred to in n. 4.

ship correspond to the basic class and topological dichotomy of this world within a time-hallowed "world's body" metaphor.

It follows that Mauler is a significant creation only insofar as he is not a conscious hypocrite,[17] but, intermittently, a sincerely sentimental philanthropist (philobovist?) who becomes a complete cynic only when (in scene x) he recognizes that "true penitence" cannot replace money. Brecht's point here is that sentimental philanthropy and religiosity are especially pernicious when sincere—in Joan as well as in Mauler.

Some new light might also be shed by such an approach on the vexed problem of empathy. The packers are totally estranged. In different ways, but with equal force, so are the workers: they are the nearest equivalent to a valid chorus that one can find on the modern stage. Obviously, it is more difficult to empathize with an Aeschylean choral collective than with individuals. However, the situation is much more complicated for Mauler and Joan. For Mauler, I think a detailed dramaturgic analysis would prove, the play demands that one should oscillate all the time (often within his single speeches[18]) between empathy and distance in order to achieve a total distance toward him at the end. The empathy is never full (for his "lofty" soul is also suspect); it should always remain in the service of distanciation. At the play's end, it should be possible for the spectator to feel he has seen through Mauler and can now hold him at arm's length.

Joan, I believe, has to be empathized with.[19] The spectator—who will as a rule be neither a big businessman nor a proletarian industrial worker—is supposed to sympathize with her and go through the learn-

[17] Ernst Schumacher, in his pioneering discussion of the play in *Die dramatischen Versuche Bertolt Brechts 1918-1933* (Berlin, 1955), pp. 443-74, seems to see Mauler as a conscious hypocrite; so, clearly, does I.M. Fradkin, *Bertol't Brekht* (Moscow, 1965), p. 102. Reports from the Dresden premiere indicate that the director took the same view. Cf. the bibliography in *Die heilige Johanna,* ed. G. Bahr, pp. 236-37. On the other side one could mention Adorno—usually unreliable when Brecht is discussed—who also seems to identify Mauler simply with a real-life *raffgierig* capitalist in his highly tendentious and simplified mention of this play, *Noten zur Literatur,* III (Frankfurt, 1965), 118-19. If one turns to the genesis of the play as explored by Grimm, Parmalee, and others, it becomes clear that in the literature Brecht read (Norris, Myers, Tarbell, Steffens, Dos Passos, London, Shaw, Bouck White, etc.) there are two psychological types of capitalists. The overwhelming majority of them (Rockefeller, Carnegie, etc.) deeply believe in the morality of their actions. A few, such as the Pierpont Morgan who gave Mauler his first name, are true cynics. Mauler changes from type 1 to type 2 within the play, roughly in scene x.

[18] For a brief analysis of Mauler's opening speech, see my essay "*Saint Joan of the Slaughterhouses:* Assumptions, Exchanges, Seesaws, and Lessons of a Drama Module," *A Production Notebook to "St Joan of the Stockyards,"* pp. 227-50. Mauler's business soul begins to dominate when Cridle asks,"How much?" (668).

[19] Brecht successively put slightly different emphases on such empathy. To begin with, he used to stress the non-Aristotelian nature of the play, but later he explicitly (though unwillingly) conceded that one should "at times" (*mitunter*) or even "largely" (*weitgehend*) empathize with Joan in the sense of my argument. Cf. GW, XVII, 1019-21; XV, 314; *Die heilige Johanna,* ed. G. Bahr, p. 171.

ing process with her. Her final stifling then will drive home the lesson, in her own words and through her supreme cognitions—just as in the case of Galileo. It follows that the empathy-versus-estrangement situation is in this play far subtler than one would expect upon reading some Brechtological glosses (including some of Brecht's earlier exaggerations). Brecht uses both empathy and estrangement in very subtle and effective dosages, differing from figure to figure and from scene to scene. Perhaps what Brecht, in the heat of battle, sometimes said elliptically we should today translate approximately as follows: "I don't want only empathy, I don't want uncritical empathy; but for some stage figures I want total distanciation, for some a balancing between empathy and distance, and for some—those I agree with, such as Kattrin, or Grusha, or Shen Te, or Joan—I want as nearly an empathy as doesn't matter." The play is written so that the spectator could learn from it: since Joan is his privileged representative inside the play, the most economical and pleasant way to do so is to empathize with her. That does not mean, as I have argued earlier, swallowing uncritically all she does and says, but it means following her general tragic curve of development; if she has led the spectator into some foolish identifications, she is going to tell him so by the time the play ends.

All such counterpoints are implicit in the basic dualistic yet subtly mediated vision of *Saint Joan*. The arrested moment of equipoise, the limbo between Heaven and Hell, the middle and yet decisive social classes that will determine the outcome of the huge social battle, the oscillating fortunes, the precarious view from atop the barricades—all of these are variants of the same basic paradigm. Finally, this play too is a seesaw between a failing society and another still unable to be born. Like Joan, Brecht, in a homologous social and ideological position, fashioned a seesaw parable. Unlike Joan, he saw from the beginning that the world stage and the stage world have to be radically altered. The task of presenting such a grim and yet vital, many-layered structure, such an axiologically empty but sensually supremely present (i.e., anti-utopian) world, demanded an almost total refashioning of the traditional dramaturgic cosmology and anthropology. Hence *Saint Joan of the Slaughterhouses* can—together with the more frequently discussed *A Man's a Man* and *Mahagonny*—stand as an impressive stage in such a refashioning, in some ways as vital in its very imperfections as any other play of our century. In it, Brecht showed how the stage could talk in iambics and yet about political economics which mean salvation or damnation. While working on what was eventually to become *Saint Joan*, Brecht is quoted as having remarked perspicaciously: "If one sees that our present-day world does not fit into drama, then drama simply does not fit into the world."[20] In this play, the world is again shown on the stage, so that the stage can again be analogous to and fit into the

[20] Elisabeth Hauptmann, "Notizen über Brechts Arbeit 1926," SF/2, 243.

world. *Welttheater* and *Theater in der Welt,* it reposes on a basis that leaves us with a final image—that of the (even now unsolved) problem and yet absolute necessity of fitting the dispossessed producers of all the values into the world stage. "Today, as always, there remain/ The poor people and the stony plain":

> Da bleiben, wie immer so auch heut
> Der steinige Boden und die armen Leut. (755)

ROUNDHEADS AND PEAKHEADS:
THE TRUTH ABOUT EVIL TIMES

Gisela E. Bahr

Roundheads and Peakheads, a parable dealing with a Hitler-like demagogue and his racial politics, was Bertolt Brecht's first anti-Fascist play. It was written in ominous times, as is evidenced by its genesis. Begun at the suggestion of stage director Ludwig Berger in November 1931,[1] it grew out of an attempted adaptation of Shakespeare's drama *Measure For Measure.* After working with Berger for a short time, Brecht decided to write his own play. He called it *Peakheads and Roundheads or Rich and Rich Make Good Company* and finished it some time in 1932. It was about to be published by the Kiepenheuer publishing company in the series *Experiments* (no. 8) when Brecht had to leave Germany in February 1933. Thereafter, the Nazis prevented the printing by destroying the plates.[2]

While in exile in Denmark Brecht revised the play to such an extent that a new version resulted from it—which he called *Roundheads and Peakheads or Rich and Rich Make Good Company. An Atrocity Story.*[3] This was followed by other plays against Fascism, such as *Fear and Misery of the Third Reich,* a series of scenes written between 1934 and 1938 on the basis of reports Brecht received about Nazi Germany, and *The Resistible Ascent of Arturo Ui,*[4] completed in 1941 after eight years of Nazi rule. Unlike these two works, however, Brecht's first dramatic attempt to deal with the Hitler regime was written in anticipation of things to come, rather than in retrospect. This is particularly true of the *Peakheads* version, which was completed before 30 January 1933,[5] but whose first scene seems to describe exactly the infamous event of that day: Hindenburg's appointment of Hitler to the Chancellorship of the Weimar Republic.

The critical reaction to the play has been quite partisan. To Western commentators, it is a work which has been invalidated by history because it deals with Hitler's racism without giving the least indication

---

[1] According to *Brecht-Chronik,* p. 53. Ludwig Berger gives an earlier date in his recollection of the project entitled, "Die Lust an der Kooperation," TH, 8/8 (1967), 27-29.

[2] On the basis of the original Kiepenheuer page proofs which Brecht had taken along, the play was eventually published in *Versuche,* 5-8 (1959), as originally planned.

[3] Hereafter *Roundheads.* This version was first published by Malik in *Gesammelte Werke,* II (London, 1938), then reprinted in all subsequent "Works" editions by Suhrkamp and Aufbau. It is the "standard" version.

[4] Using drafts from the thirties, Brecht as late as 1953-1954 tried once again to depict Hitler as a Ui-like gangster in *Turandot or The Whitewashers' Congress.* Hitler also appears in *Schweyk in World War II* (1943).

[5] The date is important. Considering the time it takes to set the type for a text of this length, to proof galleys, carry out the corrections, and provide page proofs—which were in Brecht's possession on 28 February—it is safe to say that the manuscript was completed before 30 January.

of his gruesome "final solution" (*Endlösung*) for the Jews. They also take issue with Brecht's "one-sided Marxist" interpretation of Fascism as a late phase of capitalism; furthermore, they object to his simplistic view of the race issue as subordinate to the class struggle.[6] Conversely, Eastern European critics tend to accept Brecht's interpretation; in general, they emphasize that his predictions have come true.[7]

Today, the capitalist nature of Fascism is rather widely accepted in the West, particularly among historians and political scientists. As for the criticism that the play has been invalidated by history, it should be acknowledged that in the evaluation of current political events, any time, any place, errors are more often the rule than the exception. In those pre-Hitler years pundits of all political persuasions misjudged the true character of the rising Nazi "movement." Those of the center and right (*bürgerliche Parteien*), e.g., lumped the Communists and the National Socialists together indiscriminately as the two parties threatening constitutional government. It was assumed, however, that an improvement of the economic situation would do away with both of them. The more Hitler clamored against "the Reds," the more he became acceptable to the Conservatives as a coalition partner. The Communists, on the other hand, saw as their main enemy not so much the Nazis as the Social Democrats whom they called "Social Fascists." Hitler's spectacular victory in the September elections of 1930, which made his followers the second strongest faction in the parliament, was discounted by the Communists as coming too late to have an impact. In their view, the capitalist system was soon to perish. According to their newspaper, *Die Rote Fahne*, 14 September had been the Nazis' climax; afterwards there could only be descent and decline.[8]

In making Hitler his target at that time, Brecht was, by comparison, ahead of the Communist strategy and showed a good deal of shrewdness and independence. Moreover, as a prognosis his play is unique among similar attempts to deal with contemporary politics. Therefore, even as

[6] Herbert Lüthy, "Vom armen Bert Brecht," *Der Monat,* 4/44 (1952), 131; Ernst Wendt, "Brechts Gleichnisse," TH, 5/6 (1964), 37; Henning Rischbieter, *Bertolt Brecht* (Velber, 1966), I, 125-35; *Brecht* (Ew), pp. 307-310. Not in the same vain: Klaus-Detlef Müller who, in *Die Funktion der Geschichte im Werk Bertolt Brechts* (Tübingen, 1967), pp. 76-82, gives a more balanced account while leaving the question of historical validity open; and with a different focus: Ulrich Weisstein, "Two Measures For One: Brecht's *Die Rundköpfe und die Spitzköpfe* and its Shakespearean Model," GR, 43 (1968), 24-39.

[7] Johannes Goldhahn, *Das Parabelstück Bertolt Brechts als Beitrag zum Kampf gegen den deutschen Faschismus* (Rudolstadt, 1961), pp. 40-72; 120-38; Werner Mittenzwei, *Bertolt Brecht. Von der "Maßnahme" zu "Leben des Galilei,"* 2nd ed. (Berlin, Weimar, 1965), pp. 154-92; Hans-Joachim Bunge, "Im Exil," Werner Hecht, Hans-Joachim Bunge, Käthe Rülicke-Weiler, *Bertolt Brecht. Leben und Werk,* 2nd ed. (Berlin, 1969), pp. 126-30.

[8] *Rote Fahne* (16 September 1930). Reprinted in *Komintern und Faschismus. Dokumente zur Geschichte und Theorie des Faschismus.* Ed. Theo Pirker (Stuttgart, 1965), p. 156.

an alleged failure it is worth investigating as an artistic document of a certain historical period. It raises a number of questions: What was the basis for Brecht's prognosis? How did he transform his notions into dramatic action? What was the function of the parabolic form for the topic in question? And what can be said about the effectiveness of the work in the fight against Fascism?

I

To judge from the amount of material concerning the play—complete manuscripts, fragments, variants, and work notes in the Bertolt-Brecht-Archiv[9]—Brecht struggled hard with his project. The following observations are an attempt to describe the relation of contemporary events to specific problems in the play. Since the differences between the *Peakheads* and *Roundheads* versions can be readily ascertained by a comparison of the published texts, this essay will focus on the stages of the play preceding and including the *Peakheads* version, i.e., it will primarily deal with the hitherto unpublished materials written in 1932.

In the first phase of the work, recognizable from the German names used (Angeler for Angelo, Klausner for Claudio, Hornberger for Überley) Brecht kept close to the action and structure of *Measure for Measure*. The development of the first scene is significant in this respect. It was rewritten several times, probably in close succession, and might well have been the decisive factor in the new direction the play took in Brecht's hands. In Shakespeare's play, the action of the opening scene strikes a somewhat whimsical note. The Duke of Vienna simply decides to take temporary leave from his post and hands the reins of government over to Lord Angelo, who is known as a man of propriety and strict morals. (Later we learn that the Duke expects Angelo to fight corruption and to re-establish respect for the law of the land). At the moment, however, the Duke's sudden departure and vague mandate leave the new Governor as uneasy as the old Councilor, Escalus; they decide to share the responsibility.

In his first draft, Brecht changed the Shakespearean text only slightly but immediately added a political emphasis: The country is bankrupt and the Duke has no solution. Angeler then is chosen as a "strong man." He is challenged to turn into action the criticism he has expressed so often and encouraged to take all necessary measures with vigor and rigor. "Anything needed to save the state is permitted," the Duke tells him. Far from being overwhelmed by the unrestricted authority delegated to him, the new Governor takes all responsibility unto himself and promises "reforms."

There is no other scene but this one in the Shakespearean model

---

[9] These materials are being prepared by the present writer for publication by Suhrkamp in the series "edition suhrkamp." They are listed in BBA-B, I, 56-75.

which in its basic structure lends itself to a comparison with the German situation at that time. Hindenburg, unable to solve the enormous social and economic problems that beset the Weimar Republic in the wake of World War I, had increasingly exercised his power to appoint Chancellors who then governed with a "Cabinet by presidential decree" (*Präsidialkabinett*) rather than by a parliamentary majority. The year 1932 saw three of them—Brüning, von Papen, and von Schleicher—serve at the President's discretion. When the National Socialists emerged as the strongest faction of the German *Reichstag* in the elections of 31 July 1932, Hitler demanded the office of Chancellor even though his party had not achieved the absolute majority. Because he was striving for unlimited powers, Hitler refused the post of Vice-Chancellor offered him by Hindenburg who attempted to keep him and the Nazi movement within the checks and balances of the parliamentary system. Nevertheless, Hitler had arrived at the "gates of power," and it looked as if it was only a question of time *when* he was to become Chancellor.

While Brecht's first draft seems to introduce simply a hypothetical Chancellor figure, a middle-of-the-roader who is noted for his "reformism,"[10] the second draft strongly suggests that Brecht had turned away from the Shakespearean model and set out to write a play against Hitler; in it Angeler appears as the inventor of a racial theory.[11]

The second draft is longer, dwells more extensively on the economic crisis, and in it the Duke appears to be more cynical. His opening lines parody Mephistopheles' speech (Prologue in Heaven, *Faust,* Part I): "From time to time I like to read the papers/ so that I know what's happening in the land." Although the Duke learns that the country has gone bankrupt, he rejects as unjust a salt tax which had been recommended to him as the only means for solving the economic crisis. Without regard for the sorry state of affairs the Duke announces his plan to leave and to delegate his power to a strong man: "a completely honest man/ whose first concern is strengthening the state/ unselfish and well-known as such." Moreover, he chooses him precisely because he is his political opponent. The Shakespearean skeleton of the scene is further fleshed out by clearly political elements. Appointing his opponent as temporary head of state is a shrewd maneuver on the part of the Duke, designed not only to appease a fierce opposition he can no longer control but also to cover up his mismanagement of the economy. It is specifically the new man's racial theory he makes use of. Dividing the populace into bad

[10] "Reform" measures are to be found in the first draft of the second scene. Here the new Governor's "emergency measures" (*Elendsverordnungen*) are being discussed in the streets, an allusion to *Notstandsverordnungen,* which, e.g., Chancellor Brüning is remembered for.

[11] Presumably the two drafts were written in close succession. In the first one, Brecht had indicated in the margin: "salt tax." In the second draft, the salt tax was added to the text as an important issue.

Czichs (Peakheads) and good Czuchs (Roundheads) provides a handy explanation for the common man of the seemingly impenetrable mechanism of economic crises. Relying on his opponent's popularity with the impoverished middle class, he orders him to impose a tax that will hit the common people hardest and for which he himself does not want to take the blame. In all other matters the new Governor shall be free to "shape the state according to his inner vision."

Also introduced in this second draft are the two antagonistic classes, the tenant farmers and the landowners. The farmers are getting organized for an uprising while the landowners have secretly been financing Angeler's-Angelo's hordes and are now pushing for the salt tax.[12] With these additions the basic function of the scene was established; in this form it was included in the first completed text, entitled *Measure for Measure or The Salt Tax* (BBA, 253). The further changes this scene underwent in the next two versions[13] were primarily designed to clarify certain points. The economic crisis and the impending revolt of the tenant farmers became more prominent issues, and the hostility of the Fascists against the rebellious farmers was emphasized more strongly; the Duke was identified as the country's biggest landowner who had a personal stake in the outcome of the conflict; and the Councilor was shown as the secret promoter of the new man. Finally, Brecht added to the Fascist rhetoric by borrowing phrases from Hitler's open letter to Chancellor Papen—printed in the Nazi newspaper *Völkischer Beobachter* (21 October 1932).[14]

While Brecht's quick adoption of such material from day-to-day politics[15] added color and topicality to the Hitler figure, this was not enough to carry the play as a whole. Rather, some nucleus of dramatic action was needed to demonstrate the concrete manifestations of the issues at stake. The first trial scene (iv) constitutes a climax. In the scene the conflicts of race and class were skilfully intertwined. The Czichish

---

[12] This part of the play, including the Callas-Calausa conflict, has no counterpart in the Shakespearean model. See below.

[13] Entitled *Rich and Rich Make Good Company* (BBA, 254) and *Peakheads and Round-heads* (BBA, 256), respectively.

[14] Some typical passages from Hitler's letter, a copy of which was found among the early drafts of the play: "Confining one's thinking to economics is the death of national idealism. . . . The willingness to endure neediness, indeed, the readiness to make sacrifices in general declines to the same extent as people, for want of ideas and tasks that are nationally and politically exciting, occupy themselves with, and are absorbed by nothing but their own materialistic matters. . . . [It is necessary] to comprehend that the German crisis is not a constitutional crisis but in the most profound sense of the word a spiritual crisis" (BBA, 266/67-82).

[15] Brecht continued to adopt such materials. Cf. Alexander Abusch who recalled a conversation with Brecht about *Peakheads* in Paris (November 1933): "As Brecht told it, he made use of the revelations from the 'Brown Book' in his play, e.g., regarding the shrewd maneuvers through which Hindenburg, on orders from the industrialists, eased Hitler into political power 'legally.'" *Literatur im Zeitalter des Sozialismus. Beiträge zur Literaturgeschichte 1921 bis 1966* (Berlin, 1967), p. 205.

landowner is charged with two crimes: the seduction of a Czuchish girl, his tenant-farmer's daughter, and the practice of rent usury. Significantly, the landowner is sentenced to death for his racial offense and not for his economic one; hence, the Fascist rowdies, who pressed the charge of racial misconduct, won their point and not the deprived tenant-farmer, who insisted on economic justice. But Brecht's efforts to produce a compelling conclusion ultimately resulted in suspending the death sentence: racism emerged as an obfuscation of the real issue, the class struggle.

Brecht took great pains to endow the Hitler-figure with a character of its own. Whether this figure was shown to be a dreamer and utopian thinker, a stubborn idealist and zealot, or a puppet at the mercy of the landowners and a cynical demogogue, the model of Lord Angelo was still there, and the real-life model never quite asserted itself—a fact that has often been criticized. Apparently, here was the limit of what even the keenest analysis of the time would yield. The specific prognosis which made the first scene a striking anticipation of 30 January 1933 was based on a discernible contemporary analogy. Such a basis did not exist for a prognostic portrait of Hitler whose true character had not fully emerged at that time. However, it is doubtful whether Brecht ever intended to provide such a portrayal (as he later did in the case of Arturo Ui). The focus which the Shakespearean model provided for his adaptation was the necessity of equal measures, i.e., equal justice for members of different classes. Brecht implicitly and explicitly questioned the validity of the concept of "equal justice" by a shift in emphasis, i.e., by showing a society torn by a persistent class struggle. Any attempt to dispense justice regardless of the prevailing socioeconomic conditions could only perpetuate these conditions and result in injustice for the unprivileged. In Brecht's view, the function of racism was precisely to obfuscate the class struggle and to preserve the exploitive economic system. Consequently, in the process of updating Shakespeare's play, Brecht chose the racial issue as the new focal point. By doing so, he abandoned his adaptation and created an original play. More significantly, he advanced from a demonstration of economic-political manipulation by means of the salt tax to the presentation of evidence that the rich are united by their class interests. In an elaborate pun Brecht not only gave a socioeconomic twist to the proverbial German saying, "gleich und gleich gesellt sich gern" (birds of a feather flock together), by changing it to "Reich und reich gesellt sich gern"; he further drew attention to the political implication of economic factors by alluding to the double meaning of "Reich." Thus the title may be read as (*The*) *Rich and* (*the*) *Rich Make Good Company* or *The Reich and* (*the*) *Rich Make Good Company*.

II

In addition to those details which are clearly relevant to the contemporary situation in Germany, a large portion of the play consists of
the conflict between the tenant farmer (Meixner-Meixenego-Callas) and
his landlord (Klausner-Calausa-De Guzman). The conflict takes place
against the background of a feudal society in a largely agrarian country
(Bohemia-Peru-Jahoo[16]). This part of the action has no counterpart in
Shakespeare's play, but it also has no overt connection to the Germany
of the thirties. In looking for an explanation for Brecht's avoidance of
parallels which would link his anti-Fascist play too closely to the contemporary situation in Germany, Brecht's essay, "Writing the Truth:
Five Difficulties,"[17] comes to mind. In it Brecht stresses that, in view of
the perilous times, "cunning devices [were needed] by which a
suspicious state can be hoodwinked." Given such a state of affairs,
"many things that cannot be said in Germany about Germany can be said
about Austria." The situation in "Austria" could be recognized as
significant for the one in Germany. Since Germany was a highly industrialized country, the agrarian "Austrian" parallel does not seem to
be applicable here. However, if one substitutes Italy for "Austria," a
new dimension is added and the connection to Germany becomes much
clearer.

In 1932 the Mussolini regime could celebrate its tenth anniversary.
Faced with the increasing disintegration of the Weimar Republic, many
Germans with a keen sense of history may have been aware of the fact
that the circumstances under which the Italian dictator had seized
power seemed also to exist in Germany—with all their ominous implications. After all, following World War I both Italy and Germany
had experienced grave crises—crises which were marked by unemployment, strikes, fights among the political parties, and a rapid turn-
over of governments, each one less capable than the other of enacting
any kind of program for lack of support in a badly split parliament.
Mussolini's fast growing "movement," a refuge for the discontented, the
social misfits, and the opportunists, terrorized the population with its
hordes. While preparing for a march on Rome, Mussolini secretly
negotiated with some government officials until he was made Prime
Minister by King Victor Emanuel III. As later in Germany, the intention

[16] "Jahoo" refers to Swift's "Yahoo" creatures in *Gulliver's Travels*. It appears in the
revised version, *Roundheads*, to replace "Peru" of *Peakheads* with a name that sounds
similar but evokes more exotic connotations. Despite the fact that the English translation by N. Goold-Verschoyle (cf. n. 20) has "Yahoo," Brecht's spelling "Jahoo" has
been retained here in order to avoid too close an identification with Swift's use of the
term.

[17] GW, XVIII, 222-39. The translation used here and in the following is that by Richard
Winston, "Appendix A," Bertolt Brecht, *Galileo* (New York, 1966), pp. 133-50. K.-D.
Müller, *Die Funktion der Geschichte*, p. 71, also stresses the relevance of Brecht's essay
for his interpretation of Fascism and, hence, *Roundheads*.

on the part of the ruling classes was to let this strong man "save" the country, and then to discard him. Hence, with the exception of the racial issue, here was a historical case of governmental powers being handed to a demagogue by a nominal regent, an example which must have sharpened Brecht's recognition of the analogous pattern in Germany.

There can be no doubt that Brecht observed Mussolini's Italy and read about it widely. Still in his library is a booklet with the "official" interpretation of the Italian Fascist ideology which, in facts and in style, not only resembles the Nazi party's program or Hitler's *Mein Kampf*, but which also provided the substance for a number of lines in Brecht's play.[18] A good deal of background information was probably provided by another publication, even though it is not now in Brecht's library. It is Alfred Kurella's book, *Mussolini ohne Maske* (Berlin, 1931).[19] As the first report on Italy by a German Communist journalist it was widely read and discussed by left-wing Germans. While there is no proof that Brecht had also read it, it is hard to believe that he did not, considering the close correspondence of some facts and passages of his play and A. Kurella's report.

The author describes Italy in 1931 as chiefly agrarian: "particularly in the South the land is still owned by members of the old aristocratic families although they take no part in the farming" (61). The owner divides his land up and gives it to farmers who are to provide the equipment and cattle and who are responsible for the upkeep of the buildings. One half of the crop is due the landowner, the other half is kept by the farmer for his own consumption or for selling. Since he always needs money badly, the farmer cannot wait for a favorable time to sell his crop but has to give it away cheaply. The entire arrangement with the landowner is feasible only for large families in which everybody, including the children, is able to help in the fields. Hence, under Mussolini child labor is on the increase (93 f.).

In order to enable the reader to compare A. Kurella's description of

---

[18] *Die faschistische Lehre. Übersetzte amtliche italienische Veröffentlichung* (Plauen, n.d.). In it Fascism is described as "a creed that has taken hold of the Italian people" (10), having brought about "a profound political, moral, and social revolution" (8). Mussolini is the "defender of the fatherland against its false sons and external enemies" who needs "the unanimous, enthusiastic sacrifice of the Italian people" (55). It is a "social obligation" to work not only for one's own self-interest but for the sake of the nation (40). The farmers, above all, "are incorruptible, have preserved the highest virtues of our race, and are the backbone of the nation" (49). To be a good Fascist means to have an "aversion against the soft and comfortable life" and "to love sincerity and abhor cunning" (10). For the Fascists, the class struggle can only be an exception, otherwise "it would bring about the destruction of wealth" (31). The modern capitalists are people "with a very great sense of personal and economic responsibility" (33). Property "is not theft" but carries "the sacrosanct right" to pass it onto one's descendants (34).

[19] Alfred Kurella, *Mussolini ohne Maske. Der erste rote Reporter bereist Italien* (Berlin, 1931). All page references in the text as to the reprint of the 1st ed., published under the title: *Kennst du das Land?* (Berlin, 1962).

agricultural conditions in Italy with Brecht's depiction of similar conditions in Peru-Jahoo, the tenant farmer Callas' testimony at the trial (scene iv) is quoted at some length:

> I can prove that the rent was exorbitant. The land is marshy: the fields are too far apart. The tools are almost useless. We've had to use the cow for carting. We've had to work all summer from three o'clock in the morning with the children helping. We don't control the prices of corn; they've been different each year, though the rent is always the same. . . . We could never earn the rent. We lived on crabapples and roots because we had to send all our corn to the market. Our children run around nearly naked. We have no money for repairs so that our house is falling to pieces over our heads.[20]

Kurella views this situation as typical of Fascist Italy, a regime which "likes to refer to itself as the system that overcame the class struggle" (17). "Fascism is agrarian," he quotes Mussolini (60), who continues, "Luckily, our farmers eat only once a day" (23). He also recalls in his report the revolt of the Italian farmers just prior to Mussolini's seizure of power, when they occupied the big estates in great numbers and stayed on them for several months. The Giolitti government, in office in the early twenties, did not intervene; in some cases Giolitti even had the courts decide in favor of the rebel farmers against the complaints of the landowners (41). At that time, Kurella concludes, Italy was closer to a socialist revolution than any other European country had been since the successful Russian revolution.

All of these elements—the plight of the tenant farmers, their occupation of the big estates, their near victory until they were crushed by an army financed by the landowners—are reflected in the play's action. Whether Brecht took his material from Kurella's book or from other sources, who would still maintain that he "invented" it?

In addition to the camouflage needed to hoodwink the suspicious authorities, as mentioned above, the Italian setting in a play on Nazi Germany provided an ingenious formula to isolate the essential factors in a complex situation. Brecht was able, without further elaboration, to typify the power structure of the Weimar Republic in its last phase. He showed it to be both capitalist in general and feudal and reactionary in particular. To be sure, the cabinets of Papen and Schleicher were dominated by longtime state officials (*Beamte*) and other nationalist-conservative groups with links to organizations like the *Stahlhelm,* to the landed gentry, and to the industrialists. After the July elections of 1932, even the Nazi faction, then the largest in the parliament, included

---

[20] The translation is from *Roundheads* which, in the passage quoted, differs only to an insignificant degree from *Peakheads*. Trans. N. Gold-Verschoyle in Bertolt Brecht, *Jungle of Cities and Other Plays* (New York, 1966), pp. 203-205.

a sizable number of aristocrats.[21] On a smaller scale, Hindenburg, with his Neudeck estate, can be seen in the vulnerable position of the land-owner-regent of the play. By selecting the agrarian Italian setting as his model, Brecht reduced the complex German scene to a much simpler pattern. He concentrated his portrayal of the Weimar Republic—soon to be followed by a Fascist regime—on the depiction of the feudal, regressive nature of its policy-making forces. He ignored the fact that, unlike Italy, Germany in the early thirties was a modern, industrialized state, and chose instead to expose the essentials of its economic system which was dominated by an alliance of industrialists and aristocrats, hence capitalist. Therefore, Brecht presented his Peru-Jahoo as a country in a pre-revolutionary state,[22] torn by social and political disorder and clearly at the breaking-point.

At the basis of Brecht's depiction was his conviction that *"Fascism can be combatted as capitalism alone, as the nakedest, most shameless, most oppressive, and most treacherous form of capitalism"* (GW, XVIII, 226-27). Thus he concentrated on the battle between the haves and have-nots, whose class conflict was obscured by the race issue. The fact that this formula was at the same time a simplification—"the parable is limping" he admitted—was, in Brecht's view, offset by the advantage to be able "to pass on the truth in an indirect manner."[23] For him the function of the parabolic form—which he adopted in *Peakheads* and further strengthened in *Roundheads*—was to show the truth in such a way that it could be understood, because only then it could be effective. "If one wishes successfully to write the truth about evil conditions, one must write it so that its avertable causes can be identified. If the preventable causes can be identified, the evil conditions can be fought" (GW, XVIII, 229).

III

As long as historical reality provided the broad groundwork whose essential features could be unravelled to construct the parable—e.g., the Italian analogy and the general pattern of delegating the power of government—the results could stand the test of time. The representation of Hitler's racial policies was a different matter.

Much later, in a conversation with Ernst Schumacher, Brecht offered

[21] In addition to counting aristocrats among its members the party enjoyed the benign sponsorship of such illustrious blue bloods as Hohenzollern Prince August Wilhelm, who went by the nickname "Auwi."

[22] Similarly, Kurella compared Italy in 1931—large farming areas with a few accidental pockets of industry—with pre-revolutionary Russia, and he associated the reactionary Fascist regime with "agriculturalization" (*Verlandwirtschaftlichung*) in contrast to Soviet Russia which stood for "industrialization," i.e., for progress.

[23] Cf. Ernst Schumacher, "Er wird bleiben" (1956), reprinted in *Brecht. Theater und Gesellschaft im 20. Jahrhundert* (Berlin, 1973), p. 17.

a half-hearted justification of his treatment of the Jewish question. This justification could hardly be taken seriously.[24] But his inability to foresee the kind of atrocities Hitler was capable of in the execution of his racism is not really the point. In fact, Brecht never intended to make a case for the Jews. He wrote: "As a Socialist, I have no conception at all of the race problem as such." What he wanted to show was not the "'Jewish question' in its political application by the Nazis" specifically, but "the political application of the race question"[25] in general. After all: "Racism has been employed for the purpose of lying to people not only by German Fascism (which, incidentally, differs in this respect from Italian Fascism) but all along by other reactionary governments, too."[26] Brecht's representation is still valid today, "if it is. seen as a parable of other kinds of racial persecution."[27] In the letter to Bernhard Reich quoted above the playwright exposes the distinction between the two races as arbitrary—not by denying the obvious fact of the existence of different races but by exposing the fallacy of attributing either qualities of superiority or inferiority to them: "The recognition of racial differences is, of course, not Fascist, just as the assertion of some Jews that there were no differences, is not anti-Fascist. It does not help the oppressed Negroes in the USA much if their equality is demanded on the grounds that they were white."[28] In explaining the desired effect of the play on the spectators to the Danish stage director, Per Knutzon, in the letter cited previously, Brecht stated: "After ten minutes they [the spectators] will see nothing but Roundheads and Peakheads, and they will laugh just as if the new Governor, in all seriousness, had divided the people into bicyclists and pedestrians."[29] Bicyclists and pedestrians, Czichs and Czuchs, "Tramecksans" and "Slamecksans"[30]; Brecht hoped to ridicule ill-founded racial distinctions and show their ultimate absurdity. "If the play is performed in the proper way," he advised the Danish stage director, "people will laugh and laughter should lead to purgation."[31]

[24] "The result of the war and the post-war period had proven that the 'Aryan' bankers and industrialists in Germany who backed Hitler had made common cause during and after the war with their Jewish counterparts in the U.S. at the expense of the exploited people in both countries." Cf. Schumacher, "Er wird bleiben," p. 17. Cf. also GW, XX, 313.

[25] Letter to Per Knutzon, probably April/May 1934, quoted from W. Hecht, H.-J. Bunge, K. Rülicke-Weiler, *Bertolt Brecht,* p. 128.

[26] Ibid., p. 127 (Letter to Bernhard Reich of 11 March 1937).

[27] André Müller, review of the Hanover production of *Roundheads,* TdZ, 18/1 (1963), 28.

[28] Cf. n. 26.

[29] Cf. n. 25.

[30] In *Gulliver's Travels,* Swift satirizes artificial distinctions by similar means: The "Tramecksans" and "Slamecksans" are two parties distinguished by the high and low heels of their shoes. As if this were not enough, Swift goes on to describe a war about the proper way of breaking eggs: by the smaller or the larger end; the defenders of the latter method were called "Big-Endians."

[31] Letter to Knutzon (cf. n. 25).

It is true, in his play about Fascism, Brecht used racism in a general sense rather than in the specific variety the Nazis practiced. Nevertheless, he strongly alluded to contemporary events and figures by endowing his new demagogic ruler with traits which were characteristic of Hitler; i.e., his rhetoric, his fierce hostility towards the Communists, the terror practiced by his street gangs, and his alliance with the capitalists. To be sure, these topical elements lent urgency to the play but, at the same time, too close a linkage to the actual situation increased the possibility that the play might be surpassed by events and become obsolete. Although for this very reason a factual representation of the Jews' persecution and annihilation in the Third Reich would have been sensationally relevant, for the Marxist Brecht, who took the long view of history, the persecution of the Jews was a surface phenomenon whose exposure would not contribute significantly to the spectators' understanding of the *real* causes underlying Hitler's rise to power. In Brecht's view, the factual representation of a phenomenon was not the same as telling the truth about it.

In order to tell the truth, as he saw it, about the nature of German Fascism, Brecht chose the form of the parable. The parable form allowed the playwright to pass on the truth in an indirect manner and permitted him to mobilize energies on the part of the audience without the use of pathos: "For the dramatist the parable is the perfect solution because it is simultaneously abstract and concrete by providing an obvious demonstration of essentials."[32] Brecht's method of making the essentials of the impending Hitler regime visible was by showing a reactionary capitalist country. In this country a dictator is trying to sap the strength of a revolutionary movement by dividing it into two races. When he does not succeed, he crushes the revolution in a bloody war financed by the capitalists; in this way the old oppressive system is preserved.

Brecht combined the two conflicts of class and race in the same two characters: the rich landowner is set against the poor farmer in claiming his rent; but as a Czuch, the farmer expects to prevail over the Czichish landowner. To make his case still stronger, Brecht assigns a double function to Callas, the farmer. Confronted with his landlord, Callas discovers that his poverty, not his Czuchish roundhead, determines his destiny: when he does as the rich do, i.e., when he claims property he has not earned, he loses. Confronted with the rebel farmers, he realizes that he should not have left them in the hope of getting his cut from the racist governor. By the time Callas is ready to correct his mistake, the revolution has been crushed; his awakening comes too late. There is an unmistakeable lesson to be learned from Callas, who was attempting to straddle the fence which separated the rich from the poor. What Brecht hoped to achieve was to instill the proper class consciousness in the

[32] Schumacher, "Er wird bleiben," p. 17.

spectators: "If one wants to obliterate [the spectators'] false consciousness and develop their right consciousness, one has to make people confront themselves . . . in order to have them achieve their true selves. This cannot be done by presenting [on stage] the likes of them . . . [rather] everything has to appear in an unfamiliar [*verfremdet*] light. The more simply this can be done, the better it is. Hence the parable is still the most appropriate form."[33]

Although the topical elements of the play appear dated, the core of the parable has stood the test of time. Significantly, Brecht, in his extensive revisions after Hitler's seizure of power (which he had correctly predicted in the early versions), tended to strengthen the parabolic aspects by adding songs and a Prologue. Brecht's tendency to avoid the purely topical can also be discerned in his not adjusting the ending of the play (which in both the *Peakheads* and *Roundheads* versions has the *rich* Czichs saved from persecution) even after the atrocities of the "final solution" had become a matter of public record. The fact that the play, in its various versions, reflects the course of political events at the time of its origin and also attempts to capture the essence of the period in a more lasting form, makes Brecht's parable both a literary and historical document.

IV

Paradoxically, during those years in which Brecht's "didactic piece against Fascism for all tongues"[34] might have been most effective in helping stem the tide of Nazism, the playwright had little opportunity to test the validity of his theories. Although Brecht's endeavors to have his play produced began as early as June 1933 and extended to places as far away from his Danish exile as Paris,[35] Moscow,[36] and New York,[37] the only production which materialized during the years of the Third Reich was a production in Danish which was directed by Per Knutzon and opened in Copenhagen on 4 November 1936. Brecht participated in an

[33] Ibid., p. 16.

[34] Abusch, *Literatur im Zeitalter des Sozialismus*, p. 205.

[35] *Brecht-Chronik*, p. 56: While in Paris, Brecht negotiated with the theatrical entrepreneur Ernst Josef Aufricht about a production of *Peakheads*.

[36] In 1935 the famous director, Erwin Piscator, explored possibilities of having Brecht's play produced in the Soviet Union. The Jewish Theater in Moscow; further, theaters in Kislodovsk and Engels (then the center of the Volga Germans where Piscator hoped to etablish a German theater) were among the prospects. In an interview published in the German-language paper *Der Arbeiter* (New York, 23 November 1935), Brecht mentioned that rehearsals of *Roundheads* had begun at the Realistic Theater in Moscow under the direction of Nikolai Okhlopkov. According to Marjorie Hoover, to whom I am indebted for this information, the playwright Sergei Tretiakov had revised the text for the production. It is not known whether the play was actually performed.

[37] *Brecht-Chronik*, p. 65: Brecht was in New York (Fall 1935) in order to supervise the Theatre Union's production of his play, *The Mother*. Again, he attempted to have *Roundheads* staged.

advisory function; as a consequence, the parable was staged in his epic mode.[38] Although the play did not achieve an artistic success, it caused a considerable political stir—as can be seen from the strong and often emotional reactions it evoked. The two groups most irritated by the play were the Catholics and the National Socialists. The Catholics protested loudly and won a point: an offensive piece of décor had to be removed. The National Socialists were less successful; they demonstrated in front of the Riddersalen Theater and one of them was arrested. Efforts to have the Justice Department intervene on behalf of the National Socialists failed.

In general, the theater critics were not disposed charitably toward the play. The parable was declared to be a Communist propaganda play in which the author merely proved "that he had neither poetic talent nor possessed any ability as a dramatist."[39] Another critical voice described the play as "a leery, stupid blasphemy and a base mockery of the catholic faith."[40] Ominously, the warning was uttered "that the writers among the [German] emigrants would do well to practice discretion."[41]

Among the voices from the audience,[42] two are particularly illuminating. There is a fireman's comment on three different performances. After the premiere, he was enthusiastic: "Simply ingenious, only too late. Five years earlier, and it [the play] might have prevented things from happening." A few days later he was cool and non-committal, and on the third occasion he flatly rejected the play as "too Communist." Simplistic as this may appear, his change of mind seems to give a fairly accurate reflection of the vacillations of public opinion. Another noteworthy reaction came from a well-to-do Jewess—who was a member of many committees aiding refugee Jews. Her rejection was very emphatic; the play was potentially dangerous, she said, because it drew "their" attention to the Jews.

Even from this random information it appears that Brecht's play had stirred up a hornet's nest and polarized the audience. Needless to say, Brecht's aim was surely not to cause an *éclat*. Rather, he wanted to "politicize" his audience in a positive sense, i.e., transform their emotions into actions against the Hitler regime. As he put it: "The truth must be spoken with a view to the results it will produce in the sphere of action" (GW, XVIII, 226). Since the play could not be performed anywhere else but in Copenhagen, its effectiveness as a political weapon could neither be proved nor disproved. After all, the Danish production

---

[38] Cf. the detailed description of the Copenhagen production in GW, XVII, 1082-1096. Abridged English version in *Brecht on Theatre,* pp. 100-103.

[39] Quoted from Hans-Christof Wächter, *Theater im Exil. Sozialgeschichte des deutschen Exiltheaters 1933-1945* (Munich, 1973), p. 93.

[40] *Zwölf-Uhr-Blatt* (8 November 1936).

[41] Ibid.

[42] Collected by Nena Asbjörn Andersen, wife of the actor who played the dictator; cf. BBA, 265/31-34.

was quite exceptional. In Brecht's view, it was due to its parabolic form that, in spite of the censor, the play could be performed at all in Denmark—a small country which had borders, as well as vital trade relations with Nazi Germany.[43] In a letter to Karl Korsch a few weeks after the premiere Brecht expressed his relief about the fact that his residence permit was renewed after *Roundheads* had been performed.[44]

Finally, eighteen years after the collapse of the Third Reich Brecht's parable was staged in West Germany. In the final analysis, the playwright who all along had emphasized the significance of the parabolic elements and attributed less importance to the topical aspects, was proved right. André Müller, in his review of the *Roundheads* premiere in Hanover (1963), observed: "Everywhere people discussed the play . . . they were comparing the action of the play with reality as they had experienced it. Paradoxically, a play by Brecht whose ending did not correspond to historical fact as far as Germany was concerned stimulated the spectators' reflections to a far greater extent than any other of his plays."[45]

[43] Cf. BBA, 327/26.
[44] *Brecht-Chronik,* p. 67.
[45] Müller, TdZ, 28.

SENORA CARRAR'S RIFLES:
DRAMATIC MEANS AND DIDACTIC ENDS

Grace M. Allen

Senora Carrar's Rifles, the one-act play Brecht wrote in 1937, was published in the *Experiments* series in 1953. To Hans Mayer the fact that it appeared in a special issue and without opus number, suggests a "secret illegitimacy"; as a source of embarrassment to Brecht, Mayer argues, it was thus set apart from the main body of his work.[1] Although Käthe Rülicke-Weiler contends there is another, perfectly good reason for this manner of publication,[2] Brecht's attitude to *Senora Carrar* appears to lend some support to Mayer's suggestion. In his notes to the play he tersely describes it as "Aristotelian (empathetic) drama"; as such it exhibited certain "disadvantages" for which Brecht proposes possible corrective measures without, however, explicating the "disadvantages" themselves (GW, XVII, 1100). Also, compared with his often lengthy commentaries on most of the plays, Brecht wrote significantly little about *Senora Carrar* and nowhere does he explain his reasons for using the "Aristotelian" mode. Given his theory and practice after formulating the "shifts of emphasis" from "dramatic" to "epic" in his notes to *Rise and Fall of the City of Mahagonny* (GW, XVII, 1009), this lack of enthusiasm for *Senora Carrar* is perhaps not too surprising.[3]

Werner Mittenzwei takes quite a different view. He claims that in *Fear and Misery of the Third Reich* and *Senora Carrar* Brecht was "testing out the capacities of the old technique again. He was trying out its effectiveness in order to ascertain which elements of the old drama were suitable for depicting the highly complicated processes of our reality, and how these elements could be combined with certain innovations."[4] In fact, he even argues Brecht could not have made the sudden transition from *Roundheads and Peakheads* to the "great masterpieces of Socialist Realism in the years 1938 and 1939, *Life of Galileo, Mother Courage and her Children* and *The Good Woman of Setzuan*"

---

[1] *Brecht und die Tradition* (Pfullingen, 1961), p. 110.

[2] *Die Dramaturgie Brechts* (Berlin, 1966), p. 247, n. 68.

[3] This refers only to the work itself, not the cause for which Brecht wrote it—the Republican struggle against Franco in the Spanish civil war. His "Address to the Second International Writers' Congress for the Defense of Culture" in Madrid (1937) indicates his keen commitment to stemming the tide of Fascism as it spread from Germany and Italy into Spain. Werner Mittenzwei (cf. n. 4) tells that Brecht (who did not go to Spain to read his "Address") commissioned Ruth Berlau, the Danish actress who later became his professional assistant and mistress, to gather material on the war while she was in Spain, and that Brecht himself made a press collection. The play was written for performance by a group of exiled German actors in Paris under the direction of Slatan Dudow, who shared Brecht's opposition to Fascism.

[4] *Bertolt Brecht: Von der "Maßnahme" zu "Leben des Galilei,"* 2nd ed. (Berlin, 1965), p. 233. Page references for further quotations from this source will be given in parentheses in the text.

without the experience he gained from writing *Fear and Misery* and *Senora Carrar* (p. 233). Hans Kaufmann, in rejecting the possibility that the "Aristotelian" structure of *Senora Carrar* is attributable to Brecht's "need to experiment," claims that it must be "grasped and judged from the intended effect and the particular nature of the subject which the writer believes capable of this effect."[5] Martin Esslin, commenting on *Senora Carrar* as a play in the "conventional dramatic form [Brecht] so despised," praises it as "very effective theater" but considers it "clearly a pot-boiler" and claims Brecht's explanatory note to the play is a tacit acknowledgement of the fact.[6] Frederic Ewen argues that with *Senora Carrar* Brecht was "sacrificing an all-important theory in the face of an emergency," but observes too, that it illustrates Brecht's "flexibility as a writer."[7]

Notwithstanding Brecht's designation of his works as *experiments,* Kaufmann's term *Experimentierbedürfnis* with its nuance of a desire to experiment for the sake of experimentation, strikes a false note. Ewen's reference to Brecht's "flexibility," however, points up a key factor in any discussion of *Senora Carrar;* for the incredible variety that characterizes the Brechtian *œuvre* undoubtedly derives from his basic principle: "The end must determine the means" (GW, XIX, 328)—a statement which in turn implies that the didactic content is decisive for the form. It may have gone against the grain with Brecht to write *Senora Carrar* as "Aristotelian (empathetic) drama," but the fact that he employed the same mode in the individual scenes of *Fear and Misery* and, to a considerable extent, in *Galileo,* bears witness to both his flexibility and his pragmatism as a writer. Indeed, the relationship between ends and means, content and form, is the basis of both Kaufmann's analysis of *The Days of the Commune* in *Geschichtsdrama und Parabelstück* (1962) and Ernst Schumacher's exhaustive study *Drama und Geschichte: Bertolt Brechts Leben des Galilei und andere Stücke* (1965). In each instance *Senora Carrar* serves as a significant example. Hence, although as theater it apparently has less to offer than most of Brecht's works, *Senora Carrar* warrants attention for the singular position it holds in the Brechtian *œuvre* as the only one of his works he formally designated "Aristotelian."

In considering the play from this aspect, the obvious approach to pursue is the fact that it is based on an "idea" from *Riders to the Sea* (1903), the one-act tragedy by J.M. Synge.[8] This work concerns

---

[5] *Bertolt Brecht: Geschichtsdrama und Parabelstück* (Berlin, 1962), p. 170.
[6] *Brecht* (E/3), p. 69.
[7] *Brecht* (Ew), p. 319.
[8] The brief prefatory note to *Senora Carrar's Rifles* is Brecht's only reference to Synge's work. So far as I know, there is no published explanation as to how he came to use *Riders to the Sea* in this way. It is in keeping, however, with his habit of using whatever source material suited his purpose. Quotations from *Riders* will be according to *The Complete Plays of John M. Synge* (New York, n.d.), with page references in parentheses in the text.

Maurya, an Irish fisherman's widow, who, having lost all her other menfolk to the sea, seeks to ensure the survival of her one remaining son by trying to persuade him to stay away from it. Although he refuses and is drowned, his death occurs not because he went fishing (as Mittenzwei's summary implies, p. 232), but because a skittish pony he was leading along the cliff road knocked him into the water. Even though she sought to protect him by human means and despite her priest's assurance that "the Almighty God won't leave her destitute, with no son living" (p. 84), Maurya does not rail against providence. As a devout Christian she accepts the unfathomable will of God: "No man at all can be living for ever, and we must be satisfied" (p. 97). Brecht's play also concerns a simple fisherman's family, but it takes place in Spain during the civil war. The father has been killed fighting against Franco, and his widow, Theresa Carrar, seeks to protect her two sons from the same fate by forbidding them to follow their father's example. Reluctantly they agree; nevertheless, one son dies at the hands of the Fascists—not by actively opposing them but by quietly fishing, as ordered by his mother. Instead of accepting his death with Maurya's pious quiescence, Theresa Carrar rails against the murderers: "They aren't human beings, they are a plague and must be burnt out like a plague" (GW, III, 1228). Then, with her remaining son and her militantly anti-Fascist brother, Pedro, she leaves to take up the fight against Franco in the name of her dead son, Juan.

Thus Brecht retains the same basic plot outline, yet he refutes Synge's tragic viewpoint. The problem of mortality and suffering underlies both plays, but whereas Synge deals with the metaphysics of fate, Brecht investigates the realities of survival. *Riders to the Sea* is a tragedy which shows Maurya ultimately resigned to the human condition; *Senora Carrar's Rifles* is a politically motivated, didactic piece that ends with Senora Carrar seeking to end a man-made threat to humanity. Therefore, not the inspiration Brecht received from a tragic plot is the reason for the "Aristotelian" mode of *Senora Carrar*. Nor should it be assumed that his intention was to attack Synge's play as a tragedy although both his theory and practice consistently oppose the tragic genre. A notebook entry written about 1932 affords another insight into his position vis-à-vis *Riders to the Sea*. Writing, significantly enough, on "Naturalist Tragedy" Brecht contends: "The arousal of tragic sensations in the spectator would, however, only be permitted if the impossibility of escape for the hero were really guaranteed, for only if one cannot make a practical suggestion for him can one participate in his pain without punishment. The inescapability must thus on no account be social, that is, an inescapability which exists in our contemporary social order. After all, our social order is not an eternal category from which one cannot escape."[9] Had Synge created a situation akin to that of

9 SzT, II, 44.

Senora Carrar's Rifles but retained his own kind of ending, Brecht would have strongly opposed it because passivity towards social evils is precisely the attitude he seeks to eradicate. However, the tragic events in *Riders to the Sea* admit of no "practical suggestion" for averting them. So, by Brecht's definition, Synge's play is "legitimate" tragedy. By the same token his own play does not constitute a polemic against the religion that is an integal part of Maurya's life. Also, even if Senora Carrar's policy of neutrality based on religion did not ensure the survival of her first son, there can be no certainty that the "practical suggestion" of eliminating the Fascist "plague" would be any more effective in the case of the second son. On the other hand, Brecht would have argued, I think, that to die resisting Franco would have served some purpose by making the advance of Fascism that much more difficult—in contrast to the ineffectual life (and death) of Juan in terms of the struggle against Fascism. And if the sons are taken as representatives of a new generation, then the "practical suggestion" might well prove effective in the end (as the result of World War II indicates). In the sphere of political realities only this kind of hard evaluation is valid, even though Brecht does tacitly admit man's ultimate helplessness in certain (non-social) contexts.

Religion is an extremely important element in Brecht's play, however, for in refusing to actively oppose the Fascists Senora Carrar conforms to the village Padre's ethic of total non-violence. The whole didactic thrust of the play is against such pacifism, yet Brecht's purpose is not simply to have the spectators endorse Theresa Carrar's final decision to take up arms. They must be induced to judge for themselves on the concrete issues involved in the Padre's position and the political neutrality to which it leads. Hence the central core of *Senora Carrar* is a debate between the Padre and Senora Carrar's brother, Pedro. The climax comes when Pedro asks whether the Padre, as a Christian, believes that Franco—who also professes to be a Christian (GW, III, 1216)—will carry out his threats of aerial bombardment, and whether the Padre believes that neutrality is a guarantee of safety. An honest man, the priest is reduced to anguished silence, caught in the dilemma of what he should answer according to his religious beliefs and what he ought to answer in the light of his knowledge of Fascism. Pressed again for an answer he replies, heatedly, "Surely you don't want me to give a guarantee?" (GW, III, 1217). When the brother asks for the third time whether the Padre believes Senora Carrar's neutrality will ensure her family's safety, he receives no answer. *"Rising in confusion,"* the priest takes his leave. Thus in the course of the debate Brecht has subtly shifted the emphasis from the ethical basis of the Padre's assurance to Theresa Carrar that her neutralist attitude is "justified" (GW, III, 1212), to the practical efficacy of such neutrality as a means of protection against the Fascists. An intermediate stage in the debate raises the question of what neutralist non-intervention actually signifies. The brother accuses the

Padre: "And while you are for non-intervention you in essence condone the bloodbath these Generals are inflicting on the Spanish people" (GW, III, 1213). This point is, of course, vital to Brecht's polemic and he gives it added emphasis through the Padre's physical gesture as he responds. *"Raising his hands high in a gesture of deprecation:* I do not condone it" (GW, III, 1213). The brother tellingly comments that this gesture resembles one of surrender. As in other matters, the priest can offer no solid arguments here either (GW, III, 1213).

Throughout this debate the Padre registers as a patently sincere man and yet there is reason to question the basis of his pacifism. He himself admits: "In many areas the lower clergy support the legally constituted government. Of the eighteen dioceses in Bilbao, seventeen have declared themselves for the government. Not a few of my fellow clergymen are at the front. Some have already fallen" (GW, III, 1212). From this it seems the Padre could, with good Christian conscience, choose to resist the Francoists. However, he also frankly confesses himself to be "personally not at all a fighter. God has not granted me the gift to call out my flock loudly and clearly to the fight for . . . *he searches for a word*" (GW, III, 1212). It seems legitimate to ask, therefore, whether he follows the commandment, "Thou shalt not kill" from deep moral conviction or because it accords so well with his own nature. In short: is the commandment possibly an excuse rather than a reason for the Padre's proclaiming non-violence as his creed?

The discussion with Senora Carrar's brother does not bring about any change in the priest's attitude, but his poor showing against the brother's relentless questions undoubtedly has an effect on the sister. For instance, later in the conversation with her neighbor, Senora Perez, she asks despairingly, "Why does the Padre keep silent when he should be talking?" (GW, III, 1223). And when her elder son, Juan, despite his reluctant neutrality, is wantonly killed by the Fascists, she realizes the ultimate futility of following the priest's way. Senora Carrar mistakenly assumes that Juan has secretly joined the Republican forces and pronounces her Biblical judgment: "They that take the sword shall perish with the sword" (GW, III, 1226). This judgment takes on grim irony when his body is brought in from the sea immediately afterwards. However, it also becomes her text for the future: the only way to end violence, she now sees, is not to eschew violence but to meet it with violence. This decision to fight, rather than passively turn the other cheek to the Fascists, indicates that *Senora Carrar,* for all its "Aristotelian" designation, has much in common with Brecht's "non-Aristotelian" drama. As he defines it in the notes to *The Mother,* "non-Aristotelian" drama "does not set out to deliver up its hero to the world as to his inescapable fate [but is intent] on teaching the audience a quite specific, practical form of action aimed at changing the world" (GW, XVII, 1036).

A pertinent question, then, is what "Aristotelian" signifies as applied by Brecht. Keith A. Dickson comments on *Senora Carrar:* "Brecht even equates the terms 'Aristotelian' and 'empathetic' without more ado. This suggests that Brecht misinterpreted the 'mimetic' nature of traditional art as badly as Plato once did, and likewise misinterpreted Aristotle's intelligent qualifications."[10] It does seem rather cavalier of Brecht to offer a one-word definition after scholars have toiled for centuries over the subtleties of the *Poetics,* but surely there can hardly be any doubt that "Aristotelian" in Brecht's usage is little more than a cipher, a convenient shorthand term of reference far removed from the scholar's appellation with its weighty philological and aesthetic import. In the second section of the group of notes headed "Critique of Empathy" Brecht tells what he accepts of Aristotle, and it is not very much. "So long as Aristotle (in the fourth chapter of the *Poetics*) speaks generally about the pleasure to be derived from the mimetic depiction and cites learning as the reason for this pleasure, we go along with him. But already in the sixth chapter he becomes more specific and limits the field of mimesis for tragedy" (GW, XV, 240).[11] And there is the rub! This limitation of the mimesis to "actions which arouse fear and pity" (GW, XV, 241), leads, of course, to catharsis; which in turn is central to Brecht's observations on "Aristotelian drama" in the first section of these notes.

There he offers *two* definitions of this dramatic mode. The first is essentially by way of delimiting and therefore defining "non-Aristotelian" drama. In this connection "Aristotelian" drama is said to mean "all drama to which the main point, as we see it, of the Aristotelian definition of tragedy in the *Poetics,* applies" (GW, XV, 240). This "main point"[12] is the catharsis that results from "the spectator's empathy with the characters who are imitated by the actors (GW, XV, 240). The second definition, which contains no reference to "non-Aristotelian" drama, is much broader in scope: "We designate drama as Aristotelian if it creates this empathy, regardless of whether it does so in

[10] "Brecht: An Aristotelian Malgré Lui," MD, 2 (1967), 111.
[11] There are other areas of agreement, of course. Cf. *A Short Organum for the Theatre,* where plot is declared to be the "soul of drama" (GW, XVI, 667) or the "heart of theater" (GW, XVI, 693). Also, it is said to be ("Notes to *Antigone*") the "heart of tragedy" (GW, XVIII, 1217).
[12] Brecht actually writes: "To us the matter of greatest social interest seems what Aristotle sets as the purpose, namely catharsis" (*GW*, XV, 240). However, after the initial reference to "main point" he says only that the "unities" are not what he means by this, then continues with the passage quoted. It seems fair to assume, therefore, that the "main point" for him is the catharsis.

accordance with the rules Aristotle formulates for this purpose or not" (GW, XV, 240).[13]

Although catharsis is not the criterion here, tragedy is not precluded from this category, since empathy induced according to the Aristotelian "rules" would lead to tragic catharsis. In this respect, then, the two definitions accord. However, the second one would also encompass non-tragic drama so long as it functions through empathy. But in that case the "Aristotelian" label becomes a contradiction in terms! We are given no specific examples of empathy induced without following Aristotle, although Brecht does note that over the centuries the manner by which empathy is induced has changed (GW, XV, 240), and that the empathy experienced by the ancient Greeks was not the same as the modern empathy with the individual in the era of fully developed capitalism (GW, XV, 240). Be that as it may, there can be no doubt that the second definition, Brecht's own, provides the basis for the designation of *Senora Carrar* as "Aristotelian (empathetic) drama." As we see from the foregoing observations, the equation of "Aristotelian" and "empathetic" was arrived at with somewhat more "ado" than Dickson recognizes.

Yet for all its designation, *Senora Carrar* is ideologically as non-Aristotelian as the rest of Brecht's Marxist-oriented drama, and its relation to true Aristotelian or tragic drama can best be stated in the words of the Philosopher during the first night of *The Purchase of Brass:* "The ancients saw the purpose of tragedy to be the exciting of fear and pity. Even today that would still be a good purpose if fear was simply understood as fear of people, and pity as pity for people, and if therefore serious theater helped to eliminate those conditions among people which cause them to fear and pity each other. For man has become his own destiny" (GW, XVI, 525-26). Recognizing the inaccuracy, or at least inadequacy, of the designation "Aristotelian," K. Rülicke-Weiler speaks of the "new Aristotelian drama" when referring to *Senora Carrar* and other such works; that is, plays in which "no fate drives the play forward—but social causes and human actions" and which "strive not for catharsis but a challenge to action" (p. 84). I do not think this solves the terminological problem (strictly speaking, "empathetic non-Aristotelian drama" might be more accurate), but the description of the ideological thrust of this kind of drama underlines how far removed it is from the tragic genre as described in the *Poetics*.

Brecht never explained directly why he wrote *Senora Carrar* in his "Aristotelian" mode, but his reasons can be deduced from the note

[13] Both of Brecht's definitions ignore the formal elements included by Aristotle in his definition of tragedy: "Tragedy, then, is the imitation of a good action, which is complete and of a certain length, by means of language made pleasing for each part separately; it relies in its various elements not on narrative but on acting; through pity and fear it achieves the purgation (catharsis) of such emotions." *On Poetry and Style,* trans. G.M.A. Grube (Indianapolis, 1958), p. 12.

"Direct Effect of Aristotelian Drama." After explicating the direct social action that resulted from a play "constructed on Aristotelian lines,"[14] he arrives at the conclusion:

> If a certain social situation is very ripe, then plays of this kind can bring about practical action. This sort of play is the spark which ignites the powder keg. If the role of perception can be relatively small, . . . the application of the Aristotelian effect is fully to be recommended. In the above situation non-Aristotelian drama would possibly have found it more difficult to trigger off direct action . . . the action which it would have had to aim at would have been more general and greater, but also less specific and presently less feasible. (GW, XV, 249)

The effective difference this passage denotes between the two dramatic modes can be illustrated by a brief comparison of *Senora Carrar* with two "non-Aristotelian" works which also have the same relation of religion to political action as their underlying theme: *Saint Joan of the Stockyards* and *The Good Woman of Setzuan*. In their goodness both Joan Dark and Shen Te wish to relieve the misery they see around them, but they succeed only in compounding the suffering and reinforcing the system responsible for it. Even though Joan in her dying moments comes to understand why her charitable efforts to ameliorate the suffering were so disastrous—"Only violence helps where there is violence/ Only people help where there are people" (GW, II, 783)—this insight is, in itself, of little immediate practical utility in the struggle against that oppressive system. Such knowledge has to be widely disseminated and the nature of the "violence" understood if the workers, who are on the right track, are to gain needed support from other social groups. Also, the repugnance towards violence felt by "do-gooders" who believe, as Joan did originally, that they are helping the poor by ladling out soup and sermons, has to be dispelled. Spectators who share Joan's initial naiveté would learn with her in the course of the action and if they accept her conclusions as to the only effective solution for ending the evils of capitalism, they will also recognize that the well-meaning Salvation Army lassies are wrong when they tell Joan as she tries to spread her new gospel before she dies: "You must be good! You must be quiet!" (GW, II, 241). Shen Te, on the other hand, remains uncomprehending to the end and clings to her pathetic trust in the "Gods" as they make their escape from the woes of mere mortals and piously exhort her to remain "good" without offering any practical solution to

---

[14] "A play constructed on Aristotelian lines which demonstrated as anti-social the prohibition of abortion in the overcrowded cities with their limited employment opportunities. The result of this play was that the working class women who saw it banded together and forced the insurance to pay for contraceptive devices." Part of this passage from GW, XV, 249, is quoted by K. Rülicke-Weiler, *Die Dramaturgie Brechts,* p. 81, who also cites Friedrich Wolf's *Cyankali* and P. Crede's § *218* as possible sources for Brecht's reference.

her predicament. If the spectator is to deal with the open questions posed in the Epilogue as to a possible answer to the problems left unresolved by the action, he must work out for himself why Shen Te's good intentions have such horrendous results. Then, on the basis of this understanding, he can arrive at the appropriate solution. Given the parabolic nature of this play, any "good" person seeking to eliminate social evils in a capitalist society could be confronted with a dilemma like that which Shen Te experiences. Thus the answers to her predicament could be applied in any comparable social situation.

In short: *Saint Joan* and *The Good Woman* help prepare the way for social action by inducing understanding of the kind of concerted effort needed, predicated on the insight into the social system afforded by the dramatic events. With these two plays Brecht fills the "powder keg" and primes the fuse in readiness for ignition. His concern is therefore primarily with the rational faculties of the audience, and the "non-Aristotelian" dramaturgy he employs to this end is derived from his "epic" scheme in his notes to *Rise and Fall of the City of Mahagonny*.

Senora Carrar in contrast, shows the heroine literally surrounded by people who seek to correct her misguided efforts to protect her sons. She has only to move out of her self-imposed isolation as a neutralist and participate in the militancy her family and neighbors have long been urging. The right way is clearly signposted for her to follow. Not lack of understanding, as in the case of Joan and Shen Te, but fear of the consequences of resisting Franco causes her to become a neutralist after actively supporting her husband in the Republican cause. The fallacy of trusting in the slender chance of short-term security and ignoring the all-engulfing consequences of a Francoist victory is clear. Hence the nature of the action required is beyond doubt, while the situation not only allows of immediate action but, by its urgency, demands it. Thus the purpose of *Senora Carrar* is to provide the "spark" that will set off the "powder keg" by inducing the audience to emulate Theresa Carrar's exemplary decision to actively oppose Fascism. Here the "Aristotelian effect" (in Brecht's terms, empathy without catharsis) comes into its own. [15]

The debate which runs through the play must therefore be experienced not simply as a clash of viewpoints; it has to be felt as a matter of vital human concern, i.e., the immediate fate of a people is at stake. The figures and the social milieu have much in common with those of *The Mother*, yet there is none of the deliberate rendering of "typical" figures found there: "What can I Pelagea Wlassowa, widow of a worker and mother of a worker, do?" (GW, II, 825). Rather, so far as limitations imposed by the brevity of a one-act play allow, Brecht

---

[15] Both Kaufmann, *Geschichtsdrama und Parabelstück*, pp. 174-75, and Peter Witzmann *Antike Tradition im Werk Bertolt Brechts* (Berlin, 1964), p. 117, argue along the same lines and group *Galileo* and *The Visions of Simone Machard* with *Senora Carrar*. Witzmann includes as well the *Antigone* and *Coriolanus* adaptations.

strives for "round" characters motivated by feelings with which the audience can readily identify: fear for one's family, abhorrence of violence, love of liberty, etc. Senora Carrar, the figure for whom Brecht is most indebted to Synge, is particularly finely nuanced. She not only endures the maternal anguish Maurya suffers but also has to thwart the efforts of those around her who seek, she thinks, to jeopardize the one chance there seems to be of safety. In the unceasing thrust and parry this involves, her nerves grow raw, she becomes suspicious and hostile. For instance, she responds to Senora Perez in a way which would be totally alien to her under normal circumstances. Later, she is full of remorse for having behaved in such a manner. Knowing she has pinned all her hopes on neutrality, the audience must feel with her as she sees the Padre, cornered by Pedro's probing questions, failing to justify his (and, therefore, her) position. Yet still she resists, clinging with an obstinacy born of desperation to her "simple calculation" that those who do nothing against the Fascists will be spared by them. These internal conflicts are mirrored in her long, emotionally charged replies to Pedro and her cunning tricks to outwit his attempts to obtain her husband's guns; her pathetic attempts to bribe the second son to stay at home; her vehemence towards Manuela, Juan's girl friend; the desperation of her curse on Juan. Even when, by Brecht's standards, the attitude of a character is wrong (as is the case with the Padre and Senora Carrar), the character as an individual is drawn sympathetically. Members of the audience who share such an attitude are not likely to be antagonized when finally it is shown to have been misguided.

If the audience, caught up in Theresa Carrar's love, resentment, despair, and shocked disbelief at Juan's death, do experience "fear" and "pity," the result will not be catharsis. For the play is intended to help eliminate "those conditions among people which cause them to fear and pity each other." The emotional reactions are qualified by the rational responses to the debate that forms the dramatic core. In the dialectic Brecht establishes, if one feels for and with Senora Carrar in the loss of her son, one must also be filled with anger at the Fascists and regret that she will not (up to this time) support action against them. And when the turning point comes, emotional support of her decision to act will be rationally sustained by the understanding the spectator has gained along with her that violence must be met with violence.

It has been shown that "Aristotelian" as it applies to *Senora Carrar* differs from the first definition of the term Brecht offers by way of delimiting and defining his "non-Aristotelian" mode. Later, in *The Purchase of Brass,* he coined for the latter type of "Aristotelian" drama the description "carousel (*K[arussel]*) type" to distinguish it from the "planetary (*P[lanetarium]*) type" (i.e., "non-Aristotelian" drama). But while he devoted himself unstintingly to explaining the performing techniques and attitudes necessary for the full implementation of the "P-type" dramaturgy as distinct from those practiced in the "K-type,"[16] what he required for his own "Aristotelian" drama is not so easy to ascertain. Comparing the performances of Dagmar Andreason and Helene Weigel in the role of Senora Carrar, Brecht writes that both follow "epic principles" in as far as "they themselves to a great extent renounced empathy with the character they were playing and so precluded empathy by the spectators" (GW, XVII, 1100-101). Yet there were significant differences. At Andreason's performances the public "obediently followed the action" and Theresa Carrar's neutrality as played by Andreason "appeared natural and fully explained by the milieu and by what one had heard of her previous history; [her opinion] could not, as it were, be otherwise" (GW, XVII, 1101). Frau Weigel, on the other hand, "through every attitude and through every sentence enabled and compelled the audience to take up a stance . . . while she herself was continuously taking one" (GW, XVII, 1101). Of the two, Brecht deemed the Weigel performance superior. Indicative of the merit of her performance for him is his comment in another context: "Actors such as *Weigel* achieved apparently complete empathy by the spectators (who said enthusiastically: 'She did not act the fisherman's wife, she was one'), and yet at the same time that critical attitude in the spectator was achieved which is so important to us" (GW, XV, 316).

This insistence that a "critical attitude" be induced in the spectator by means of acting reinforces the tempering of emotional responses with rational evaluations which the text intends. It reminds us, too, of Brecht's argument, in connection with his "non-Aristotelian" drama: "A completely free, critical attitude by the spectator, concerned with purely earthly solutions to problems, is no basis for a catharsis" (GW, XV, 241). Clearly, then, the empathy of Brecht's "Aristotelian" drama is far removed from that induced by drama ancient or modern which is either defined in, or derived from, the *Poetics*. His comment during a rehearsal of Strittmatter's *Katzgraben* by the Berliner Ensemble in 1953 is possibly the best indication of Brecht's didactic intent in *Senora Carrar:* "Mere empathy may induce the wish to emulate the hero, but hardly the ability to do so. In order that one can rely on the [hero's] outlook, it must be adopted not merely impulsively but also at a rational level. In order that a correct action can be imitated, it must have been so comprehended that the principle can be applied to situations which may not be exactly the same as the one depicted. It is the task of the theater to

---

[16] The most comprehensive and systematic comparison occurs in *The Purchase of Brass, Second Night* (GW, XVI, 543-45).

present the hero in such a way that he stimulates conscious, not blind emulation" (GW, XVI, 813-14). [17]

As theory this all seems clear enough, but the task of the actor in realizing these goals is less easy to grasp—even if one grants that the complexities of the actor's art are not readily comprehensible to the layman. What puzzles me in particular about Frau Weigel's performance as described above, is that, although by and large she did not strive for empathy and so precluded empathy by the audience, she nevertheless achieved a seeming total empathy by the spectator. Moreover, she too, according to the *Dramaturg* speaking on the third night of *The Purchase of Brass,* had problems: "Even Weigel broke into tears at certain points on certain evenings, quite involuntarily and not to the benefit of the performance" (GW, XVI, 600). One specific passage cited is her cursing Juan because she thinks he has gone off to fight the Fascists whereas, in fact, he has just been gunned down by them. But, claims the *Dramaturg,* her tears were not those of the character she was playing; rather, she as actress was weeping at the character (GW, XVI, 601). Even so, it is hard to imagine that the audience would not empathize with her at this point (and so with the character), just as they would have done with any equally talented performer of the conventional acting school. Instances such as this can turn theory on its head.

It is certain, however, that in the final analysis the primary instrument of the political didacticism is empathy, that the dynamics of the play are emotional. Of necessity, therefore, the dramaturgy is the type described in the notes to *The Threepenny Opera* as "school drama" *(Schuldramatik),* in which "the playwright has to put everything he wants to say into the action" (GW, XVII, 992). No narrator, songs, projections, films or other "epic" narrative devices are allowed to break the dramatic momentum, and the structure causes the action to sweep on to its emotional climax. True, on one occasion children at play outside the Carrar's cottage chant a ditty mocking the elder son's supposed cowardice (GW, III, 1204); on another, Pedro draws attention to the sound of lorries passing by full of International Brigade troops who can be heard singing their national songs (GW, III, 1206); and during the Padre's visit a Francoist propaganda broadcast is heard. But these devices are fully integrated into the action. Indeed, the broadcast serves as starting point for the discussion between Pedro and the priest; the content of the tirade becomes a focal point of Pedro's attack on pacifist

[17] Presumably by this time Brecht had cleared up the doubts he had early in 1941 as to whether "empathy" could be kept separate and distinct from "suggestion"; in short: "whether an act of empathy (i.e., an act of self-suggestion) can be performed without suggestion for the spectator" (AJ, I, 226, 228). In 1941 Frau Weigel did not think it possible.

neutrality (GW, III, 1211-14). Because the play has only one act, the Aristotelian "unities" are necessarily observed.[18]

What, then, of the "disadvantages" of this "Aristotelian" dramaturgy to which Brecht refers, without explanation, in his notes to *Senora Carrar*? Werner Mittenzwei argues, "[Brecht] could not adequately depict the social causes of the civil war, the economic-political relationships, through the plot. The constellations within the scene, the action of the characters did not tell enough for him about the class position of the individual figures, their material interests and struggles" (pp. 237-38). Hence, in Mittenzwei's view the purpose of the Prologue and Epilogue, which Brecht later added, was "to render clearer the social and political events" (p. 235). True, the new material does deal almost exclusively with such issues, yet I do not think it substantiates Mittenzwei's main point.

The setting of both the Prologue and Epilogue is a French internment camp; Senora Carrar, her son and Pedro are inside the wire, and two French soldiers, one of whom is reading a newspaper, are outside. In the Prologue an item in the newspaper sparks off a discussion about international politics; during this discussion the Spanish situation is compared to that in Czechoslovakia—President Beneš had been forced to renounce possible Russian assistance against Hitler because the Czechoslovakian landowners threatened to revolt if he invoked the treaty providing for such aid. Pedro comments: "The forces of oppression are international."[19] But lest there be any doubt as to what this means, Brecht has one of the soldiers spell it out in detail (the speech is quoted in full so that the style and tone may be noted): "You mean the one nation is attacked from the inside, then the big people open the door and let foreign invaders in so that they will help them [the big people] and the other nation is attacked from the outside by foreign invaders and then the big people [there] open the door and help them in the attack?" (p. 391). Another theme is then introduced when the second soldier asks what point there is to fighting since the people are defeated whether they fight or not. The question is left hanging until the Epilogue when Pedro confidently asserts the Carrar family will be free, "because she there [i.e., Senora Carrar] knows now why it's necessary to fight" (p. 392).

These additions were not published. Mittenzwei claims this was because Brecht realized them to be a "didactic supplement, in fact just a clarification of his political intent" (p. 235). They are, indeed, and as such they diverge completely from the tone of the main text. There, with the aim of mustering international support, Brecht had presented op-

---

[18] The "unity" of time is so strictly observed that the play's duration is exactly the baking time of the bread Senora Carrar puts in the oven at the beginning of the action and takes out just before setting forth with her menfolk at the end (GW, III, 1197, 1228).

[19] Mittenzwei, *Bertolt Brecht*, p. 391. He gives the full text of these additions, pp. 390-92.

position to Franco as action in the name of humanity against inhumanity, as fighting against the "Generals."[20] Even the political significance of the term "Generals" has to be deduced from the Padre's affirmative answer to Pedro's question as to the legality of the government which the "Generals" are trying to overthrow (GW, III, 1214). There is no overt reference to any political "ism" because Brecht's predominant concern was to enlist support for the Republicans from as wide a spectrum as possible, which meant cutting across party and class lines, as well as international boundaries. Needless to say, the main text is not entirely devoid of ideological implications, but Brecht presents them in such a way that they are likely to evoke a sympathetic rather than an antagonistic response from a bourgeois audience. The Red Flag, which Senora Carrar treasures as a memento of her dead husband, might normally be expected to cause bourgeois eyebrows to be raised. However, the heroism of Carlo Carrar (and of Senora Perez' daughter, who also died opposing Franco) is set in such a positive light, and his widow has such claim to our sympathy, that this uneasiness could be quickly allayed. The same holds true in regard to the International Brigade; their presence in the country was well known outside Spain; hence, their passing through the village could be taken as simple dramatic realism. Further, the convoy is heard just as Senora Carrar is reminding her son to be grateful that he still has all his limbs intact. At this point, an audience hearing the ominous thunder of artillery in the background is vividly reminded of the dangers these volunteers face. Their readiness to stake life and limb might well persuade the audience that both the men and their cause are worthy of support. Only politically aware spectators of leftist persuasion would be likely to realize the political import of Theresa Carrar's reasoning about Juan's fatal cap: "It was the cap that did it. . . . It's shabby. No gentleman wears anything like that" (GW, III, 1228). The specifics of the class struggle with which Brecht, the Marxist, is usually concerned, take second place in *Senora Carrar* to the more immediate and pressing need of the moment—the creation of a United Front against Fascism.[21]

This tactical circumspection is quite at odds with the overtly propagandistic tone of the Prologue and Epilogue, where, as Mittenzwei observes, the political content is explicated in all clarity. Only a leftist audience would not be likely to react negatively to this material, and it

[20] Until shortly before the premiere the title was to be "Generals over Bilbao" (Mittenzwei, p. 228).
[21] Although Brecht never doubted that the workers formed the vanguard of opposition to Fascism, he also recognized the vital need to involve other classes and social groups. Hence, for example, his "Address to the Second International Writers' Congress for the Defense of Culture," where he concludes his appeal in terms appropriate to the interests of that particular group: "Culture, all too long defended only with intellectual weapons, attacked however with material weapons, itself not only an intellectual but also and especially even a material matter, must be defended with material weapons" (GW, XVIII, 250).

was for just such spectators that Brecht made the additions. The occasion was a performance at Västerås, Sweden, in August 1939, for Social Democrat trade unionists.[22] K. Rülicke-Weiler states the framework was added as a result of discussions as to whether the work had been invalidated by the outcome of the war in Spain (p. 84). More decisive, in my opinion, is the fact that one could readily deduce from the general political climate in Europe that war was imminent. With the additions, the text had become a polemic against neutrality not only towards Franco, but towards Fascism in general. Thus, Fascism was now seen from the vantage point of a broader ideological perspective: it was the ultimate and most destructive manifestation of capitalist class warfare. The suggestion of an international capitalist-Fascist conspiracy made in the Prologue (linking Franco in Spain with Hitler in Czechoslovakia) and the inference drawn by Pedro, were intended to bring home to the Swedish workers that to continue their traditional neutrality under the present circumstances would be tantamount to signing Sweden's death warrant. Here as in the *Lehrstücke* the basic aim is to teach the correct political attitude, and the method is akin to what Andrzej Wirth aptly terms "the teaching by unequivocal assertions" of those works.[23] In passing, the stylistic similarities between the *Lehrstücke* and the additions to *Senora Carrar* may be noted. Following W. Mittenzwei, one may assume that the Prologue and Epilogue allow Brecht to treat the social causes of the Civil War and the economic-political relationships more fully. However, the "disadvantages" of the "Aristotelian" mode did not necessarily preclude a treatment of socio-economic factors. Hence, the new material was not primarily intended to overcome a disadvantageous mode of dramatic presentation but designed as an adjustment both to the changed circumstances in the summer of 1939 and to the specific audience for whom Brecht was writing—new circumstances which necessitate extending the didactic scope of the original text to cover the new issues.

The "disadvantages" are, I suggest, of two kinds and closely related. First, if the audience is to be moved to emulate Senora Carrar's exemplary action at the end, the full horror of the situation must be made clear; yet, if empathy is to be induced (particularly in a work of only forty-five minutes playing time), nothing can be allowed to break the dramatic momentum. Hence, all the events which could engage the spectators' feelings have to be conveyed through the spoken word—the anguish of Carlo's last hours as he flees, mortally wounded; the execution of Republican fighters who had been forced to surrender; the

---

[22] Entries in AJ, I, 51, 52 (May 1939) show Brecht's active interest in this kind of theater while he was in Sweden: "Discussions with an emigré German actor, Greid, who is organizing acting groups for the Social Democrats here." *"Speech to lay* [worker] *actors on the art of observation* [i.e., 'Address to Danish Actors . . .']. In connection with conferences on setting up amateur theater groups for the Social Democrat trade unions."
[23] "Über die stereometrische Struktur der Brechtschen Stücke," SF/2, 357.

bombardment of civilian refugees on the road; the desperate situation at the front and the geographic vulnerability of the Republicans as they fight, literally, with their back to the ocean. Such grim realities would be little known to audiences outside Spain; at that time visual news coverage was still in its infancy as compared to today—when television brings war directly to us at the dinner table. In *Riders to the Sea* the same limitation prevails, of course, but it does not present the same problem. The dangers of the sea and death by drowning are familiar to any audience; thus imagination can give substance to the spoken word. For Brecht the only solution lay in the use of features such as he suggests in his notes to *Senora Carrar:* a documentary film showing "the events in Spain" or some other "propaganda" item to supplement the play. Second, the powerful impact of Juan's body being borne in from the sea, combined with the fact that his mother's change of mind occurs immediately afterwards, could create the danger of the audience viewing her decision in a purely personal frame of reference. On the play's own terms this is legitimate (Theresa explicitly states she is going to fight "for Juan"), but it could reduce the drama's effectiveness in gaining support for the Republican political cause. Terrible as this particular mother's individual loss was, Brecht's concern was the greater issue of defeating Fascism. The battle against Fascism could only be waged effectively if its necessity was fully understood. Thus the inclusion of films, etc., as suggested by Brecht, would broaden the conceptual horizons of the audience by drawing attention to the general struggle. In 1939, when Brecht was striving to educate his audience about the politicoeconomic background to the then imminent war and to the class interests involved, he did not insert the new material into the main body of the text by means of "epic" devices because the need for empathy still obtained. However, the formal framework provided by the additions allows the events of the play to be seen from the perspective of the current international situation, so that the story of Senora Carrar might serve as a guide for other neutralists when Fascism began to march again—which was the case only weeks after the Västerås performance.

Nevertheless, just a few months before the performance, a diary entry records Brecht's misgivings about the one-act play. On 25 February 1939, in a note relating to the original version of *Galileo,* he describes *Senora Carrar* as "all too opportunistic" (AJ, I, 41). Since he passes the same judgment on *Galileo* and further deplores it as "technically a great step back," the faults he finds with this work can help us understand the somewhat cryptic comment on *Senora Carrar.* Regarding *Galileo* he notes that "everything should be more direct, without the interiors, the 'atmosphere,' the empathy. And everything set up as planetary demonstrations." "Planetary," as Brecht defined it in his notations for *The Purchase of Brass,* denotes "theater only for the purpose of teaching, simply just the movements of people (also of the emotions of people) set up as models for study, the functioning of social connections shown, so that society can intervene" (GW, XVI, 1*). The contrast between this, Brecht's ideal, and his "Aristotelian (empathetic) drama" is pinpointed by H. Mayer's comparison of the salient aspects of *Senora Carrar* and an earlier play, *The Mother:* "The transformation of Pelagea Wlassova was demonstrated, didactically interpreted, through an epic report rounded off, as it were, in the manner of an oratorium; . . . the transformation of Senora Carrar takes place within the interior of a traditional stage setting, only the figures themselves are involved, the most important elements of the action are depicted, not reported."[24] "Opportunistic" would seem, therefore, to denote Brecht's more facile, undemanding approach in *Senora Carrar*—an approach which exploits the particular poignancy of the setting and the action to achieve its didactic goal. But if the frankness of the diary comment is the measure of Brecht's regret at having been forced by the exigencies of the situation in 1937 to adopt such an approach, it hardly betokens the "secret illegitimacy"[25] of which Mayer speaks.

Germane to this discussion is the fact that when Brecht wrote this work a vigorous literary-aesthetic debate was starting in *Das Wort,* an emigré journal of which he was co-editor; the debate concerned essentially what kind of literature could most effectively galvanise and increase opposition to Hitler. The problem to be resolved was not so much a question of *what* values were to be conveyed, but *how* they were to be conveyed. In other words, the approach chosen would in large measure determine the reception of anti-Fascist literature by the broad public who were to be educated as to the true nature of Fascism.[26] Georg Lukács, the eminent Hungarian Marxist critic, forcefully prescribed the giants of nineteenth-century bourgeois realism, particularly Balzac and Tolstoi, as models. Brecht rejected Lukács' position with equal force and expressed his belief that "realism is not merely a literary matter, but a great political, philosophical, practical matter" (GW, XIX, 307). Further, Brecht charged that "to make realism a matter of form, to tie it to one (and indeed an old) form, is to make it sterile. Realistic writing is not a matter of form. All formal elements which hinder us from thoroughly investigating social causality must go; all formal elements which help us to thoroughly investigate social causality must be brought in" (GW, XIX, 291). The diversity of forms Brecht developed made him appear a "Formalist" (GW, XIX, 339) according to the standards propagated by Lukács as well as those adopted

[24] H. Mayer, *Brecht und die Tradition,* p. 111.
[25] Cf. n. 1.
[26] No exhaustive discussion of the "Realism" debate is intended here; rather, only those problems which have a bearing on *Senora Carrar's Rifles* will be briefly mentioned. For Brecht's statements, cf. GW, XIX, 286-381; for a recent assessment of the controversy between Brecht and Lukács, see Lothar Baier, "Streit um den Schwarzen Kasten. Zur sogenannten Brecht-Lukács-Debatte," TuK, 37-44.

later by the German Democratic Republic—where the official doctrine of Socialist Realism held sway. Such an assessment totally ignores his insistence that the realism of a work must be judged from its content, and the fact that the form of any of his works always derives from the content! Both in exile and in East Berlin Brecht adamantly opposed any prescriptive approach, even in his own theory. Thus he notes in his diary on 12 January 1941: "In any consideration it should never be forgotten that *non-Aristotelian theater* first of all represents only *one* form of theater. It serves certain social purposes and has no usurpatory significance so far as the theater in general is concerned. I myself in certain productions can use Aristotelian theater alongside non-Aristotelian" (AJ, I, 225). Likewise in a note entitled "On the Application of Principles" Brecht, looking back on his two decades in the theater, observes that because "almost every new task necessitated new methods" he did not adhere unswervingly to his own theoretical principles (GW, XV, 314) but avers in conclusion that the one he never knowingly broke was: "To subordinate all principles to the social task we had undertaken to perform with each work." Far from representing Brecht's "sacrificing an all-important theory in the face of an emergency,"[27] as F. Ewen suggests, *Senora Carrar* exemplifies his adherence to this overriding principle. But considering the fact that Brecht championed the new in the face of Lukács' insistence on the old, it seems likely he would view his "Aristotelian (empathetic) drama" with the same reservations he expressed about his *Galileo* on 30 July 1945: "Concerning the form, I don't defend this piece very strongly" (AJ, II, 747).

The modest one-act play nevertheless has its rightful place alongside the plays for learning, operas, parables, history plays, chronicles, folk plays and adaptations—the *experiments* that mark Brecht's unceasing preoccupation with the relationship between socio-didactic ends and dramatic means, content and form. Inspired by the "idea" from Synge and owing something to Aristotle, *Senora Carrar* is, in the final analysis, the product of Brecht's political commitment which drew its "aesthetic" and its "ethics" from the "needs of the struggle" (GW, XIX, 349).

[27] *Brecht* (Ew), p. 319. Cf. also n. 7.

FRANCIS BACON, *GALILEO,* AND
THE BRECHTIAN THEATER

Ralph J. Ley

If asked to come up with both an epigraph and a eulogy for Brecht's theater, one might readily suggest the following aphorism from Francis Bacon's *Novum Organum,* since it points up not only the rationale underlying Brecht's aesthetic methodology but also the reason it is frequently misunderstood: "Even to deliver and explain what I bring forward is no easy matter; for things in themselves new will yet be apprehended with reference to what is old."[1] One could as aptly have chosen the New Testament reference to new wine in old skins if Bacon had exerted no more than an incidental influence on Brecht. Yet it is very likely that after Marx (and Hegel) no other writer has been of greater help to the playwright in the formulation of the practical side of his theater. No examination of the technique of *Verfremdung* could attempt to do full justice to a proper understanding of the Brechtian methodology without coming to grips with the influence exerted by the English philosopher. Such a confrontation permits us to see that the problem of the Epic Theater is a problem of epistemology, of inculcating a new way of thinking which is thoroughly Marxist.

Before examining the relationship between Bacon and the Brechtian theater, it might be helpful to present a somewhat superficial scheme of Brecht's conception of the epochal nature of history. It is not offered as an explanation of any sort, but simply as a device by which one may visualize at a glance the analogical and ambitious use Brecht made of history to clarify the epistemological problem inherent in Marxism as a new way of thinking. It anticipates the argument that the key to a proper understanding of Brecht's methodology lies in grasping the connection among the *organa* of Aristotle,[2] Bacon, and Brecht. Anyone familiar with these works, as well as Brecht's *Life of Galileo* and "The Experiment," may already discern this connection from the Scheme of Parallelisms on the following page.

---

[1] *Novum Organum, The English Philosophers from Bacon to Mill,* ed. Edwin A. Burtt (New York, 1939), p. 33 (Book I, aphorism xxxiv).

[2] Aristotle's work is actually six treatises on logic collectively entitled *Organum* in Byzantine times. In these works Aristotle established logic as a separate science and "discovered, isolated, and analyzed the fundamental form of inference, namely the syllogism" (Frederick Copleston, S. J., *A History of Philosophy.* I: *Greece and Rome* [Westminster, Md., 1948], p. 284). However, he failed to systematize rules for an inductive method that could firmly establish general principles.

Epoch I	Epoch II	Epoch III
feudalism	capitalism	socialism
status quo	first scientific revolution	second scientific revolution
Organum	*Novum Organum*	*Short Organum*
Aristotle	Bacon	Brecht
deduction	induction	dialectic
transcendental realism	vulgar materialism	historical materialism
theology - philosophy	philosophy - science	science - sociology
Ptolemy	Copernicus - Galileo	Einstein
God in the middle	science in the middle	man in the middle
science of God	science of nature	science of man
church - aristocracy	middle class	working class
serf	proletariat	human being
Summa Theologica	*Wealth of Nations*	*Capital*
Bible	*Origin of Species*	*Communist Manifesto*
maternalism	individualism	collectivism
Dante	Elizabethans	Epic Theater

In Brecht's *Life of Galileo* the gullibility of peasants denounced as stupid by an aristocratic landowner and champion of the status quo is regarded as a virtue by the protagonist. Galileo shares their curiosity about a rumor that a pear was seen growing on an apple tree. His interest follows naturally from his pronouncement in the opening scene that a new age is dawning for mankind; man must approach the sacred cows of the old order with a mind swept clean of prejudice and preconception—an attitude personified in the scientist's young pupil, Andrea, who dares to call the most learned man of his time stupid. In such circumstances gullibility is transformed into the childlike naivety of human beings who are once more able to marvel because the long-accepted and the taken-for-granted are *seen* under the aegis of a "concupiscence of the intellectual eye," a phrase felicitously coined by an historian of philosophy[3] to describe the new feeling of wonder and awakening that seized the leading spirits of the seventeenth century. In his stage directions to the actor assuming the role of Galileo, Brecht said shortly before his death that the scientist must be played like a man from Mars who marvels at everything.[4]

This quality of naivety is inextricably bound up with any age characterized by fresh intellectual beginnings and a new way of scrutinizing reality. Bacon, whose writings Brecht utilized in writing *Galileo*,[5] aphoristically emphasized this point when he drew an analogy between the new intellectual temper of his own age and the Christian revolution

[3] Robert Heiss, *Der Gang des Geistes: Eine Geschichte neuzeitlichen Denkens* (Bern, 1959), p. 31.
[4] Käthe Rülicke, "Leben des Galilei: Bemerkungen zur Schlußszene," SF/2, 283.
[5] See Ernst Schumacher, *Drama und Geschichte: Bertolt Brechts "Leben des Galilei" und andere Stücke* (Berlin, 1965), pp. 40-41.

in thinking, which itself called for the eyes of childlike faith, albeit of a different kind: once the Idols of the Mind are overcome the entrance into the kingdom of man, founded on the sciences, is not unlike the entrance into the kingdom of heaven, which none may enter except as a little child.[6] Marx considered gullibility the most excusable of human vices.[7] And Einstein himself was endowed with the Baconian *Weltanschauung* vis-a-vis the common sense notions buttressed by classical physics. "Why," Einstein asked, "is it any more strange to assume that moving clocks slow down and moving rods contract, than to assume that they don't?"[8]

Almost in desperation Brecht applied the notion of Baconian naivety to his theater in his last years as director of the Berliner Ensemble. Having become increasingly vexed at the fact that his methodology was being misinterpreted and misunderstood, especially by the East Berlin critics, he explained the difficulty in terms of a problem of knowledge, and the solution to this problem in being able to comprehend that the practice of his theater was naive. At the same time he alluded to the epistemological difficulties encountered by those who missed the basic naivety involved in grasping Einstein's theory of relativity.[9] Three years later, in the month of his death, he gave his theater, called by him at various times epic, philosophical, and historicizing, its tentatively final appellation, "Dialectical Theater," which he explained in terms of a descriptive definition of the *V-Effekt:* "The telling of a story on stage is in the last analysis also a 'dialecticizing' of the events. In everyday life habit of course usually kills off anything vivid in the observed events. Correct observation, too, is a 'dialecticizing,' a starting up again."[10] He then equated this dialectical methodology with the concept of naivety, which for him was the direct opposite of naturalistic form, a form canonized by the aesthetic doctrine of Socialist Realism and detrimental to the effect he wished his theater to have on its audiences: "In its entire operation our way of performing is naive, . . . in our performances we narrate the fable, a direct story. Artistic effects, ideas—these can or must emerge at the same time, but our real concern is precisely the narrating of a remarkable event."[11]

This seeming digression on the idea of naivety, which Brecht did not explicitly formulate until after his return from exile, is important because it raises a question which is central to a proper understanding of Bacon's influence on Brecht's Marxist methodology: what has the scientific way of thinking, the Baconian naivety, to do with Hegelian

[6] *Novum Organum,* p. 48 (I, lxviii).
[7] See Erich Fromm, *Marx's Concept of Man* (New York, 1961), p. 257.
[8] Cited in Lincoln Barnett, *The Universe and Dr. Einstein* (New York, 1952), p. 58.
[9] GW, XVI, 815-16.
[10] Cited in Manfred Wekwerth, "Auffinden einer ästhetischen Kategorie," SF/2 (1957), 266.
[11] Cited in Wekwerth, 268.

logic? Actually, the scientific outlook in terms of which Brecht has consistently described his technique of *Verfremdung* does not run counter to but rather complements the historical dialectic. For both methods of thinking have a common element, their bitter opposition to a world held together by the common sense notions based on its particular way of thinking. The first step to truth via scientific experimentalism and Hegelian logic is an attitude which regards no long-established canon of law or fact as sacred *per se*. It was Brecht's belief that the epistemological opposition encountered by Marxism in questioning the capitalist ordering of society was, all things being equal, no different from the oppugnancy of the representatives of law and order, whether divine or secular, toward the cosmological innovators of the seventeenth century. The historical accuracy of Brecht's equation is not the issue here. The fact is that this analogy between two related ways of thinking, each of which opposed the status quo of its epoch, did guide Brecht in the ultimate formulation of the theory and practice of his theater as revealed in the *Short Organum*. It was implicit in his thinking as early as 1930 and received its most perfect artistic expression in *Galileo*.

Now it is certainly true that if Brecht had not placed his rather considerable talent in the service of Marxism the shock effect of his theater could be defined largely in terms of his early and continuous addiction to science. Thus in the period 1926-1929, when Brecht's theater was more sociological than activistic, he could say that although the epic theater appeals to the *ratio* rather than to the emotion of the spectator, it would be completely wrong to deny this theater all emotional appeal. For that would be like trying to deny modern science all emotional appeal.[12] However, the unity of form and content expounded in Brecht's early attempts to theorize about his theater was not achieved until the scientific outlook was subsumed under historical materialism. Writing from hindsight in 1939, Brecht was able to point out the essential dichotomy between content and form which, theoretical formulations notwithstanding, had plagued his theater in the late twenties. *The Threepenny Opera,* he was forced to admit, cannot be construed as epic theater in the strict sense. The character of the play is two-pronged; instruction and entertainment are at odds with one another.[13] Shortly before his death he summed up the difficulty in one sentence: "The terrible thing is: without the application of dialectic 'epic' cannot be obtained."[14]

The analogy between the scientific outlook and historical materialism as related ways of thinking expresses, however, only the negative or, if you will, critical side of their union in the practice of the Brechtian theater. What was probably of even greater moment for Brecht in the

[12] GW, XV, 132.
[13] GW, XV, 293-94.
[14] Quoted by H. J. Bunge, "Über eine Neuinszenierung der Dreigroschenoper." *Bertolt Brechts Dreigroschenbuch,* ed. Siegfried Unseld (Frankfurt, 1960), p. 134.

formulation of this analogy was that in their revolutionary aspects one also complemented the other. For the first scientific revolution, made possible by a new way of thinking, had as its goal the transformation of nature into a ready servant of mankind. The second scientific revolution (Marxism) is intent upon transforming society into a form which can unconditionally actualize the potentialities of plenty uncovered by science. The first revolution had a momentary glimpse of this future Kingdom of Man but lost it by becoming subservient to the status quo.

Both the critical and revolutionary aspects of the first age of science were spelled out by Marx and Engels; thus they were easily available to the mind of Brecht in the late twenties and early thirties. Copernicus, Bacon, and Descartes are depicted as emancipators from the status quo and adherents of a new, critical form of thinking. In this regard, the palm is clearly awarded to Bacon, the first theorizer of vulgar materialism and "the real founder of . . . all modern experimental science," which "consists in applying a *rational method* to the data provided by the senses."[15] Bacon is given credit for foreseeing vaguely the second scientific revolution and being in some sense a precursor of Marx himself, for he "anticipated an alteration in the form of production, and the practical subjugation of Nature by Man, as a result of the altered methods of thought."[16] Engels indicated the form which the struggle between the established order and the innovators had to take at that time, the very form Brecht utilized in *Galileo*, in which the Church is not regarded as an instrument of oppression by itself but rather as a typification of reactionary authority.[17]

Both aspects of the analogy between the two scientific revolutions express themselves at the outset of Brecht's Marxist period. Thus under the banner of historical materialism the mechanics of *The Baden Play for Learning* (1929), representatives of the science of nature whose goal has been perverted under capitalism through ignorance and exploitation, are urged to undergo a rebirth which will weld the two revolutions, of nature and of man, into a gigantic effort to establish the classless society.[18] One year later Brecht expressed the critical side of the analogy in what may well be the first descriptive definition of the *V-Effekt*, rendered six years before he found the proper label for his technique of estrangement. In the Prologue and Epilogue of *The Exception and the Rule*[19] he interfused the epistemological factors common to both the experimental method and the Hegelian logic. The spectator is even called upon to assume an attitude of naive astonishment.

[15] K. Marx and F. Engels, "The Holy Family, or Critique of Critical Criticism," *On Religion* (Moscow, n.d.), pp. 63-64.
[16] K. Marx, *Capital* (New York, n.d.), p. 426, n. 1.
[17] F. Engels, "Ludwig Feuerbach and the End of Classical German Philosophy," *On Religion*, p. 262; GW, XVII, 1110.
[18] GW, II, 610-11.
[19] GW, II, 793, 822.

To the end this double analogy guided Brecht's thinking on the theoretical and practical aspects of his theater. The problem of winning the world over to a rational ordering of society remained for him a problem of knowledge. The analogy served as the example *par excellence* that history can repeat itself, that an imperfect society can be dialectically transformed through a change in the fundamental thought-processes of mankind. What is needed is a way of thinking that is on the one hand historical and critical and on the other advocates a revolution in the social order. The twofold nature of the analogy is consistently pursued in the "Address to Danish Actors from the Working Class" (1934), "Theater for Pleasure or Theater for Instruction" (1936), "Estrangement Effects in Chinese Acting" (1937), "On Experimental Theater" (1939), and "Short Description of a New Technique of Acting" (1940).[20] In the *Short Organum* (1948) the basis for Brecht's theater of activism finds its most articulate expression.[21] Brecht again stresses the connection between the revolutionary nature of the two ages of science and calls for a new epistemology which combines the attitude of wonderment typical of a Galileo with the principal epistemological weapon of Marxism, the dialectic of history. The *V-Effekt* is the artistic tool for nurturing the critical faculty which is the *sine qua non* for revolutionizing society. The epistemological solution proffered is that of the Prologue and Epilogue of *The Exception and the Rule*. Theory and practice, ideology and methodology, content and form are thus declared to be an indivisible and rigidly defined compound, whose constituent elements are the dialectic of materialism as system and method.

In Brecht's double analogy the influence of Bacon, present from the outset of the playwright's pronouncedly Marxist phase, was, of course, based on the historical situation in which the philosopher did battle with the firmly entrenched upholders of the status quo and which later became a key element in *Galileo*. This work holds a singular position among Brecht's dramas not only because it depicts with greater clarity and force than any other play the kernel idea of Marxism as a system, an artistic feat made possible by concretizing the analogy initially used by Marx himself with respect to the humanitarian goals of the two revolutions. Its uniqueness is due in far greater measure to the fact that *Galileo* has as an integral part of its subject matter the methodology which is at the core of Brecht's Marxist-oriented plays, i.e., the technique of *Verfremdung* in the guise of a new way of thinking. In short, methodology is both aesthetic form and ideological content. The experimental method, as was indicated, assumes the same epistemological starting point as the dialectic. For it demands a critical-naive *tabula rasa* willing to question existing reality even in the face of overwhelming intellectual opposition from the vested interests. This method not only

[20] GW, IX, 764; XV, 263-65; XVI, 627-29; XV, 295-302; XV, 347, 355, respectively.
[21] See especially GW, XVI, 670, 681-82 (aphorisms 19, 44, 45).

forms a portion of the play's content, but, as the author insisted, shares equal billing with that part of the plot which depicts Galileo's struggle for and failure to achieve what Brecht regarded as the equivalent of the Marxist goal of the Kingdom of Man.[22]

In the first scene there is an implied confrontation between the time-honored method of formal logic systematized by Aristotle (as much the heavy of this play as he was of Brecht's ideology and aesthetics!), which secured the unity of medieval thought in theology, philosophy, and the natural sciences, and the new inductive-experimental method formulated by Bacon and practiced by Galileo. The direct confrontation between the Aristotelian and the Baconian ways of thinking occurs in the fourth scene. Here for the first time this critical aspect of the analogy is linked up with its activist side. The theory and practice of the epic theater are actually played out on stage. On the one hand, the science of nature and the science of man encounter the status quo held together by the metaphysics of Aristotle. On the other, the logic of Bacon and Hegel opposes the logic of Aristotle, the ontological premises of which delimit and help justify both capitalism and its "culinary" theater in the Brechtian scheme of things.

Galileo has invited a theologian, a philosopher, and a mathematician to glance through his telescope and confirm with their own eyes the existence of the satellites of Jupiter. They refuse to do so unless Galileo is able to demonstrate to them both the possibility and the necessity of their existence. Their reasoning is sound within the limits of their metaphysical and physical world outlook. For "common sense" tells them that the very existence of such "stars" runs counter to a first principle of science and philosophy. Stars *cannot* be in the heavens circling the planet Jupiter because every celestial body is obviously attached to an impenetrable crystalline sphere. They *need not* be in the heavens because the order of the Creator, which eschews the superfluous, would be impugned. Galileo must prove his point deductively but within the confines of a system of logic which works hand in glove with the established order. Confronted by such "ignorance," he is helpless. An intellectual impasse results. Brecht makes it clear that a particular way of thinking is the obstacle which keeps even intelligent and sincere men from discovering new truths precisely because it is the most effective bulwark of the old order of reality. For what is at stake is not the relatively unimportant question of the existence of a few moons but rather the whole medieval outlook, which was inexorably tied to the existence of the crystalline spheres.

[22] GW, XVII, 1109-1110. Whether Brecht's contention holds true for the later versions, in which Galileo's crime against society is more heavily emphasized, depends on the extent to which one regards the scientist's self-analysis (GW, III, 1339-41) as extrinsic to the work as a whole. For a discussion see M.A. Cohen, "History and Moral in Brecht's *The Life of Galileo*," CL, 11 (1970), 80-97.

When his opponents make it clear that they will not employ his method of probing reality, since doing so would reflect on the unquestionable authority of Aristotle as metaphysicist and logician, Galileo's answer is an appeal to time as the final arbiter of truth, coupled with a threat and a prophecy which bring out the activist element in the analogy between the two ages of science. It was at this point that Brecht paid silent tribute to Bacon's *Novum Organum,* the contents of which correspond to the efforts of Galileo in this fourth scene, as indeed in the plot as a whole, to make popular a new way of thinking directly opposed to the disputatious methods of reasoning borrowed from Aristotle, and to proclaim the advent of the Kingdom of Man. The following dialogue forms the focal point for the transition to the revolutionary side of Galileo's activities:

> THE PHILOSOPHER (grandly): If Aristotle is to be dragged into the mud here, an authority whom not only all the scientists of the ancient world but also the eminent fathers of the Church themselves acknowledged, then to me at least a continuation of this discussion seems superfluous. I refuse to engage in pointless discussions. Basta.
> GALILEO: Truth is the child of time, not of authority. Our ignorance is endless, let us diminish it by one cubic millimeter. Why do we still want to be so smart now when we can finally be a little less stupid! I have had the unimaginably good fortune to get hold of an instrument with which one can view a small corner of the universe somewhat, if not much more closely. Use it. (GW, III, 1269-70)

In a section of his work in which he discusses some of the reasons why science has made little progress since the time of the ancients, Bacon charges that even in his day men are still mistaken as to the end of science ("that human life be endowed with new discoveries and powers"[23]) and the means, preferring an appeal to authority to the experimental method:

> Again, men have been kept back as by a kind of enchantment from progress in the sciences by reverence for antiquity, by the authority of men accounted great in philosophy, and then by general consent. . . . And with regard to authority, it shows a feeble mind to grant so much to others and yet deny time his rights, who is the author of authors, nay rather of all authority. *For rightly is truth called the daughter of time, not authority.* It is no wonder therefore if those enchantments of antiquity and authority have so bound up men's powers that they have been made impotent (like persons bewitched) to accompany with the nature of things.[24]

The notion of truth as part of an historical process which will in the

---

[23] *Novum Organum,* p. 56 (I, lxxxi).
[24] Ibid., p. 58 (I, lxxxiv; my italics).

course of time reveal itself because it is synonymous with reason and is, of course, impossible to separate from the essential role time plays in Marx's concept of the epochal nature of history. By itself, Galileo's assertion that truth is the offspring of time is sheer Baconianism, but the statement is placed by Brecht at that crucial juncture where activist implications of the scientific revolution made possible by the new way of thinking are introduced to complement the critical side of the analogy. Thus Galileo tells the representatives of the hierarchical order:

> The moons of Jupiter do not reduce the price of milk. But they were never seen before and yet they do exist. From this the man in the street concludes that lots of other things might exist, if he would only open his eyes! . . . It is not the movements of a few distant stars that cause Italy to prick up its ears, but the news that teachings regarded as unshakable have begun to totter. . . . (GW, III, 1270)

The scene with the little monk and the carnival episode (especially in the later versions) remove all doubt that the most imperturbable of all these teachings is the hierarchical conception of both the physical macrocosm and the social microcosm. For the first time in recorded history the "Great Order" which divides the race into rulers and ruled, oppressors and oppressed, is in imminent danger of being seriously questioned: "Obedience was man's cross from the start!/ Who wouldn't like to be one's own master?" (GW, III, 1315). There is thus implicit in Galileo's activist pronouncement of the fourth scene the concept of history which forms the central thread of the *Communist Manifesto*. Such an interpretation of history is inseparable from the notion of time as a dialectic process which insists that the greatest stability is found side by side with the greatest instability, that the point of maximum quantitative accumulation is also the signal for an abrupt qualitative change. These changes are always transitions from one set of oppressors to another during the pre-historical phase of human development. Real history begins when the oppressors are permanently overthrown. These two eras of history, subject to the change that only the reasonableness of time can effect, were epitomized by Brecht in two distinct versions of the concluding refrain of the poem "Ballad of the Mill Wheel," itself expounding the idea that all authority is subject to time. The original version of 1933-1934 depicts the type of change that occurs in pre-history.

Freilich dreht das Rad sich immer weiter	Still the mill wheel turns and turns forever.
Daß, was oben ist, nicht oben bleibt.	What is uppermost remains not so.
Aber für das Wasser unten heißt das leider	While the water underneath in vain endeavor
Nur: daß es das Rad halt ewig treibt. (GW, III, 1007)	Does the work but always stays below.[25]

[25] From *Roundheads and Peakheads*, trans. N. Goold-Verschoyle, Bertolt Brecht, *Jungle of Cities and Other Plays* (New York, 1966), p. 253.

The later version, whose date of composition is unknown, speaks of the sudden negation of the pre-historical phase of man's development:

> Denn dann dreht das Rad sich nicht mehr weiter
> Und das heitre Spiel, es unterbleibt
> Wenn das Wasser endlich mit befreiter
> Stärke seine eigne Sach betreibt. [26]

From the brief analysis of the fourth scene of *Galileo* it becomes clear why Brecht found it sufficient to refer to this play and no other in illustrating the practical side of his theater in the *Short Organum,* representing as it does the ideal expression in dramatic form of both the ideological foundations and methodological principles on which his theater rests. The historical analogy was at the core of Brecht's Marxist *Weltanschauung.* It was proof that the reasonableness which he equated with Communism must in the end emerge triumphant from its seemingly insurmountable epistemological obstacles. In all of this Brecht's debt to Bacon is considerable. Just how considerable becomes evident from an examination of the close intellectual affinity between the philosopher and the playwright from the beginning of the latter's Marxist period. The results of such an examination more than suggest that Brecht was a twentieth-century Bacon turned Marxist.

When asked in 1949 whether the methodology of the epic theater could be applied in a practical way to classical, romantic, and naturalist dramas, Brecht replied in a manner which left no room for doubt that what distinguished his theater from all others was its activist character, which combined both ideology and form as integral components of his stage productions. His reply was an elaboration of his pithy remark of 1931 [27] that form is authentic only to the extent that, it is synonymous with a specific content: "An epic method of performing is not equally applicable to all classical works. It seems it can be most easily applied, that is, can most readily promise results in the case of works like those of Shakespeare or the early plays of our classicists (*Faust* included). It depends on how these works are geared to the social function—the representation of reality for the purpose of influencing reality" (GW, XVI, 717).

It is on the question of activism that Brecht's quarrel with Aristotle stands most clearly revealed. Man must be depicted as both active and passive agent within a concrete historical situation, able to determine it and determined by it. Brecht felt strongly that any other depiction of man's role on the stage amounted to obscenity. It was an insult to the

[26] *Gedichte,* 9 vols. (Frankfurt, 1960-1965), III, 240. Neither this nor a third version which is to be found in *Selected Poems,* trans. H. R. Hays (New York, 1959), p. 90, and is similar in import to the second, is included in GW. ("For then the wheel no longer continues to turn, and the serene game is discontinued when the water pursues its own affairs with liberated strength.")
[27] GW, XVIII, 173-74.

dignity of men living in an age of science which provided the material conditions for forging a decent life. The drama of the scientific age had, *ethically speaking,* to be totally materialistic. In other words, extrinsic determinations based on an unbridgeable transcendentalism usually labeled "fate" or on the supposedly irremediable defect of character encased in a social vacuum had to be ruthlessly expurgated. Hence in Brecht's revision of *Antigone* the idea of tragic fate is converted into the activistic concept of man as the master of his destiny. This radical change in the ideological base of the play makes plain the main bone of contention between Brecht and Aristotle, a quarrel which goes far beyond the confines of the *Poetics* and confronts the metaphysicist on his native grounds: "As for representational style, we are at one with Aristotle in the opinion that the center piece of tragedy is the fable, even if we are at odds about the purpose for which it should be performed" (GW, XVII, 1217). The purpose Brecht had in mind is peremptorily stated in the notes written for the Greiz production of the play in 1951: "In the conception of the ancients man is more or less blindly delivered up to fate, he has no power over it. This conception B. B. has replaced in his adaptation with the view that man's fate is man himself. This change is very great. . . ."[28] Three years earlier, in the *Short Organum,* Brecht had excoriated as anachronistic (and indecent) both the Greek and Elizabethan theaters.[29] But he regarded the latter as ideologically superior. For it at least depicts its protagonist as someone who takes "fate" into his own hands, even if he does not know what to do with it. Man regains a semblance of his dignity because he has within him the potential for controlling his destiny. Here the beginnings of a materialistic totality are visible.

In the early thirties, when he first began to elaborate on the activist nature of his theater, Brecht referred to the materialism of Bacon as an essential ingredient in any theater that attempts to come to grips with the real world of the flesh-and-blood individual. It was this ingredient which both the Elizabethan and his own theater had in common, marked as they were by a rejection of idealistic or metaphysical determinations. The following explication of this point, written in 1931, indicates that in the critical years when the theoretical foundations of the epic theater were being laid, Brecht was already thinking in terms of the analogy between the kind of individualism that Bacon was advocating and the revolutionary side of his own theater. The specific subject under discussion was the Elizabethan dramatic form:

> All the force of this type of drama comes from the accumulation of resistances. The desire for a cheap, ideal formula does not yet determine the arrangement of the material. It is animated by a certain something of that Baconian materialism, and even the in-

[28] *Stücke,* XI, 112.
[29] GW, XVI, 676-77 (aphorism 33).

dividual still has flesh and bones and resists the formula. But wherever materialism is found, epic forms arise in the drama, generally and most often in comedy, whose focus is always more materialistic and "lower." Today, when the human being must be comprehended as "the ensemble of all social relationships," the epic form is the only one which can comprise the processes that render to drama material for a comprehensive picture of the world. Even the human being, and I mean the human being of flesh and blood, can be comprehended only through the processes in which and by which he exists. The new methodology must methodologically accommodate the "experiment" within its form. (GW, XVII, 998-99)

In that same year Brecht launched a stinging attack on the bourgeois art forms. He accused their practitioners of fostering an Aristotelian-medieval conception of reality and employing the syllogistic reasoning of the Peripatetic, hamstrung by its tautological conclusions. At the same time he called for an application of the experimental method developed by Bacon for the provocation of reality, alluding however to the fact that this method, though of great value for the technological revolution, had failed to bring about any radical changes in the humanistic sciences.[30]

In specifically referring to the Baconian methodology and advocating it as an ideal means of combatting the Aristotelian ontology and logic, Brecht had fashioned the critical side of an analogy with which he hoped to surmount the epistemological obstacles to the ideology he professed and strove to inculcate in his audiences. Thus it can be surmised that by 1931 he had formulated *in semine* the first principles, as it were, of the *Short Organum*. The case for Bacon's influence is strengthened when one considers the manner in which Brecht chose to publish the theoretical writings in which he first explicitly connected the philosopher's methodology with the experimental nature of his theater. Bacon had launched his literary career with the publication in 1597 of a work simply entitled *Essays*, written like his later *Organum* in an aphoristic style that broke radically with the prevailing Elizabethan literary tradition of copiousness. As one Bacon scholar described this innovative style: ". . . the stark aphorism challenges readers to pit their observations against the writer's and thus add to the ultimate attainment of truth. The provisional 'scientific' attitude here implied is borne out by the fact that Bacon called these sketches merely *Essays*, i.e., tentative explorations."[31] Brecht ambitiously initiated his career in print as a Marxist in 1930 with the publication of his works in large, cardboard-bound volumes imitative of science folios, under the collective title *Versuche* ("Experiments"), "certain important works which were of an

---

[30] GW, XVIII, 198-204, especially 201.
[31] Hugh G. Dick, ed., *Selected Writings of Francis Bacon* (New York, 1955), p. xvii.

experimental nature," as Elisabeth Hauptmann, Brecht's long-time collaborator, defined them.[32]

Whereas the nod to Bacon implied in the format and title of the *Versuche* seems subtle (what Brechtologist has ever specifically alluded to the connection?)[33], the debt of gratitude is more bluntly acknowledged in Brecht's literary tribute to the Englishman, a short story written upon completion of the first version of *Galileo* in 1939. The tribute lies in the fact that its title is "The Experiment"[34] and that it is essentially a retelling of the play from the standpoint of the two scientific revolutions and a new way of thinking. Among the major points of concordance, based on the sequence of events in "The Experiment," are the following: (1) Both Bacon and Galileo are failures as men partly because society is unjust; (2) both have also betrayed and hampered the cause of science; (3) their last years are lived out in disgraceful retirement but their addiction to scientific investigation is as strong as ever; (4) each has a young disciple whom he treats with respect and carefully instructs in the scientific method; (5) both scientists are protagonists of the Brechtian maxim that truth is concrete—Galileo when he admires Horace's sense of beauty in refusing to substitute in his eighth satire the word "table" for "toilet," and Bacon when he teaches the stable boy not to describe an insect as ugly; (6) both are aware of the fact that nature, as the object of the sciences, cannot be separated from ethics once the question of the use of things made by humans is raised (actually the street-singer makes this point explicit in the first version; in the later versions Galileo denounces the "new morality" of Andrea: science for the sake of science); (7) both Galileo and Bacon celebrate the advent of a new age and a new way of probing reality in the presence of their pupils; (8) in both works Latin is a symbolic prop of the established order zealously safeguarded by the clergy as the representatives of authority *per se*; (9) both men risk their lives in the interest of science—Galileo exposes himself to a plague and Bacon succumbs to the elements; (10) Galileo shatters the Aristotelian principle that form determines capacity for floating in water, a notion whose correctness had simply been taken for granted for two millenia. Bacon and the stable boy undertake to dispel the common-sense belief that a week-old frozen chicken is inedible because its insides "naturally" decay; (11) In their final days the words of Andrea depicting the effect of the Ptolemaic system on men's minds ("But we are so boxed up"; GW, III, 1232) become ironic reality for Galileo and Bacon. The former is the prisoner of the Inquisition, the

---

[32] *Versuche*, 1-4, p. 2.

[33] But cf. Reinhold Grimm's essay, "Naturalism and Epic Drama," in this volume, p. 20.

[34] GW, XI, 264-75. In May 1939, Brecht made what may well have been his first public presentation of the theory of *Verfremdung*. He called his lecture "On Experimental Theater" (GW, XV, 285-305). See Reinhold Grimm, "Vom Novum Organum zum Kleinen Organon: Gedanken zur Verfremdung," *Das Ärgernis Brecht*, ed. Willy Jäger and Hans Oesch (Basel and Stuttgart, 1961), pp. 45-70, especially p. 50.

latter of the doctors who in their insistence that the windows in the bedroom of the mortally ill philosopher be kept tightly shut represent the old order of things; (12) Galileo's distinction between *Glotzen* (staring without comprehending) and *Sehen* (perceiving) is repeated in "The Experiment"; (13) in surroundings hostile to his scientific experimentation Galileo resorts to trickery to enable him to carry on his work (the telescope incident of scene two) and Bacon's young disciple also practices deception when he encounters obstacles; (14) *Galileo* (in the first and final versions) and "The Experiment" end on a positive note: the last words of both works make it clear that the new way of thinking will prevail.

If Bacon's influence is in evidence at the genesis of Brecht's Marxist theater, it is even more decidedly visible at what one might term the culminating point of his theorizing, i.e., when he undertook a somewhat systematic and tentatively final formulation of his theater in the *Short Organum*. We have already discussed the contents of this work in connection with the analogy Brecht made between the two ages of science and the dramatic realization of that analogy in *Galileo*. Both works are parts of a single whole, of an identical affirmation and negation. They are ideologically based on the Marxist vision of the second scientific revolution as the complement and completion of the first. But prior to this in the logical if not in the real order, they advocate a new way of thinking which attempts to negate the main obstacle to the realization of Marxism, namely an older way of thinking grounded in the metaphysics and epistemology of Aristotle and equated with the "sin" of ignorance. In this sense Brecht's *Short Organum* cannot simply be regarded as counterposing the *Poetics* of Aristotle. Yet this is the point critics of Brecht have consistently emphasized. In fact, the only Brecht scholar who has up to now called detailed attention to Bacon's influence on the *Short Organum*[35] does not advance beyond the idea that this work is the antithesis of the *Poetics*. The *Organum* of Aristotle, the real villain in the piece, is not mentioned. For this reason it is important to understand precisely where the influence of Bacon's chief philosophical work on Brecht lay. For the *Novum Organum* is an attempt, through the formulation of a new methodology, to discredit a work which laid down the fundamental rules for syllogistic reasoning, in Bacon's day the main stumbling block to the establishment of the Kingdom of Man. The fact remains that Brecht did not call his culminal theoretical work the "New Poetics" or "Short Poetics" or "Anti-Poetics." He chose to call it "Organum" and thereby placed it squarely within the philosophical tradition of two of the most influential works in the history of Western epistemology.

Even a cursory reading of Bacon's work reveals the fact that for him as for Brecht in the *Short Organum* the main concern is one of effecting

[35] Grimm, "Vom Novum Organum zum Kleinen Organon."

a radical change in hitherto unchallenged mental operations for the purpose of recasting the goals of society. The opening words of *The Great Instauration* (of which *Novum Organum* formed the second and only completed part of Bacon's attempt "to commence a total reconstruction of sciences, arts, and all human knowledge, raised upon the proper foundations")[36] focus on the epistemological problem, epitomized in the concept of ignorance as *the* intellectual sin. The remedy for ignorance amounts to a negation of the formal logic of the first *Organum*. Bacon wished to introduce "a kind of logic; though the difference between it and the ordinary logic is great; indeed immense." It differed from the logic in vogue in three ways, "in the end aimed at; in the order of demonstration; and in the starting point of the inquiry." The end was of course ultimately to "command nature in action," the method of demonstration induction, and the starting point an examination of "those things which the common logic takes on trust."[37] In explaining this point, Bacon came close to giving a descriptive definition of the *V-Effekt,* suggestive of an illustration twice employed by Brecht (Galileo staring at the oscillations of a pendulum with the eyes of a Martian)[38]: "Nay, in my judgment philosophy has been hindered by nothing more than this, that things of familiar and frequent occurrence do not arrest and detain the thoughts of men, but are received in passing without any inquiry into their causes; insomuch that information concerning things which are not known is not oftener wanted than attention concerning things which are."[39]

The confrontation between the Baconian experimental method and the logic of Aristotle is as direct and implacable as that described in the fourth scene of *Galileo*. The first principles of science canonized by the authority of Aristotle must be subjected to a radical process of questioning. Only when the tautological stranglehold of the old way of thinking has been broken[40] can there be a new beginning in the search for truth: "It is idle to expect any great advancement in science from the superinducing and engrafting of new things upon old. We must begin anew from the very foundations, unless we would revolve forever in a circle with mean and contemptible progress."[41] The resolution of the epistemological problem, is, however, merely a means to an end. Once the understanding has been "emancipated and come as it were of age," then

---

[36] "The Great Instauration," *The English Philosophers from Bacon to Mill,* p. 6.
[37] Ibid., pp. 15-17.
[38] See GW, XVI, 627, 681-82. Cf. Grimm's assertion ("Vom Novum Organum zum Kleinen Organon," 60) that the *Novum Organum* may be regarded as the first work to provide a philosophical foundation for *Verfremdung.*
[39] *Novum Organum,* p. 79 (I, cxix).
[40] Cf. GW, XVIII, 200, where Brecht levels a similar charge against the methodology of the "Aristotelian" theater.
[41] *Novum Organum,* p. 33 (I, xxxi).

there cannot but follow an improvement in man's estate, and an enlargement of his power over nature. . . . For creation was not by the curse made altogether and forever a rebel, but in virtue of that charter "In the sweat of thy face shalt thou eat bread," it is now by various labors (not certainly by disputations or idle magical ceremonies, but by various labors) at length and in some measure subdued to the supplying of man with bread; that is, to the uses of human life.[42]

Apparently without being fully aware of it, Bacon transformed the curse set on mankind in *Genesis* into a potential blessing. In raising the question of bread for his neighbor, he had unwittingly touched upon what for Marxism purports to be the primary ethical question, since it sees itself as the conscious scientific or rational (Brecht was right in equating the terms) attempt in history to fulfill the dream of bread for all made possible by the unleashing of the first scientific revolution. It is good to remember that whenever he applied his favorite Baconian dictum to his brand of theater and his conception of realism, Brecht had in mind not only the science of nature but also the science of man: "Only he who obeys nature has dominion over her" (GW, XIX, 368).[43] He knew, however, that the Marxist revolution cannot succeed where, analogously, the Baconian did until the primary obstacle is overcome: ignorance of the nature of society. Perhaps this idea is most forcefully (and somewhat sadly) expressed in a section of *The Purchase of Brass* (written c. 1939) dealing with "the ignorance of the many." Here the critical side of the analogy, the epistemological factor that determined more than anything else the experimental methodology of the epic theater—the word "organum" means a method for communicating knowledge—is implicitly but inextricably linked to the revolutionary side, which determined its ideology:

> Because human beings know so little about themselves, their knowledge of nature helps them so little. They know why the stone falls this way and not that way, but why the man who flings it acts this way and not that way they do not know. So they can cope with earthquakes and not with their fellow humans. Whenever I sail away from this island [in the Danish province of Svendborg], I fear that the ship may go down in a storm. Actually I do not fear the sea but rather those who might possibly fish me out. (GW, XVI, 525)

[42] Ibid., p. 123 (II, lii).
[43] For variations, cf. GW, XVI, 921, and XIX, 378.

THE ALIENATED WOMAN: BRECHT'S
THE GOOD PERSON OF SETZUAN[1]

John Fuegi

It is a lamentable fact that in the long history of world drama relatively few dramatists of major international rank have been very much concerned about the specific problems of women in a world dominated by males. To be sure, there is no dearth of exceptions, particularly if one is inclined to take into account German drama. In looking for dramatists in whose works women play a more or less central role, Euripides, Shakespeare (e.g., Portia and Lady Macbeth), Racine, Ibsen, Shaw come readily to mind—not to mention the long line of German dramatists which includes Lessing, Goethe, Schiller, Kleist, Grillparzer, Hebbel, Hauptmann, among others. We must now, I feel, add to this list of exceptions the work of Bertolt Brecht. Though Brecht's very earliest plays such as *Baal, Drums in the Night, In the Jungle of Cities, The Life of Edward the Second of England, A Man's a Man,* and even *The Threepenny Opera,* are very much male-dominated plays with women playing relatively minor and often completely exploited roles, it is a remarkable fact that many of the later major plays, including several of those on which Brecht's world reputation now rests, have a woman as *the* central figure. The list of such plays is long and includes *Saint Joan of the Stockyards,* major scenes of *Fear and Misery of the Third Reich, Senora Carrar's Rifles,* the character of Begbick in *A Man's a Man, Mother Courage and Her Children, The Good Person of Setzuan,* the ballet *The Seven Deadly Sins of the Lower Middle Class, The Visions of Simone Machard, The Caucasian Chalk Circle,* and four adapted works, Gorki's *The Mother,* Sophocles' *Antigone,* Anna Segher's *The Trial of Joan of Arc at Rouen, 1431,* and the Soviet dramatist Sergei Tretiakov's consciously liberationist piece, *I Want a Child* (the latter, unfortunately, still not easily available in print).[2] It is

---

[1] The title of Brecht's play, *Der gute Mensch von Sezuan,* has been translated by Eric Bentley and Maja Apelman as *The Good Woman of Setzuan.* Under this title, the play has been published (first in 1948), performed, and become known in the U.S. In choosing the word "person" for *Mensch* I wish to draw attention to Brecht's use of a term which is devoid of the connotations of sex. Cf. also *Brecht* (W), pp. 50-51: *The Good Person of Szechwan.*

[2] According to a note in *Brecht* (W), p. 64, Tretiakov's play (*Die Pioniere* or *Ich will ein Kind haben*) was translated by Ernst Hube and adapted by Brecht. A copy of Brecht's adaptation is available in manuscript form in Berlin (BBA, 662). Inexplicably, there is no reference to this text in the otherwise very complete BBA-B, I. Brecht's adaptation was published as a duplicated manuscript for the use of stages (Freiburg im Breisgau: Max Reichard, n.d.). The play deals with a Soviet woman who picks out a man to father a child for her and she is most explicit in telling all candidates for fatherhood that she has no interest whatsoever in marrying them. For details on Tretiakov's personal views of "women's liberation" in the USSR in the thirties (a subject to which he was completely dedicated), see A. E. Chesterton's fascinating book: *Sickle or Swastika?* (London, 1935).

190

not without significance that a large number of these plays with women at their center were written by Brecht in collaboration with either Elisabeth Hauptmann, Ruth Berlau or Margarete Steffin; moreover, many of these plays were intended to provide major roles for Brecht's wife, the great Austrian actress, Helene Weigel. So important were women such as Hauptmann, Berlau, Steffin, Weigel, and others in Brecht's professional life and so clear is the role of women in many of his major plays that there is obviously scope here for a booklength study on this subject.[3] In the following short essay, however, I shall largely confine myself to that play which seems to me to be a paradigmatic instance of woman's alienation in a male-dominated society, Brecht's *The Good Person of Setzuan*.

From Brecht's notebooks[4] we know that he first began work (in the late twenties in Berlin) on the theme of a prostitute who disguises herself as a man. From the earliest sketches it is clear that the action of the story (not yet cast in play form) was to take place in Germany and was to be an economic study (from a Marxist point of view) of the counter measures taken by an unusually ingenious prostitute to disguise herself as a man. In this way she hoped to circumvent reliance on a pimp and to avoid her double exploitation by the capitalist system in general. The earliest title for this sketch (which exists in a number of widely divergent variants) neatly sums up Brecht's objectives in writing it. The title, *Die Ware Liebe*, with its punning play on *wahr* (true) and *Ware* (goods for sale) manages to simultaneously suggest two possibilities often deemed to be mutually exclusive. The sketch is about "true love" and, at one and the same time, "love for sale." Everything about the various versions of this *Love for Sale* sketch points to the Brecht of the late twenties, the Brecht who had recently begun an intensive study of Marxist economic theory, and the Brecht who had explored the same shabby demimonde atmosphere of Berlin in two major operas of this period, *The Threepenny Opera* and *Rise and Fall of the City of Mahagonny*, both of which, paradoxically, are not set in Berlin. Only some ten years later does Brecht return, however, to the theme of the prostitute who disguises herself as a man. In this next version, written in exile in Scandinavia in 1939, 1940, and part of 1941, in collaboration with Ruth Berlau and Margarete Steffin, Brecht produces the story in a

---

[3] For an autobiographical sketch of Brecht's personal treatment of women in the twenties, see particularly Marieluise Fleißer's short story, "Avantgarde," *Gesammelte Werke*, III (Frankfurt, 1967), 117-68. In addition, on the basis of some documentary evidence and personal conversations with Marieluise Fleißer and Elisabeth Hauptmann, I believe a strong case could be made for the contention that Brecht had a pronounced tendency to exploit the work of both his male and female collaborators. For a detailed analysis of how Brecht failed to acknowledge E. Hauptmann's contribution to an important work of "Brecht," see my forthcoming article, "Molière and Brecht. The Authorship of 'Brecht's' *Don Juan*," CLS (1974).

[4] AJ, I, 45, 94, *et passim; Materialien zu Brechts "Der gute Mensch von Sezuan*," ed. Werner Hecht (Frankfurt, 1968), pp. 11-30.

way more clearly recognizable as *The Good Person of Setzuan*. He now casts the sketch in play form and its locale is clearly China.[5]

Very consciously, *The Good Person of Setzuan* opens in an imitation of the style of highly conventionalized Chinese drama. The plot is expounded ·in narrative style directly to the audience by Wang, the waterseller. Wang sketches the locale of Setzuan and announces that three gods are expected to arrive in the city shortly. With the appearance of the gods Wang attempts, with little success, to find them lodgings. Finally, the prostitute, Shen Te, agrees reluctantly and with considerable financial sacrifice to give the gods her own room for the night. As a direct result of her kindness to them, the three male gods present Shen Te with one thousand silver dollars and enjoin "the good person of Setzuan" to use this money to do good. Through the tobacco shop that she purchases with this money, Shen Te proceeds to do her level best to attempt to be and to do good, but the greediness and sheer numbers of those in need of help make it obvious that one good person with one thousand dollars is totally incapable of turning the tide of want in Setzuan. Taken advantage of on every side, particularly by her fiancé, Sun, and threatened with the loss of her modest capital and with it the loss of any real chance of doing good, she invents (at the prompting of others) a stern business-*man* "cousin," Shui Ta, who then constantly claims that he is serving the absent Shen Te's interests. Only as she is willing to give up herself as woman, it would seem, and become literally and figuratively the male Shui Ta is the "good person" taken seriously by the business community and is left alone by the needy who had flocked to the compassionate Shen Te. At the metaphysical level the moral is profoundly disturbing: it is suggested (and the echoes of Goethe's *Faust* are particularly strong here in the play[6]) that only by doing evil can one do good. Appalled at such heresy but themselves offering no solution to the dilemma of Shen Te-Shui Ta, the gods exit in indecent haste at the play's close. As they leave, they mouth counsels of goodness that clearly cannot be observed in Shen Te-Shui Ta's Setzuan. An actor then steps

[5] For an excellent preliminary account of Brecht's interest in China and Chinese philosophy, see Anthony Tatlow's essay, "China oder Chima," BH, 1 (1971), 27-47. Cf. also A. Tatlow, *Brechts Chinesische Gedichte* (Frankfurt, 1973).

[6] A separate study needs to be done on the strong and positive influence of Goethe's *Faust* on this play by Brecht. We know that Brecht later became extremely interested in the so-called *Urfaust* of Goethe. To mention only some of the more obvious parallels between Brecht's play and Goethe's *Faust* we may note that both plays draw on the Biblical story of Job and the Lord's lament that no good people are to be found on earth; both plays present the divine endorsing of a person who might be seen as far from holy in conventional or earthly terms (Margaret in *Faust I* and Shen Te in *The Good Person*), both plays use literally and metaphorically the notion of two souls residing in the breast of each play's complex central character. Though it is obvious that some of these parallels are clearly intended as parodies of Goethe's masterpiece, the basic question of how to do good without doing evil is as serious and central in Brecht's play as it is in Goethe's.

forward and asks the public to search for a way out for Shen Te-Shui Ta's universal and timeless dilemma.

Faced with the split[7] in Shen Te's character demanded by the economics of Setzuan, a frequent and valid approach to this play has combined psychological analysis of Shen Te's clearly schizoid personality with Marxist-oriented analysis stressing the impossibility of "solving" the problem of the good person without a radical socialist reshaping of her society. These analytic postulates make excellent sense as a reading of the play but they seem to leave largely untouched the concrete and specific problem of the total alienation of *woman* in Setzuan's savage capitalist milieu.

Once one begins to think of Shen Te's dilemma as not only that of a good *person* but also as that of a good *woman* specifically then one can begin to fully appreciate Setzuan's savagery. The play is based very obviously on a series of societal clichés. As a woman in general and a prostitute in particular, Shen Te is characterized as "one who cannot say no" (GW, IV, 1494).[8] She responds directly and emotionally to need with little heed of long-range consequences.[9] As the play opens, she is literally and figuratively a sex object rather than a person. In one particularly brutal and explicit speech made to Shen Te directly when she is disguised as the male cousin Shui Ta, her fiancé reveals how totally sexist is his own thinking. He says, and we must remember that this is said of (and in a sense *to*) the woman he is supposed to love:

> What certain people think of their female relatives and the effect reasonable lectures are supposed to have on them has always surprised me. Have you ever heard of the power of love or the itch of the flesh? You want to appeal to her reason? She has no reason! Rather, the poor animal has been mistreated her whole life long. When I put my hand on her shoulder [a little later he will say "on her breast"] and say to her: "You're going with me," she hears wedding bells and wouldn't recognize her own mother. (GW, IV, 1545)

Even more disturbing than Sun's male views of Shen Te (the woman) made known to Shen Te herself disguised as Shui Ta is the fact that his prediction as to her behavior is actually proved correct shortly thereafter. When Shen Te next sees Sun, the text reads: SHEN TE, *trembling:* "What do you want?" SUN: "That you go away with me" (GW, IV, 1552). Without further ado, Shen Te goes off with Sun, saying as she

---

[7] For an account of the high incidence of such split characters in Brecht's plays, see Walter H. Sokel's essay, "Brecht's Split Characters and His Sense of the Tragic," *Brecht* (D), pp. 127-37.

[8] For contrast to the cliché views of Setzuan's inhabitants, in *A Man's a Man* Brecht presents a man who cannot say no. In the Setzuan play we must not confuse Brecht's view of women with those of the characters in the play.

[9] It is important to note that only Shen Te acts in this manner and that the male Shui Ta is thought by the inhabitants of Setzuan to be completely incapable of such behavior.

goes, to the rich and middle-aged barber Shu Fu, who is interested in purchasing her affections: "He [her cousin, Shui Ta] is wrong, I feel it." The scene closes with her poetic declaration:

> I will go with him whom I love.
> I will not calculate the cost.
> I will not meditate on whether it is good.
> I will not seek to know whether he loves me.
> I will go with him, whom I love. (GW, IV, 1552)

As rigorously as in any neoclassical tragedy, reason is pitched here against feeling, but unlike the neoclassical drama where characters, male or female, feel *within themselves* the tug of both feeling *and* reason, Brecht's poetic metaphor of the split character makes Shen Te as woman virtually a personification of feeling, while Shui Ta as a man is made virtually a personification of reason or calculation. The poetic metaphor achieves its full force only by the complete exploitation of societal pre-judgements (whether Chinese[10] or Western) of the "nature" of men and of women. Only by "masking" Shen Te are relations between the sexes in Setzuan literally unmasked.

Sun's nakedly explicit and self-conscious sexist analysis of Shen Te made to the masked Shui Ta is indicative not of a personal eccentricity of his but of the general thinking of other characters in the play. It is of the greatest importance to note that when Shen Te (still as a woman) attempts to abandon her former role of sex object and establish herself in the tobacco business as an independent entrepreneur, Sun is not the only societal force working vigorously against her liberation. The rich and vicious barber, Shu Fu,[11] is willing to help her tobacco business only (as he tells both Shen Te and Shui Ta) in direct exchange for sexual favors. So Shen Te, in order to avoid selling herself, must, paradoxically, once again contemplate offering her body for sale—though she had promised herself after receiving the gift of the three gods: "I said to myself, for one whole year I'll have nothing to do with a man" (GW, IV, 1525). In order to succeed in business Shen Te is left two major and alienating options by her sexist society. Either she can remain true to her own "nature" as woman, i.e., in terms of the play, a constant prey to feeling and by necessity a sex object; or she can totally deny herself as a woman with natural feelings and must "become" a man. Should she wish to attempt to work out a third option (as she actually endeavors to do in the play), she is immediately thrust into another alienating, stereotyped role. She can literally and figuratively give up her tobacco business (as

[10] Cf. n. 5 above.
[11] To underscore Shu Fu's viciousness, Brecht has Shu Fu deliberately smash Wang's hand immediately before he makes protestations to Shen Te of his interest in the plight of the unfortunates of Setzuan. Cf. GW, IV, 1548-49.

Sun insists she sell it and give him the proceeds as a condition of marriage) and devote herself exclusively to furthering Sun's career as a pilot in Peking.[12] In the final analysis, and for complex moral reasons, she is unwilling to resign herself to such a supportive role. Consequently, Sun, insisting on marriage only on *his* terms, rejects her out of hand. Thrown back then on her own resources by Sun, the now pregnant Shen Te must rely ever-increasingly on her male disguise to keep the tobacco business afloat.

It is perhaps the crowning irony of the play that it is precisely the fact of Shen Te's pregnancy which explicitly and finally alienates Shen Te from her biological role of woman and which demands the total metamorphosis of the woman Shen Te into the man Shui Ta. Shortly after she discovers that she is pregnant, she is told of a hungry child who has been discovered raiding garbage cans. Shen Te immediately swears that that will never happen to her expected child. She declares explicitly:

> What I have learned in my school, the gutter
> Through blows and deception, now
> This will serve you, son, to you
> I will be good but will become a tiger and wild animal
> To everyone else, if it has to be. And
> It must be. (GW, IV, 1573)

Instantly the otherwise mild Shen Te becomes now, almost permanently, the ruthless Shui Ta. Clearly, in the world of Setzuan, the instinct of motherhood triggers unbridled savagery against everyone else.[13] Now all restraint is removed on Shui Ta as "he" seeks to expand "his" tobacco holdings into a manufacturing and chainstore enterprise, employing, among others, child laborers, an enterprise designed to magnificently support Shen Te's child. Ironically, the major capital to support Shui Ta's ever expanding business is provided Shen Te-Shui Ta—who had greeted her original small business as an end to her life in prostitution—by Shu Fu explicitly in consideration of favors that the barber expects to get from Shen Te "upon her return." Shen Te, as imagined by the prostitute in Brecht's earliest sketch set in Berlin, has actually become her own pimp![14] Brecht, piling irony upon irony, has

[12] There is even a strong suggestion in the play that Sun is so completely intent on the exploitation of Shen Te to serve his own egocentric ends that he plans to take her money and then simply leave her behind while he goes off alone to Peking. Cf. GW, IV, 1545.

[13] It is a significant fact in Brecht's work that biological motherhood is often linked with unbridled savagery. Perhaps the best example of this is Mother Courage who is willing to become a tiger in the defense of her offspring. Equally important, however, is the fact that in Brecht's play, *The Caucasian Chalk Circle,* the biological mother of the child in the play is seen explicitly as being far less kindly than the child's adoptive mother. In each instance, however, a fullscale analysis of the role of woman would have to be placed in an economic context in which the relationship of woman to a capitalist society would be extensively analyzed.

[14] See *Materialien zu Brechts "Der gute Mensch,"* p. 18.

Sun who had refused to work *with* the "female" Shen Te *equally* in her original tobacco business, now working on a unequal basis *for* the "male" Shui Ta.

But the artificial world of the disguised Shen Te begins to collapse as her pregnancy advances. The stratagem that was necessitated by the pregnancy is destroyed by the pregnancy. Finally, Shui Ta, suspected of having murdered the too-long absent Shen Te, must face the wrath of the gods with which the play began. Wearing the clothes of Shui Ta, she despairingly tears off her mask to reveal to the gods the face of Shen Te and stands before them simultaneously as the male and female, bad and good, Shen Te *and* Shui Ta. It is with this final image which shows us simultaneously the thesis of Shen Te with her antithesis Shui Ta that metaphorical synthesis is achieved in the play. Finally we are shown that Shen Te-Shui Ta is neither a cliché image of woman, nor yet a cliché image of man but a person (*Mensch*) full of human complexity and perplexity. For that fleeting instant an actual person stands before the gods in Setzuan. This person is neither wholly "good" in any abstract metaphysical sense, nor wholly "bad" in the same sense[15]: Shen Te is simply a human being. But as such may one be permitted to wonder if she, in the agony of her predicament and in the recognition of her predicament, has not come closer to concrete, heroic, and active goodness than either the gods or the crowded populace of Setzuan? As a person, despite every crushing social attempt to constrain her in a mold of traditional female conformity, she has sought to liberate her*self* from all such self-alienating restraints; if she must finally fail (and there is a strong suggestion that she must), this is no indictment of her efforts but it is certainly a savage indictment of a society which has so little scope for *persons,* good or bad. As the audience thinks of the societal solution that the Epilogue with threefold urgency tells us, "must, must, must" be found, we cannot help but see Setzuan as all places everywhere where women must give up themselves in a hopeless attempt "to become themselves." Whether this can only be achieved in a Marxist-oriented society (as in present day Setzuan!)[16] or whether a non-Marxist society is capable of creating a non-alienating social frame for women is for you, a person, in the spirit of the open-ended Epilogue, to think about.

[15] One is particularly reminded here of Aristotle's description of the characteristics of an ideal central figure in tragedy.

[16] Present day productions of the play in East Germany often suggest that the problems dealt with in *The Good Woman* are no longer to be found in Communist China.

196

PART III

BRECHT: WRITER BETWEEN IDEOLOGY AND POLITICS

Andrzej Wirth

So far, critics who wished to explore Brecht's politics and ideology had to rely to a large extent on his plays, poems, and fiction. Now, with the posthumous publication of two works of a clearly political character, the situation has changed. In *Me-ti. Books of Twists and Turns* (1965),[1] written between 1934 and 1956, Brecht uses his favorite Chinese cipher code and the cover name of a classical philosopher from the fifth century B.C. in order to express his ideas. *Writings on Politics and Society* (1967)[2] is a collection of essays and notes which were penned from 1919 until 1956. Although the two books mentioned do not provide a complete documentation of Brecht's political and ideological development, they do offer sufficient material for my interpretation of the relationship between ideology and politics in Brecht's thought. Thus, it is not absolutely necessary to have recourse to Brecht's works which are of a more literary nature.

According to the definition provided by *The Shorter Oxford English Dictionary* I use the word "ideology" here in a broader sense: as a "manner of thinking characteristic of a class or an individual," and the term "politics" also in a broad sense as actions or practice deriving from this manner of thinking.

Brecht's interest in or rather addiction to ideology as reflected in these two works presents an immediate problem to the critic. Young Brecht showed no inclination toward "visionary theorizing" as I call the utopian layer which is an unavoidable component of each ideology. He began with the radical rejection of any kind of ideology and of any kind of didacticism as well. In 1919 he wrote in his notebook:

> The snake in Paradise was the first teacher; she wanted to "teach" men what is good. Revolutionaries belong to the teaching profession; that is to say, the insignificant revolutionaries, the ones who get rid of the Kaiser and introduce Communism; and the conservatives who fight them are also teachers. . . . But the free man has no principle when it comes to such indifferent matters. The absolute pacifist and the absolute militarist—they are the same kind of fool. (GW, XX, 6-7)

In 1928, shortly after Brecht's conversion to Marxism, in a note entitled "Copyright Reserved!" he states his position on the Spartacus uprising: "We all suffered from a lack of political convictions, and I, moreover, from my old inability to be enthusiastic" (GW, XX, 25).

The title and the last sentence of this note ("I don't like to think about

---

[1] Published in Bertolt Brecht, *Prosa*, V (Frankfurt, 1965). Also in GW, XII.
[2] First published in GW, XX (1967) and then in an almost completely identical hardcover edition the following year by Suhrkamp.

it [i.e., lack of political convictions]") express in a Brechtian self-critical, ironic manner his tendency to suppress his youthful attitudes toward ideology and politics. Therefore, we must approach Brecht's self-interpretations after his conversion to Marxism with caution. His confession from 24 August 1920 stresses even more his indifference toward ideology: "Again and again, I forget my perceptions; I just cannot make up my mind to learn them by heart. . . . What will I do when I am old . . . how miserably I'll be living out my life . . . with my damaged ideas, which will be no more than arrogant cripples" (GW, XX, 10).

This indifferent attitude to ideological systems characterizes the pre-Marxist period in Brecht's development. There is, however, an element in the pre-Marxist Brecht which made the transition to ideology and the obsession with it possible, i.e., the element of compassion for the suffering of an underdog: ". . . I demanded a kind of reassurance in order to sanction passion; perhaps I was afraid that compassion without hope could senselessly destroy a man" (GW, XX, 96). In order to achieve conditions in which mercy and compassion would be possible, Brecht dedicated himself to a merciless ideology of class struggle. It was a cold way of rationalizing human-oriented compassion: "Contrary to many of my comrades in the struggle, I arrived at my Marxist position in cold blood, so to speak. This is probably due to the fact that I originally studied science. Arguments enthused me more than appeals to the emotions, and experiments swayed me more than experiences" (GW, XX, 96).

This "cold-blooded" approach to Marxism was a trap, as we shall soon see. Ideology, expelled through one door as an irrelevant appeal to emotions, entered triumphantly through another and was embraced by Brecht as science. The phrase "The Scientific Age," which sounds like a delayed echo of the Enlightenment, was used by Brecht as a pseudonym for ideology. Other pseudonyms followed, such as "The Great Method," "The Great Order," etc. By using terminology of this sort, Brecht believed that he remained loyal to his favorite saying: "One should look upon ideals with gloom" (GW, XX, 313).

The move toward ideology masked as science was made easier because of the inherent tendency of Marxism to conceive of itself as a definitive scientific philosophy. The militant terminology of Marxism seemed to satisfy both Brecht's longing for *principia* and the needs of his polemical temperament. His predilection for polemics, which can hardly be overemphasized, may be ascertained from the following fragment from 1946: "Basically, I am looking for a harmless theme which gives me the opportunity to take a position . . ." (GW, XX, 300). At times, Brecht carried his principles as ideologist to the extremes of a kind of *Stellungnehmerei,* positional warfare.

The assimilation of Marxism led Brecht to redefine many of his earlier concepts. The state as a social institution which in 1920 was defined by him by means of a scatological metaphor (GW, XX, 8), was accepted after 1926 as a necessary tool of social change (GW, XX, 68). This idea of the state as a dictatorship of the proletariat found further exemplification in Brecht's interpretation of the Paris Commune in 1871 whose failure he explained in terms of its inability to apply terror to the enemies threatening its existence. Brecht's defense of the Soviet Union and Ulbricht's Germany was based on his conviction that both states represented the dictatorship of the proletariat which Brecht considered the most advanced form of government.

Brecht's view of didacticism, which was so negative in his pre-Marxist period, was modified after 1926. "The learner is more important than the lesson" (GW, XX, 46), Brecht states now. The lesson as ideology is understood here functionally as an aim in itself. Perhaps this statement from his period in exile explains Brecht's own early attitude toward ideology as a sanction for compassion. The value of an ideology would then lie in its ability to comfort an individual and not in its truth. From an orthodox Marxist point of view such a concept would be sheer heresy, as Brecht later realized.

Brecht's Marxist reasoning developed in a peculiar style—a style not unlike that of analytical philosophy involved in linguistic critique. Such a style was Brecht's means of avoiding to conceive of a utopia as utopia; he was unwilling to recognize the utopian character of socialist ideology, just as he was unwilling to see ideology in it: "One cannot say in the workers' state of Russia liberty rules. But one can say there, liberation rules" (GW, XX, 103). Liberty came to mean liberation for him, and, therefore, a process unverifiable through existing political reality. On the other hand, instead of employing the future tense in describing the socialist program, he uses the present. He consciously confuses present-day reality with projections into the future; he states rather than postulates: "In socialism the worker is the leader of production and—it must be said over and over again—of a totally different production, not only of a production with new leadership" (GW, XX, 95).

This statement from his polemic with the Fascism of the thirties is political nonsense: neither the workers in the Soviet Union nor the German workers of the Third Reich had a decisive voice in the character and the direction of production. In polemicizing against Fascism Brecht confronts conditions created by it with the socialist utopia—understood here as an existing condition. When he is confronted with the existing reality under socialism, Brecht translates this reality into a process and, in doing so, escapes any kind of verification of his theories. The existing lack of freedom becomes unreal as a condition; the real is process only, and this process points to liberation.

Brecht's early Marxism is closely related to his interest in Chinese *mores:* "I don't study Chinese customs from the Chinese themselves, of whom there are enough specimens here [in Santa Monica, California] as well as in New York, but from a little book; I have no idea, of course, whether it is very dependable. For my more or less frivolous purposes it suffices just as well to have such a book as to have such customs" (GW, XX, 299-300). One way to understand Brecht's ideological casuistry would be to occasionally substitute *Das Kapital* for the small book.

Brecht's desire to use means of stylizing can be attributed to the fact that he was not a systematic thinker. His ideological reasoning oscillates between ideology stylized as science and ideology as ethics. Brecht's peculiar motivation to find in ideology justification for his own feelings of compassion expresses itself openly in this case. The phraseology of the "Scientific Age" and of the "Great Order" is accompanied by the phraseology of happiness and goodness, of "right" and "wrong," of "good" and "bad". Thus he writes: "Comrades, our friends, the Negroes are not socialists, but they are unhappy people. We have feeling for them, and we wish that they, like us, having been unhappy, may become socialists" (GW, XX, 87).

Wishful thinking, masked as objective science, and projected into politics, produces judgments determined by tactics and silences genuine ethical considerations: "As far as the trials go, it would be all wrong to take a stand against the government of the [Soviet] Union, which instigated them, simply because such a stand would very soon turn automatically into a stand against the Russian proletariat, which is today threatened with war by world Fascism, and against its socialism which is in the process of growing" (GW, XX, 111).

Brecht's rigid Marxist attitude led him to insist on such historically incorrect observations as: "Before Hitler and his accomplices subjugated [other countries] . . . they subjugated the German people. . . . They subjugated the German people by means of police terror and propaganda, just as they subjugated foreign nations by means of military power and false promises" (GW, XX, 282-83).

These words were written in 1943; strangely enough we do not hear about Auschwitz in this context. The same attitude does not allow Brecht to see in Hitlerism a successful appeal to German nationalism; engulfed by Marxist terminology, he prefers to speak exclusively of economic determination. Ignoring the evidence he describes the reality of the Third Reich as dominated by hunger and unemployment; further, he interprets the Nazis' achievement of full employment (*Arbeitsbeschaffung*) as a measure designed to promote war (*Kriegsmaßnahme;* GW, XX, 220).

Thus economic determination is rendered absolute. Consequently, the liberation of man is understood as a liberation of production: "Men must liberate production, strip it of its chains—then they will be free" (GW, XX, 261). This is probably the most important sentence for an understanding of Brecht's attitude towards Marxist ideology. Most critics seem unable to grasp that Brecht meant this somewhat paradoxical statement to be taken literally, not metaphorically.

Brecht postulated the application of dialectics to destroy ideologies (see GW, XX, 157), but his own ideology remains unscathed. His use of dialectics is brilliant indeed. Brechtian dialectics, however, are more a vehicle of style than of insights. The insignificant dialectic word "almost" and its use by Brecht require separate study ("*Almost* an age of justice," the Singer calls the rule of Azdak). There is also the dialectic juxtaposition of "neither-nor." "He was neither wanting in appetite, nor insatiable," Brecht states about Marx. This distinction is dialectic in the sense that it interprets the transition between qualities as fluid. The diction of a practical man, who is careful not to exaggerate and who sees life in its contradictory complexity, is audible here. It is a voice not without its charm.

In Brecht the attitude of a practical man struggles with the posture of a self-styled Hegelian *Besserwisser,* as can be seen from his reiterating Hegel's famous dictum: "What is rational becomes real, and what becomes real is rational" (GW, XX, 77). Brecht needed to go only one step further to reach his ideal as formulated in "Goals of the Society of Dialecticians" (ca. 1931): "Behavior as logic. The order of business as order" (GW, XX, 148). The opposition between capitalism and socialism is that of disorder and order; life is understood as an organization of processes which determines one's very existence.

Brecht emerges from his posthumously published political writings not as a builder of a consistent ideological system, but first of all as a polemicist. He seems to be more concerned with exposing the false concepts of his opponents than with establishing the truth. His thoughts are too complicated to be explained by means of the immanent method, i.e., on the basis of his Marxist social theory. This does not mean, however, that the importance of his Marxist theory of social life is only marginal. On the contrary, the newly published materials[3] offer evidence against all attempts to understand Brecht as an undogmatic skeptic (as Reinhold Grimm did); as a liberal humanist, superficially involved in the Marxist rhetoric (as Martin Esslin did); as an advocate of a century-old plebeian tradition (as Hans Mayer did); or as a discoverer of the truth with the help of Marxist theory (as Ernst Schumacher did). The new materials prove that Brecht took his Marxist convictions seriously, and that they play a central role in his reasoning. Of crucial importance here are the transitions from the pre-Marxist period to Marxist indoctrination; from Marxist orthodoxy to a less dogmatic perception of Marxist theory. Unfortunately, the documentation of these transitions still remains incomplete and very unsatisfactory. In particular, there is hardly any documentation for Brecht's earliest period and that for the

---

[3] The recently published AJ also belongs into this category; however, although AJ was not available when this essay was written, my views are confirmed by many of the statements in AJ.

period 1919-1926 is completely sparse.

Brecht's political notes in *Me-ti* and *Writings on Politics and Society* appear a little old-fashioned; they resemble those of an Encyclopedist fighting for the Enlightenment. Brecht in his political prose is a kind of delayed German *Aufklärer,* who in the area of ideologists and expert editorial writers decides to perform a very complex and highly specialized task on his own. Among the "Five Difficulties" in "Writing the Truth" (GW, XVIII, 222-39) in our time he did not mention his personal difficulty which can be defined as the fear of being inconsistent. As a matter of fact, in the attempt to be consistent Brecht did not always serve the cause of truth. By emphasizing the primacy of economic considerations, Brecht did not sufficiently distinguish between Hitler's state and Western democracies (cf. AJ, II, 823); in *Fear and Misery of the Third Reich* he portrayed imaginary hunger and unemployment; in *Roundheads and Peakheads* he interpreted racial persecution as a perverted class struggle; in the poem "Freedom and Democracy" (GW, X, 943-49) he denounced the parliamentary system as a device of warmongers.

On the one hand, Brecht's most deeply rooted theoretical prejudice concerned the connection between capital and military dictatorship. On the other hand, he wrote: "Those dictatorships which act against these conditions of an economic nature [i.e., conditions perpetuating exploitation] must be supported and endured [because they] destroy their own roots" (GW, XX, 102). Undoubtedly, for Brecht one such dictatorship which had to be endured was that of Stalin. Nevertheless, there is no simple answer to the question of Brecht's Stalinism—at least the answer is not as simple as Hannah Arendt seems to imply.[4]

If we examine references to Stalin in the material under discussion in general, and in *Me-ti* where Stalin appears as Ni-en in particular, we will discover that its author is actually doing what the Stalinists did: he supports the Stalin-Hitler pact; he seems to prefer Stalin to Trotsky (Totsi); he defends the Stalinist constitution; and he writes a eulogy for Stalin.

In the thirties Brecht translated politics into ideology by simply taking it for granted that politics are identical with ideology. If different ideologies produce the same policy, as in the case of the Stalin-Hitler pact, he merely interprets it to the advantage of the ideology he sympathizes with (cf. GW, XII, 428).

The Chinese allusion—a kind of cipher language—used in Brecht's *Me-ti* lends it the character of a historical parable rather than that of a political comment. Capitalists become master blacksmiths (*Schmiedeherren*), while the workers—the blacksmiths (*Schmiede*)—and their conflicts are projected into the realm of undefinable ancient history.

[4] Hannah Arendt, "Quod licet Jovi. . . . Reflexionen über den Dichter Bertolt Brecht und sein Verhältnis zur Politik," *Merkur,* 23 (1969), 527-42, 625-42, 1083-84.

The terms Brecht substitutes for Marxist terminology are at times misleading, such as in the example cited above where the depiction of the Soviet Union suggests a rather feudalistic system.

The apology for the Soviet State under Stalin is based on fantastic assumptions; for example, Brecht infers that the production of goods for all had as an accompanying factor the restriction of freedom; the industrialization and collectivization under Stalin is not taken into account at all! (cf. GW, XII, 438-39).

It is obvious that in discussing Brecht's convictions we have to consider not only their content but their structure and form of expression as well. The content is determined by Brecht's excessive intellectualism which he called his "cold-blooded" approach to Marxism. Brecht projected his intellectualism into both ideology and into politics. Only from this perspective can one understand his criticism of the Stalin trials: "Me-ti blamed Ni-en because he [Ni-en] demanded too much trust from the people in his trials against his enemies in the Union" (GW, XII, 538). Only if one is aware of how much emphasis Brecht placed on equating politics with reason does one realize how serious Brecht's criticism is. In a similar vein Brecht describes in a short note the negative impact of Stalinism, i.e., the destruction of the ability for dialectic thinking (GW, XX, 326). In Brecht's idiom such a statement expresses extremely strong condemnation.

As an outright condemnation would not fit Brecht's diction of understatement, Stalin appears in his political writings not as the father of nations, the greatest general, linguist, and noble builder of human happiness—which the international chorus of Stalin sycophants claimed him to be. Rather, in Brecht's perception, Stalin resembles his own countryman Governor Abashwili as seen by the Singer in *The Caucasian Chalk Circle*. Brecht proposes to call Stalin not great but useful. And he adds: "Ni-en used to appear as a Kaiser. The backwardness of the country Su [Soviet Union] . . . still showed itself in that" (GW, XII, 538).

The most sensitive issue of the Stalinist construction period, the dispute between Trotsky and Stalin, is presented not without epic humor:

> About everything which was done in the country Ni-en said: "I accomplished that," and To-tsi said: "I advised against that." In reality a lot happened which To-tsi wanted and a lot which Ni-en didn't want. Whoever influenced the course of events was satisfied; but the dissatisfied naturally also influenced the course of events. To-tsi referred continually to Ni-en's vast power, and Ni-en hardly spoke of anything but To-tsi's vast power. The one group of Tuis called Ni-en, the other group To-tsi, father of nations and the deprivator of nations. And all the Tuis called each other Tuis in the worst sense of the word. (GW, XII, 522-23)

The epic humor and historical manner of detachment which Brecht mastered in *Me-ti* developed into a new style of political reasoning.

This style is highly dialectic and, therefore, according to Brecht's own definition, cannot be called Stalinist. Dialectics at work can be seen from the following statement in which the inner tensions of the Soviet Union are explored: "The prisons were still overcrowded, twenty years after the Union assumed power and there were death sentences and trials everywhere, in which even old members of the Club [*Verein*] were involved. Great wars with bourgeois countries lay ahead" (GW, XII, 524).

Brecht's preoccupation with the Soviet dictator culminated in his eulogy for Stalin, a masterpiece in which ambiguity and precision are not contradictions: "The heartbeat of the oppressed of the five continents of the Earth—including those who liberated themselves and all those who fight for peace on earth—must have come to a stop as they heard: Stalin is dead" (GW, XX, 325).

Brecht's perception of Stalin and Stalinism as illustrated in the newly published materials allow us to respond to the question Hannah Arendt[5] poses: Brecht was not a Stalinist. As stated before, he was, above all, a Hegelian *Besserwisser,* who conceived of and reacted to Stalin and Stalinism not as an isolated phenomenon but as a part of the contradictory historical process.

The new reading of Brecht's posthumously published political writings must proceed from the assumption that the playwright was, indeed, serious in what he said. So far attempts have been made to correct his political views (Hans Mayer, Ernst Schumacher) or to forgive him his Marxism because of his apparent longing for liberal humanism (Martin Esslin). Further, among the so-called "revisionists" in Eastern Europe there was a tendency to use Brecht as an advocate for the cause of "socialism with a human face"—a socialism propagated by, e.g., the ideologists of the pro-Dubcek movement in 1968. Our new reading does not encourage an interpretation of Brecht as an advocate of such a socialism. Rather, the first conclusion we have to draw is that Brecht was entirely serious about his Marxism—notwithstanding the fact that it was his very own version of Marxism—and that it did, indeed, exercise great influence upon his writings. Second, Brecht did not harbor any illusions about the role of the individual in society—regardless of whether the society was new or old. In one of the most brilliant aphorisms in *Me-ti,* Brecht engages in a skilful play on words to demonstrate that formerly privileged individuals were ultimately "eaten" (*verspeist*) by those at whose expense they lived. As the aphorism is untranslatable, the German version is given here: "Die Einzelnen, sagte Me-ti nachdenklich, hatten früher etwas Kostbares, d.h. sie waren, wie sie waren, auf Kosten der andern. Waren sie so köstlich, so kosteten sie auch. Kost kostet, das besagt aber auch, daß sie verspeist wurden" (GW, XII, 541).

[5] Cf. n. 4.

Brecht had no illusions about the freedom of an individual under capitalism *or* socialism: "Whether one says, better to be not free in a good country than free in a bad one . . . whatever one says, one cannot say that one is free . . . The individual is cramped from all sides; everywhere he must give way, give in, give up. [Only] the collectives have been liberated; they now can move freely" (GW, XII, 540-41).

Just as there is no evidence of the "socialism with the human face" in Brecht's political writings, there is also no evidence of his interest in a socialist democracy. In fact, Brecht's hatred of democracy characterizes his political ideology precisely because democracy means capitalism to him. In Brecht's view, Hitler came to power by manipulating democratic freedoms; Fascism is a product of the capitalist democracy. While in exile as a guest of Western democracies, Brecht, the enemy of democracy, found himself in a dilemma. He had become involved in a tactical alliance with the strategic foes of Communism—although he took care to be allied with the more progressive forms of democracy (cf. AJ, II, 823).

In vain one searches Brecht's political-literary remains for traces of revisionism. To be sure, neither revisionism nor orthodoxy are terms applicable to Brecht—despite the fact that in his reasoning he often expresses orthodox points of view. His occasional criticism of the Ulbricht government is rather marginal; thus he does not take notice of the most blatantly negative aspects such as the overgrown system of the secret police which dominated the party apparatus and the political prisons. Just as one can assume on the basis of his posthumously published political writings that Brecht did not pay any attention to Fascism before 1933, but after 1933 saw Fascism lurking everywhere, so some of his mildly critical remarks about the Ulbricht government do not appear until the Berlin uprising of 1953. Therefore, the prognostic ability in politics does not seem to be one of his strong points.

Günther Grass's criticism of Brecht's political behavior in his semi-documentary play *The Plebeians Rehearse the Uprising* exposed the significant gap between the generations. Grass's criticism made it obvious that Brecht, the ideologist, aside from the originality of his style, belongs to the fading post-World War I generation, who believed in socialism as a panacean alternative to capitalism. Grass represents a post-World War II generation who believes in a middle-of-the-road position and treats both capitalism and socialism with the same skeptical caution. It is obvious that no communication is possible between the two generations. But the voice of still another generation can be heard more and more clearly in both Europe and America. This generation favors either-or solutions again, and therefore Brecht's reasoning may attract them.

To summarize: Brecht underwent an evolution which is still inadequately documented to allow definitive scholarly insights. His initial position was extremely anti-ideological and anti-political, a kind of nihilistic anarchism which implied a rejection of both ideology and politics. Around 1926, he assimilated Marxism in a very anti-dialectic, ultra-leftist reading by equating ideology and politics with science. Starting with the early forties—the transition is gradual and very difficult to trace because of the lack of a precise chronology of most of the political notes—Brecht now moves toward a more balanced kind of Hegelianism and emphasizes a dialectic approach to man and history. In this area, he achieves his personal style as ideologist and political writer; *Me-ti* is the most representative example of this achievement. The doctrinaire attitude of the middle period now gives way to a kind of "detached engagement."

Brecht seems to be the first political writer who manages to veil his engagement by using stylistic devices suggesting detachment. Dialectics, as a method of exposing contradictions, led him to a new style of political reasoning, an example of which may serve as a fitting conclusion: "The decision of the Club in Su [Soviet Union] to realize the *Great Order* weighs like a nightmare on the people of Su. The progressive tendencies are tripping up the people. Bread is thrown with such vehemence at them that many are killed. The most prosperous of institutions are created by scoundrels, and quite a few virtuous people block progress" (GW, XII, 524).

BRECHT'S MARXISM AND AMERICA

David Bathrick

> Died: Bertolt ("Bert") Brecht, 58, slight, bespectacled German playwright (librettist for Kurt Weill's *Threepenny Opera*) who, according to ex-Communist Arthur Koestler sold Marxism "with great brilliance and intellectual dishonesty" to "the snobs and parlor Communists" of Europe; of a heart attack; in East Berlin. (*Time*, 27 August 1956)

In one sense, it is all there in its most popular and truncated form: Brecht of *The Threepenny Opera;* Brecht the Commie; a *Time* "Milestone" which deflates the political and artistic endeavors of a lifetime. An American tribute. But, of course, it is not all there. Rather, this obituary represents one aspect of the complicated process by which an author is evaluated and received into an alien, in this case, "alienating" culture. Brecht's coming to terms with capitalist America was a love-hate struggle which involved in a fundamental way his move to Marxism during the most formative years of his political-aesthetic development. If his relationship to America was an ambivalent one, this society's response to Brecht, i.e., "the Americanization of Bert Brecht,"[1] is an even more complicated and at least as painful process—which tells us as much about ourselves as about the playwright.

Dialectical materialism constitutes the groundwork of Brecht's art. Yet the failure to understand its unique character and its relationship to his creativity have led to the severest distortions at the hands of a culture all too eager to equate the teachings of Marx with the worst excesses of his would-be followers. Most prior treatments of Brecht's reception in America have centered first on the artist and have dealt with his ideology as a separate entity, peripheral to the "poet within."[2] This paper purports to invert such an approach by assuming that ideological-political factors are inseparable from his art and that they are, indeed, at its very center. The exploration of the reception process clearly shows the importance attributed to these factors. By focusing on the political reception of Brecht in this country we are forced to confront the hidden and not so hidden assumptions underlying our own aesthetics. If such an emphasis relegates conventional, non-political cultural taste to a secondary concern, it conversely suggests an historical

---

[1] Lee Baxandall, "The Americanization of Bert Brecht," BH, 1 (1971), 150-67.
[2] Ulrich Weisstein, "Brecht in America: A Preliminary Survey," MLN, 78 (1963), 373-96. Weisstein's study treats thoroughly the first decade and a half of Brecht's reception in America.

understanding of the role of literary fashion.

This analysis will attempt to answer two fundamental questions: 1) What are the political contours of the Brecht image in this country, and how does it change over the years? 2) What are the forces within the social and cultural life of our society which have helped shape that image? This study does not claim to treat Brecht's reception in its entirety, but it focuses specifically upon those intellectuals who, as producers of culture, have been pivotal in popularizing his image. Rather than present a complete compendium, I have concentrated upon critical writings which are both instrumental and paradigmatic in the process of mediating the political Brecht to a wider audience. In the course of this investigation there emerged four periods of Brecht reception which paralleled roughly four cultural-historical periods of American life. I have consequently chosen to organize this study around the following divisions: the radical Thirties (1933-1939); the struggle against Fascism (1940-1947); Cold War culture (1948-1959); re-emerging Politics (1960-Today).

Brecht's Marxism was born during a time of revolt and debate within the once enclosed ranks of Marxian theory. In a sense, it is a product of these times. His two most important mentors—Karl Korsch and Fritz Sternberg—were viewed by the party as heretics and expelled for their efforts. Yet, despite their heterodoxy, the work of Korsch in particular exhibits, at the same time, its own kind of orthodoxy. Thus it stands with Georg Lukács' *History and Class Consciousness* as the progenitor of a now long line of thought which looks back to Hegel by seeking to relocate the subjective moment within a dialectical relationship of theory and practice. Brecht is a part of this tradition, and his dialectical theory of theater with its emphasis on consciousness contains major refutations of certain mechanical aspects of Soviet Marxism.[3] Still, for all its nurturing in European classical idealism, Brecht's thought also sends one of its taproots deep down into Anglo-American traditions. Again Korsch provides the link.[4] Unlike Lukács, a student of both *Lebensphilosophie* and German idealism, Karl Korsch's path to Hegelian Marxism emerges from the positivist, anti-dialectical and pragmatic tradition of Fabian socialism, a tradition to which he returns in part after his emigration to the USA in the forties. In this light it is also interesting that the one theoretical American Marxist closest to Brecht and Korsch, Sidney Hook, was known for his efforts along with Max Eastman and Walling to reconcile pragmatism with dialectical materialism, Dewey with Marx. Hook met Brecht in Berlin in 1929 at

---

[3] See Heinz Brüggemann, *Literarische Technik und soziale Revolution. Versuche über das Verhältnis von Kunstproduktion, Marxismus und literarischer Tradition in den theoretischen Schriften Bertolt Brechts* (Hamburg, 1973).

[4] See Minaly Vajda, "Karl Korsch: Marxism and Philosophy," *The Unknown Dimension: European Marxism since Lenin* (New York, 1972), pp. 131-46. Vajda, a student of Lukács', discusses critically Korsch's positivism.

some meetings held by Korsch,[5] and it is obvious that Korsch's influence at this point is seminally important for the development of both men.

For all three men Marxism was not a *Weltanschauung* but a "methodology of science" in which historical, logical and natural elements are connected. All three stressed the active side of Marxism as a critical theory of social change; as "the self-conscious, theoretical expression of the practical activity of the working class engaged in struggle."[6] The emphasis upon learning through doing and the instrumental nature of knowledge is central to Brecht's theories of the *Lehrstücke* which draw importantly on Watsonian behaviorism and the thought of John Dewey.[7] Potentially, then, Brecht's theoretical predilections placed him closer to America than one might think and make the distortions of his politics—reducing them simply to ideology and *Weltanschauung*—one of the tragic aspects of his reception in this country.

Yet, for all the theoretical affinity, Brecht did not share with Hook or Korsch their intense disdain and rejection of the Soviet Union, and we see elements emerging in Brecht's complicated relationship to international Communism under Stalin which were to further complicate Brecht's reception in this country by both the right and the left.[8] From his earliest days, Brecht's criticism of official Communist bureaucracies was legion. Yet although he never was a member of any Communist party, he remained in a fraternal working relationship with official Communism—despite his professions of intellectual disdain and very serious political, theoretical, and artistic deviations. Brecht maintained his association with Communism, not out of an alleged "choice of evils," but simply because he believed that with all its inherent structural weakness, the international working class struggle offered the only viable means for a better future. The injection of this child of European Communism into a body politic clearly unsympathetic toward such a tradition was bound to call forth the kind of distortions it did.

I. 1933-1939

Although two plays, *The Threepenny Opera* and *He Who Said Yes* were produced in New York as early as 1933, it was not until the 1935 production of *The Mother* by the leftist Theatre Union that Brecht was first thrust into the foreground of cultural interest in this country. Appropriately, *The Mother* was a play suited to bring to the surface all the

[5] See Sidney Hook, "A Recollection of Bertolt Brecht," *New Leader,* 43 (1960), 22-23.
[6] Sidney Hook, *Towards the Understanding of Karl Marx: A Revolutionary Interpretation* (New York, 1933), p. 222. Hook has since dissociated himself from this earlier phase of his thought.
[7] See Hansjürgen Rosenbauer, *Brecht und der Behaviorismus* (Bad Homburg, 1970).
[8] Hook, "A Recollection of Bertolt Brecht," 23. Hook describes evicting Brecht from his apartment in 1935 because of Brecht's support for Stalin's show trials.

attendant problems of Brecht's reception.[9] From Brecht's very first confrontation with Paul Peters' translation of the play through the endless battles with the director, Victor Wolfson, concerning the Theatre Union production to the nervous and mostly unfavorable critical reception, there prevailed a scale of reactions ranging from total miscomprehension to outright hostility. Much of the concern for the play was confined initially to the left, and the vehemence of the response itself gives evidence of the cultural upheavals and transitions in the months of 1935 which preceded Brecht's arrival in the New World.

Due both to the formation of an international United Front against Fascism and to the changing nature of domestic politics resulting from the success of the New Deal, the year 1935 occasioned an important switch in the policies of the American Communist Party. Most immediately, there was a move away from a narrowly defined, highly militant emphasis upon class struggle to an indiscriminate, all-inclusive policy attempting to embrace larger sectors in collaboration against Fascism. For some members of the literary left, this signaled the end of "left literary infantilism"[10] or the "RAPP period in American literary Communism"[11] and the opportunity to encourage experimentalization and liberalization in the arts. Paradoxically, such a conclusion was an inversion of the emphasis laid down by Georgi Dimitrov in the 1935 conference of Soviet writers which was to become a guideline for the new position: "I must admit . . . that I have not always the patience to read our revolutionary literature. I cannot read it and I do not understand it; I am not a specialist. But in so far as I know the masses, the workers and their psychology, I must say no, this will not meet with much approval from the workers."[12]

When Matthew Josephson writing in *New Masses* (30 April 1935) comments that "Dimitrov is somewhat unjust to numerous excellent works, but his warning is timely," he chooses to ignore Dimitrov's obvious swipe at modernist art and interprets his statement as an attack which is primarily directed at excessive revolutionary partisanship. This emphasis upon non-partisanship within the American left helps explain the problems *The Mother* encountered in its reception—a play unequivocating in its call for proletarian struggle. Upon his return from the First International Writers' Congress for the Defense of Culture, held in Paris in 1935, literary Communist Mike Gold rejoiced at the gloriousness of international writers "taking their place among the leaders of humanity" and railed at a small group of "Trotskyite

[9] See Lee Baxandall, "Brecht in America, 1935," DR, 12 (1967), 69-87. Reprinted in *Brecht* (M), pp. 33-60.
[10] Matthew Josephson, "For a Literary United Front," *New Masses,* 16 (30 April 1935), 22.
[11] John Chamberlain, "The Literary Left Grows Up," SR, 12 (11 May 1935), 3.
[12] Reprinted in *New Masses,* 16 (16 April 1935), 21.

pathologues living in a self-centered world helpful to the enemy."[13] Gold could well have been talking about Brecht; in fact, Brecht's controversial "Address" (GW, XVIII, 241-46) at the conference was openly anti-capitalist, divisive, and ran directly counter to the United Front. A similar "latitudinarianism" lay at the philosophical root of the Theatre Union—an effort to build a consciously working-class theater in the tradition of the New Playwrights and the Theatre Guild which would at the same time mute the clarion call of militancy in an appeal to a broader sector of interests.

The contradictions and tensions of the United Front policy were carried over into the whole production-consumption process of *The Mother*. Brecht lists six major revisions in the production, all of which diluted the political content of the play.[14] Yet, the real problem of the ideological reception did not center on its ideological content, traditionally understood, but on the cognitive-aesthetic politics of its form. Brecht himself criticized the overly "naturalistic" style of the production which in eliciting sympathy and catharsis reduced a classical historical event such as the political development of a mother to an everyday happening. He faulted the Theatre Union for not having the courage to carry the play through with the proper style (GW, XVII, 1076-1077). Many of the reviews noted a mixture of styles and even the *Daily Worker* took the Theatre Union to task for not doing the play in the Brecht-Eisler fashion.

Although valid, the above explanations focus too specifically on the 1935 production and ultimately fail to locate the problem of reception in an unresolved ambiguity at the core of Brecht's art. On the one hand, there is the notion of drama as a "play for learning" (*Lehrstück*): an emphasis upon the open, tentative and heuristic presentation of ideas; upon learning through involvement, through active, critical, testing participation. The quintessence of the "play for learning"—Brecht realized this only in theory, never in practice—is the very opposite of "didactic," for it requires that the audience not accept action and characters as finished products, but rather as unhewn attitudes and behaviors which must be tested; as models for critical experimentation. Opposed to the *Lehrstück* is the drama as *Thesenstück*, as a "thesis play" which focuses less on questions and more on answers—on final conclusions and ideological premises.[15] These two contradictary dramatic modes coexist

---

[13] Cited in Daniel Aaron, *Writers on the Left* (New York, 1961), p. 321.

[14] These changes included the omission of the scene in the country and the copper collection scene; the omission of revolutionary slogans; and the changing of the song "Praise of Communism" to "Praise of Socialism." Cf. "Criticism of the New York Production," (GW, XVII, 1048-1052), and Baxandall, "Brecht in America" (n. 9) for a discussion of these revisions.

[15] For a discussion of the *Lehrstück* emphasizing these two types of drama see Reiner Steinweg, "Das Lehrstück—ein Modell des Sozialistischen Theaters," *Alternative*, 16 (1971), 102-116.

to a lesser or greater degree in all of Brecht's political plays, whether in the works he specifically referred to as *Lehrstücke* or in the "epic" *Schaustücke* (*Mother Courage, Galileo,* etc.) of the later years. In some instances, we find elements of both learning and thesis drama in one and the same scene or speech.

A look at scene iv of *The Mother* reveals aspects of both. As a thesis scene, the mother and the audience are presented with a lesson in political economy: Pelagea Vlassova learns from her son Pavel and the other young revolutionaries about the contradiction between private ownership and social production and about the difference between possessing a table and owning a factory:

> PAVEL: . . . there is a big difference between whether a table or a factory belongs to you. A table really can belong to you. So can a chair. Nobody is hurt by it. Suppose you feel like setting them on a roof; what harm can it do? But when a factory belongs to you, you can hurt hundreds of men with it. In this case you are a man who owns others' tools; and you use them to get use out of men. [16]

In simple language, Brecht explicates the intricacies of the labor theory of value. Yet the main focus of this scene is not on the *answers* of Pavel and the revolutionaries but on the hard common-sense *questions* of the mother. "Why don't you think Mr. Suklinov should cut the wages he pays you just as he pleases? Is it or isn't it his factory? . . . But what happens when he says he doesn't need you any longer?" [17] Brecht himself remarked about this scene: "She [the Mother] receives her first lesson in economy with the attitude of a great realist. With considerable energy, which is not meant to be unfriendly, she fights those who oppose her in the discussions; she opposes them as idealists who do not want to accept reality. She demands that proof not only correspond to truth but also to probability" (GW, XVII, 1039).

Central here is the language of the experiment: critical attitude, proof, inquiry. In the figure of the mother we observe the behaviors and attitudes of a person confronted with different situations and engaged in the process of investigation—an attitude which Walter Benjamin has called "the step-by-step advance of ordinary common sense." [18] It is in this sense that *The Mother* is a sociological experiment, representative of both a "play for learning" and Brecht's unique brand of Marxism.

[16] Bertolt Brecht, *The Mother,* trans. Lee Baxandall (New York, 1965), p. 62.
[17] Ibid., pp. 60, 61.
[18] Walter Benjamin, *Versuche über Brecht* (Frankfurt, 1966) p. 42.

The unresolved tension between *Lehrstück* and *Thesenstück* is apparent also in the American response to *The Mother*.[19] Merely as a "thesis play," i.e., restricted to its discursive ideological character, the message seemed a crude and somewhat obvious transmittal of the ABC's of Communism. A sampling of criticism reveals a fixation on this aspect of the performance: "[The play] should be classed as an entertainment for children for it is a simple kindergarten for Communist tots. . . ." (GW, XVII, 1058); "Wanted to make straightforward Communist preachment out of compelling source . . . affected, didactic, dull, pretentious. . . ."[20] Even the positive review by M. J. Olgin in the *Daily Worker* obviously understood the play in its stricter ideological sense as an agit prop call to action: "It was Brecht's plan to have a spectacle representing the dramatic story of present-day class struggle which would culminate in the victory of the proletariat. He planned his play on a grandiose scale."[21]

In his controversial book *Was Europe a Success* (1932), Joseph Wood Krutch excoriated all Communist literature as "clarion call," "opiate," "propaganda" or "dreams" and concluded that the real business of literature demanded "disinterestedness." Ironically, Krutch was one of the few critics to understand the stylistic intentions of *The Mother:* "The effect of all this is the achievement of a sort of guileful guilelessness and a sort of a pseudo-naiveté."[22] We see in these two kinds of responses—both Krutch and Brooks Atkinson of the *The New York Times* appreciated the politics of style without the politics; conversely, the *Daily Worker* fixated on the proletarian message—the beginning of a dialectical separation which was to haunt the Brecht reception down to the present.

II. 1940-1947

Brecht's "Address to the First International Writers' Congress" (1935) concluded with the call for class struggle as the means of ending Fascism: "Comrades, let us talk about the distribution of property

[19] The only American article written during Brecht's first visit to the United States which came to terms with Brecht's intentions was obviously the result of collaboration with the playwright himself. Eva Goldbeck in *New Masses*, 16 (31 December 1935), 27, stresses the centrality of the *Lehrstück* for Brecht's entire thinking about drama at that time: "Significantly, the most fully developed and popular form of this new dramaturgy is called the Study play (*Lehrstück*)." Here the *Lehrstück* is not yet understood as a separate category, but it is the most highly developed form of Brechtian drama. Shortly thereafter, in an interview, Brecht was to say of the *Lehrstück*, "the nearest equivalent I can find in English is the learning play." Cited in Reiner Steinweg, *Das Lehrstück* (Stuttgart, 1972), p. 48. Brecht was later to exclude *The Mother* from this category, showing his own ambivalence toward the work and underlining its unresolved stature between *Lehrstück* and *Schaustück*.
[20] E.J.R. Isaacs in TA, 20 (1936), 13.
[21] "Mother: The Theatre Union's New Play," *Daily Worker* (29 November 1935), 5.
[22] *The Nation* (4 December 1935), 660.

(*Eigentumsverhältnisse*)" (GW, XVIII, 246). By the time of the Second Congress, held in Madrid two years later, Brecht had modified his position to conform with that of the United Front. Now he urged "an all-encompassing, untiring struggle against Fascism on the broadest possible scale" (GW, XVIII, 251). This shift in political emphasis is reflected in Brecht's creative work, which in turn affected the reception process in the U.S. In 1935 the playwright had left New York uncompromising in his political stance, if somewhat sobered after having had to haggle with the American left. In 1941 Brecht returned to the United States and established his residence in Southern California—which he called the "mortuary of easygoing" (AJ, I, 291). His journal (*Arbeitsjournal*) for this period is a document of political and intellectual exile. Not once does he mention substantive political exchange with members of the American left. Much of his critical political thought during these years consists of vicious and somewhat pathetic assaults upon the Frankfurt School—Theodor Adorno, Max Horkheimer, Herbert Marcuse and other "Tuis" of the Hegelian left. Moreover, his journal reveals growing doubts concerning the hope of a militant workers' movement in advanced capitalist countries or the viability of Marxism in America.[23] More importantly, running throughout the journal is equivocation on Brecht's part concerning the wisdom of waging class struggle at a time when the political priority was clearly the fight against Fascism.

An information bulletin issued by the Embassy of the USSR in 1942 described Brecht as that "well known German anti-Fascist writer" (AJ, I, 484)—a description which precisely fits his image in the USA during the following years. Poems from his collection *Songs, Poems, Choruses* (GW, IX, 423-58), first published in Paris in 1934, appeared in a number of leading periodicals, including *Time*.[24] In 1943 Eric Bentley's translations of scenes from *Fear and Misery of the Third Reich* began to appear. First, *The Nation* published *The Jewish Wife* (11 September 1943); one year later five scenes, entitled *The Private Life of the Master Race*, appeared in *Theater Arts* (September 1944) together with a major article by Bentley on Brecht; and in 1944 seventeen scenes were published by New Directions. Bentley's translation also provided the text for the New York production of *The Private Life* (June 1945) under the direction of Brecht's close friend Berthold Viertel and a cast of German artists in exile. The reviews of the play reveal a marked change in critical attitude toward Brecht's partisanship since the 1935 production of *The Mother:* "Eric Bentley and Brecht are forceful. They have con-

---

[23] "The special opportunity which Marxism could avail itself of in Europe is missing here. The sensational uncovering of [shady] business deals undertaken by the bourgeois state caused Marxism to have the special effect of enlightening [people]—an effect which is not possible here. Here a state exists which was established by the bourgeoisie itself; hence this state does not for one moment feel ashamed of being bourgeois" (AJ, I, 373).

[24] "Ballad of the German Soldier's Bride," *Time*, 41 (1 February 1943), 30.

tempt for the Nazis and make no bones about it." Brecht is no longer considered "didactic, . . . obvious . . . [or] pretentious"[25]; now his anti-Fascist sympathies are clearly in keeping with the prevailing ideological climate. The critic of *The New York Times,* Lewis Nichols, even finds that the play is not agitational enough; his plea for relevance is particularly astounding considering the time of its production: "Now that the panzers are lying in junkpiles, the play has an air of history. It sounds like the echo to a call to arms rather than the call itself."[26]

It is significant that *The Private Life of the Master Race* was one of the two works from the Brecht canon which was most often performed in the United States up through 1947, and Eric Bentley's extremely influential writings on Brecht at this time clearly reflect the kind of bias implied by such an emphasis: "No single work of Brecht's is more important than *Fears and Miseries of the Third Reich*. . . . It will probably be his best known piece."[27] Here and in an earlier review of *The Trial of Lucullus* Bentley advances two positions which are important for the evaluation of Brecht in the United States. The first contains an assessment of Brecht's drama. He differentiates two major categories—the "didactic" plays (*Lehrstück*) and what he calls the "documentary" plays (e.g., *Fear and Misery*). He designates the latter play, i.e., the least revolutionary, as Brecht's most "ambitious" work. By elevating a comparatively minor play to a position of importance, Bentley helps make Brecht more palatable. The once antagonistic Marxist is now welcomed for his more "historical" and documentary concerns; the stringency of the epic form—so disturbing and baffling in 1935—is now watered down as "hybrid": "the point was that epic, dramatic and lyric elements could all be used. So could all the styles the dramatist needed."[28] The understanding of Brecht as primarily an anti-Fascist and the interpretation of one of his least representative, most Aristotelian works as typical for his entire *œuvre* was an inevitable and necessary consequence of the war and United Front politics to which Brecht temporarily adhered.

Less necessary, it seems to me, is Bentley's second point dealing with Brecht as a political artist. Here, his concern is to separate Brecht from the legacy of the "red decade in American letters" and his obvious paranoia concerning the propagandistic aspects of Brecht's work anticipates the coming difficulties of the Cold War culture: "We fear the politics because we associate political drama with our own abortive proletarian literature of the now despised thirties. But Brecht's political emphasis was never a phase or fad."[29] With this Bentley begins another separation process central to Brecht's reception in this country; he

[25] NYT (13 June 1945).
[26] NYT (17 June 1945).
[27] "Bertolt Brecht and His Work," TA, 27 (1944), 511.
[28] Ibid.
[29] "Brecht: Poetry, Drama, and the People," *The Nation*, (31 July 1943), 131.

begins to salvage Brecht for the intellectuals in order to preserve him for literary posterity. Bentley's explication of Brecht as a modern poet draws upon, develops, and popularizes a side of Brecht first presented to Americans in 1941 by Clement Greenberg's important contribution.[30] Bentley rightly emphasizes the plebeian *Volkston* element which is not folk art, but uniquely and synthetically Brecht. He draws an interesting comparison between the philosopher William James's writing on music and Brecht's theories of audience response. And finally he places him both poetically and linguistically in a popular tradition that goes back to Luther and Hans Sachs.

But Brecht's poetic elevation contains also political nullification; Bentley's divorcing of Brecht from the "poets of the Mike Gold mint," which is certainly valid as an aesthetic judgment about certain aspects of engaged art in the thirties, implies political repudiation. In Bentley's presentation, Brecht's work as an artist is not understood as concrete political activity rooted in a specific historical struggle. By rescuing him from "our own abortive proletarian literature of the now despised thirties," he attributes the same universal significance to him as a revolutionary which he had attributed to the poet before. This is not to impute to Bentley a vulgar rejection of political art. He is, in fact, careful to stress "that from the artistic point of view political emotion is just as good a basis for a poet as any other. . . ."[31] But this very emphasis upon politics as inspiration betrays Bentley's premises. By focusing upon political art as emotional impetus, he severs the subjective side of the poetical-political creative process from the conditions that might be affected by that process, and thereby relegates Brechtian art to the realm of Kantian aesthetics. Brecht's art, for Bentley, is ultimately disinterested. It is not functional; it is not a force in the process of change. For, as he makes clear at the conclusion of his review of *The Trial of Lucullus,* even great democratic art does not and cannot interact dialectically in a productive remaking of an imperfect world. But, paradoxically, such art can only exist in an imperfect world: "The prerequisite of a great popular art, as Whitman and other realistic democrats have allowed, is a great populace and not a people drugged by opiates every bit as strong as religion. Until this condition is fulfilled, Bertolt Brecht will be important only to the intellegentsia; *after* it is fulfilled, paradoxically enough, propaganda will be gratuitous."[32]

In conclusion, Bentley attempts to make Brecht fit for society as both a poet and as a revolutionary. His final words reveal the attitude underlying his attempt; moreover, they indicate the direction and emphasis of Brecht's reception in this country in future years.

[30] "Bertolt Brecht's Poetry," *Partisan Review,* 8 (1941), 114-27.
[31] Bentley, "Brecht," *The Nation,* 131.
[32] Ibid. 132.

II. 1948-1959

Fittingly, Brecht's final day in the United States was spent as a participant in what was subsequently recognized as the opening ceremonies of the Cold War culture. The trial of the Hollywood film industry by J. Parnell Thomas's senate committee was merely a more overtly aggressive phase in the process through which American policies for containing Communism on a global scale were sustained and given coherence by an ideological framework of implicit and explicit beliefs about history and values. For both McCarthyian demagogues and the Cold War liberals the content, if not the style of their views bespoke shared assumptions about the "Free World," its cultural contours and ideological enemies. For literary America it meant a turn to the right; the repudiation of the radical thirties; the expunging of Howells, Dreiser, Mark Twain, Thomas Wolfe and other socially progressive writers from the center of the canon; the elevation of Henry James as a primary writer; the depoliticizing or repoliticizing of Faulkner and Melville; the glorification of the twenties. The alternatives of this direction were twofold in the case of the Brecht reception. One could either accept the integral unity of his politics and his art, i.e., write him off or repudiate him as a Stalinist; or one could divide and conquer, i.e., attempt to salvage the poet in him by denying the significance of Marxism for his art. The former approach, while opportunistic, required too blatant a denial of his artistic achievement; hence, Brecht criticism in this country began to be founded on the latter—systematic denials and conscious misinterpretation of his politics.

The development of testimony before the Thomas committee set the tone for both these directions in the Brecht reception. For the "executioners" it was back to the *Lehrstück*, in this case *The Measures Taken*. Brecht's work came under attack not as a "play for learning" but as the most explicit statement of his politics. In *The Measures Taken* a young comrade is voluntarily put to death for his inability to complete the directives of a collective. In his interrogation Mr. Stripling pointed straight to the interpretive approach to this play which was to dominate and guide the approach to Brecht's Marxism:

> MR. STRIPLING: Mr. Brecht, will you tell the committee whether or not one of the characters in this play was murdered by his comrades because it was in the best interests of the party?
> MR. BRECHT: No, it is not quite according to the story.
> MR. STRIPLING: Because he would not bow to discipline he was murdered by his comrades, isn't it true.[33]

Brecht's response to this query, both in the hearings and in theoretical treatments of the play was an unequivocal no. *The Measures Taken* is

[33] *Thirty Years of Treason,* ed. Eric Bentley (New York, 1971), p. 212.

not about an ethical problem, concentrating on an end result, but an *Übungsstück*—an exercise to explore the problems of false consciousness. Taken as a "thesis" play, a final answer, the solution becomes primary—an ideological justification for death at any price. This is precisely the line of argument pursued by Ruth Fischer in her book, *Stalin and German Communism* (1948). As an authority on German Communism, her description of Brecht as "minstrel of the G.P.U. [i.e., the former Soviet Secret Police]" was representative of the general understanding of Brecht's Marxism even among those critics who found her indictment of Brecht too harsh.

R. Fischer's depiction of the role of Communist Party discipline which Brecht embraces as a palliative in order to escape the turmoils of his chaotic and nihilistic early years anticipates in essence an entire line of interpretations fostered by the intellectual climate of the Cold War. It includes such critics as Arthur Koestler,[34] Herbert Lüthy,[35] Peter Heller,[36] and Martin Esslin whose Freudian interpretation was to become very influential.[37] R. Fischer writes: "From this over-all negation, from this cynical withdrawal from all values, from this bitter empty nihilism, Brecht collapsed into the polar opposite—the adoration of the discipline and hierarchical order of the German Communist Party. Hypnotized by its totalitarian and terrorist features, he became the most original poet the party ever possessed."[38] Regarding the complicated genesis of Brecht's Marxism, R. Fischer omitted the fact that Brecht himself was allied with the very left oppositional and heretical elements which had led to her own expulsion from the German Communist Party in 1926; that he was in conflict with the cultural commissars of the League of Proletarian Revolutionary Writers[39]; that he was relentless in his criticism of party bosses; indeed, that his whole relationship to party bureaucracy had been a strained and uneasy one. Nevertheless, R. Fischer maintains: "Brecht had not been drawn to communism in its original form . . . he was hostile to it as long as it was a democratic organization."[40] Rather than deviation Fischer finds that Brecht's works (and here she concentrates almost exclusively on the *Lehrstücke*) "are the reflection of the transitional period [of German Communism] and its finished product the Stalinist party."[41]

Importantly, Fischer's book laid the groundwork for *all* the American Cold War approaches to Brecht's politics. For those who would impute

[34] Arthur Koestler, *The Invisible Writing* (London, 1954) pp. 42 ff.
[35] Herbert Lüthy, "Of Poor Bert Brecht," *Encounter,* 7/1 (July 1956), 33-53.
[36] Peter Heller, "Nihilist into Activist: Two Phases in the Development of Bertolt Brecht," GR, 28 (1953), 144-55.
[37] *Brecht* (E/1). Cf. also below.
[38] *Stalin and German Communism* (Cambridge, Mass., 1948), p. 616.
[39] For a discussion of Brecht's relationship with "Bund proletarisch-revolutionärer Schriftsteller" (BPRS), see Helga Gallas, *Marxistische Literaturtheorie* (Neuwied, 1971).
[40] Fischer, *Stalin,* p. 615.
[41] Ibid., p. 616.

to him unswerving party loyalty, Brecht's *The Measures Taken* represents the climax of his career and, at the same time, the most "revealing work of art in the entire communist literature."[42] For those who tended to rescue his art from the politics, to downgrade the importance of the politics, the *Lehrstücke* were viewed as transitional works. Yet in both instances—for those who viewed Brecht primarily as a Communist poet and for those who did not—the attitude toward the nature of his politics is strikingly similar. The *Lehrstücke* are didactic—a "glorification of the anti-Christ"; Brecht's politics are Stalinist, but they do not matter for his art. Moreover, he is in conflict with the "aesthetics" of the Kremlin and that is good. This second Cold War approach to Brecht finds its most popular expression in an article by William Becker in the *New Republic,* which appeared shortly after the 17 June 1953 East German uprising:

> But for us, the important point which usually is missed in all the talk about Brecht's "position" is that one cannot demonstrate any necessary connection between Brecht's political position and his aesthetic one, that Brecht is not, by any sensible definition of the term, a Communist playwright. That one may deplore his political commitment, and still learn what he has to teach about theatres, seems an obvious thing to say.[43]

It was particularly easy for Becker to deplore Brecht's political commitment in the belief "that his political position as rendered through his plays and theories has not fundamentally altered since the days when *The Three Penny Opera* was the greatest popular success in modern German history."[44]

Once the separation between art and politics had been made, the possibilities for praising Brecht, the artist, were infinite. The growing Brecht cult in the United States—even in the early fifties—is clearly an indication of this phenomenon. Between 1948 and 1956 there were approximately thirty-seven Brecht productions given in the United States: fourteen of these were of *The Good Woman of Setzuan,* eleven of *The Caucasian Chalk Circle,* five of *The Threepenny Opera.* The only *Lehrstück* produced was a performance of *The Exception and the Rule* at Dartmouth College. Clearly, the "Humanist" Brecht is most easily located in the parable plays and the massive interest in these works indicates a trend which can be traced in Brechtian scholarship within the Universities as well—save the poet from his political self. Paradoxically, there is a double character to this rescue operation. Bentley is indeed correct in emphasizing that it was the little theater movement which kept interest in Brecht alive at a time when he enjoyed less

---

[42] Koestler, *The Invisible Writing,* p. 43.
[43] *New Republic,* (26 October 1953) 16-17.
[44] Ibid.

popularity[45]; just as Weisstein rightly points to the role of little journals in promoting Brecht the poet.[46] In both instances, however, such a promotion was at the expense of the whole man.

IV. 1960 - Today

The recent focus on Brecht as a political artist is directly connected to the repolitization of society as a whole due to the social upheavals of the sixties: the civil-rights movement, the student movement on the campuses, the struggle against the involvement of the United States in Vietnam. The emergence of a New Left in the United States brought with it a reconsideration of cultural values and a search for models deemed more relevant to the social realities of contemporary life. If those seizing on Brecht as one of these models often perpetuated the images and myths about him which they hoped to refashion, they nevertheless opened the way to appreciating the politics at the center of his art.

Yet this revitalizing of the political Brecht is a decidedly limited, if growing phenomenon, and it would be highly misleading not to interpret the mainstream of Brecht's reception in the sixties as a continuation of earlier developments. The publication of two major works on Brecht in English during the years 1959-1960 gave impetus to the growing Brecht cult among intellectuals and academicians, at a time when the question of whether to perform Brecht's plays or not generated a heated debate in the Federal Republic of Germany.[47] John Willett in his *The Theatre of Bertolt Brecht* accepts Brecht's Marxism as integral to his political and artistic development but, at the same time, remains painfully ignorant about the nature of that Marxism and the extent to which theory penetrates and informs even the less obviously agitational pieces. While excepting *The Mother* and *The Measures Taken*, Willett states: "[Brecht] wrote little that can be seen as specifically Communist."[48]

Martin Esslin, on the other hand, clearly recognizes the centrality of the problem, and it is his book[49] which draws together Anglo-Saxon strands of the Brecht reception into a coherent pattern of interpretation based on a Freudian theory of personality. His thesis is a familiar one, for it is found recurrently as the explicit or implicit basis for numerous American studies of Brecht. According to Esslin, Brecht's Communist phase necessitated the acceptance of vulgar Marxist orthodoxy, a strait jacket which bound him to the dictates of intellectually inferior party functionaries as a preventive for his creative self-destruction. Poet and

---

[45] "Brecht on the American Stage. Three Notes," *Bulletin of the National Theatre Conference,* 10/2 (1948), 3-8.

[46] Cf. n. 2.

[47] André Müller, *Kreuzzug gegen Brecht* (Berlin, 1962).

[48] *Brecht* (W), p. 78.

[49] Both the first British, *Brecht* (E/1), and American versions, *Brecht* (E/2), are to be considered here.

Marxist are at odds, and if the Marxist prevails in Brecht's own mind, the poet ultimately wins, not only in Esslin's study but in the myriad of works based on this convenient separation as well: "Yet the deeper needs of his personality made it impossible for Brecht to argue on any lines other than rational considerations of political or propaganda expediency. The poet deep within always had to hide behind the Marxist."[50]

Robert Brustein also bases his interpretation on the two souls in Brecht's breast. He presents an elaborate system whereby the realist (Marxist) is juxtaposed in the creative process to the romantic (existentialist). Again, Communism, the ever present Freudian hero-super-ego arrives to save Brecht from his "obsession with the darker side of man . . . a self which is essentially morbid, sensual, anarchistic . . . to dissolve the nightmare of absurdity."[51] For Brustein, Brecht is underneath it all an existentialist. In a refreshing departure from the Freudian interpretations, Frederic Ewen shows Brecht's political-aesthetic development as a part of the cultural and political history of modern Germany. Moreover, his measured and informative treatment of Brecht's life in the German Democratic Republic is based on information and not on anecdotal polemic. However, he too conceives of Dialectic Materialism essentially as ideology and does not understand its methodological implications for Brecht's art.[52]

In the nearly forty years of Brecht reception in the United States, we note the use of a variety of shibboleths to portray Brecht's philosophical orientation: nihilist, Stalinist, anti-Stalinist, Communist, humanist, anti-Fascist, democrat, minstrel of the G.P.U., existentialist under the skin—the interpretations proliferate with changing conditions and the tastes of a given age. Yet running below the superficially conflicting sympathies and judgments of the critics, there emerges a surprising unanimity on key premises despite the critics' ideological variance. Generally speaking, these break down into three categories:

1. One group of critics propounds the theory of the separation of art and politics, art and nature, art and work. These opposites are posited as totally incompatible; they are considered autonomous, non-interactive realms. Ever since Hegel's pessimistic pronouncements concerning the end of art, European aestheticians have been thrashing at the relationship between art and life. Those fighting for a fusion of the two often shared with their opponents the same biases concerning art—which was considered to be a reflective, static entity outside the artist and outside of history. Brecht attempts to build an aesthetic based on machines and production; he advances the notion of art in an active, changing and dialectic relationship to the world. An axiom of the

[50] *Brecht* (E/2), pp. 231-32.
[51] Robert Brustein, *The Theatre of Revolt* (Boston, 1962), p. 232.
[52] *Brecht* (Ew).

Brecht reception in this country has been to affirm the separation of the two realms and thus *a priori* disregard one of the cornerstones of Brechtian art.

2. Another group of critics adheres to psychological reductionism. They believe that Brecht was suffering from neurosis and that his move to Communism arose from a deep compensatory need for authority and final answers in a world of flux and chaos. In point of fact, the opposite is true. Brecht's relationship with Korsch, Sternberg, and Benjamin, whatever his inner disposition, grew out of questions, not easy answers; actually, his ruthless inquisitiveness took him light years beyond the kinds of facile solutions that Brustein and others claim he found in Communist dogma.

3. Finally, there is the claim that Brecht's politics represent ideology and *Weltanschauung*. However, for Brecht the theater was primarily an institution for the demonstration of pedagogical exercises, not for the proclamation of didactic messages and preconceived judgments. In fact, Brecht did not shrink from asking challenging questions about the nature of Marxism itself.

In arriving at an understanding of the reasons for the political distortions of Brecht's work and in looking for ways to change this situation, we come to see the connection between his reception and the infrastructure of our own institutions. Unless the core of Brecht's drama is understood as method, his more obviously "ideological" plays will always be held up as merely doctrine, monolithic in their answers, dated in their themes. This has been the fate of the *Lehrstücke*, even at the hands of those who are sympathetic to Brecht's Marxism. Conversely, those plays which are not as overtly political run the opposite risk; namely the risk of being defused into universal statements of human existence which divest them of political content. Ultimately, the fate of Brecht's works in this country will depend on whether a favorable climate, which is tolerant of the premises of his art, can be created. Although Eleanor Hakim in *Studies on the Left*[53] engages in a somewhat senseless polemic against Eric Bentley's introduction to *Seven Plays*,[54] her article, together with Lee Baxandall's review of the same edition of Brecht's plays,[55] represent pioneering work in this direction. Hakim and Baxandall take seriously the entire tradition in which Brecht's art was conceived and put into practice. The annual publication of *Brecht Today* (1971 ff.), organ of the American based Brecht Society, is continuing those efforts. By far the most discerning contribution on Brechtian aesthetics to appear in the United States is Darko Suvin's article, entitled "The Mirror and the Dynamo."[56] If Suvin discerns too

---

[53] "Brecht: A World Without Achilles," *Studies on the Left*, 2/2 (1961), 59-72.
[54] *Seven Plays by Bertolt Brecht*, ed. Eric Bentley (New York, 1961).
[55] "Brecht's Theater of Transformation," *Studies on the Left*, 2/1 (1961), 93-99.
[56] DR, 12/1 (1967), 56-67. Reprinted in *Brecht* (M), pp. 80-98.

much Blochian utopianism in Brecht and plays down the importance of production and contradiction, his essay is the first to cement aesthetics and politics, to demonstrate the totality of aesthetic vision. It is only on the basis of such contributions that a serious discussion of Brecht can be begun.

In 1935, Brecht's play *The Mother* confronted America with a new kind of drama—the result was controversy and, ultimately, profound misunderstanding of the playwright's political-aesthetic intentions. In the more than thirty-five years since that time neither *The Mother,* nor the "plays for learning," nor the political Brecht have fared much better in an environment often openly hostile to his Marxism. In the fall of 1973, The San Francisco Mime Troop opened a two-year run of *The Mother* which is to tour much of the United States with final performances in New York. The response to that tour and to the generally reviving interest in Brecht's *Lehrstücke* throughout this country will continue to tell us as much about ourselves as about Brecht.

BRECHT'S WORKS IN ENGLISH

A SELECT BIBLIOGRAPHY

No attempt has been made to provide a complete list of English renderings. Rather, this bibliography is primarily intended as an aid to the reader who wishes to avail himself of fairly recent and, for the most part, comparatively easily accessible translations of those works discussed in this volume.

I. Collected Plays

1. *Baal; A Man's a Man and The Elephant Calf. Early Plays by Bertolt Brecht.* Ed., introd. Eric Bentley. New York: Grove Press, 1964.
2. Brecht, Bertolt. *Collected Plays.* Vols. I, V, IX. Ed. Ralph Manheim and John Willett. Vintage Books. New York: Random House, 1971-1973.
   Vol. I: *Baal; Drums in the Night; In the Jungle of Cities; The Life of Edward the Second of England;* Five One-Act Plays.
   Vol. V: *Life of Galileo; The Trial of Lucullus; Mother Courage and Her Children.*
   Vol. IX: *The Tutor; Coriolanus; The Trial of Joan of Arc at Rouen, 1431; Trumpets and Drums; Don Juan.*
3. Brecht, Bertolt. *The Jewish Wife and Other Short Plays.* Trans. Eric Bentley. New York: Grove Press, 1965. [*The Jewish Wife; In Search of Justice; The Informer; The Elephant Calf; The Measures Taken; The Exception and the Rule; Salzburg Dance of Death;* "What Was He Killed For?"]
4. Brecht, Bertolt. *Jungle of Cities and Other Plays: Jungle of Cities; Drums in the Night; Roundheads and Peakheads.* Trans. Anselm Hollo, Frank Jones, N. Goold-Verschoyle. New York: Grove Press, 1966.
5. Brecht, Bertolt. *Plays.* 2 vols. London: Methuen, 1960-1962.
   I: *The Caucasian Chalk Circle; The Threepenny Opera; The Trial of Lucullus; The Life of Galileo.*
   II: *Mother Courage and Her Children; St. Joan of the Stockyards; The Good Person of Szechwan.*
6. *Parables for the Theatre. Two Plays by Bertolt Brecht: The Good Woman of Setzuan and The Caucasian Chalk Circle.* Rev. English versions by Eric Bentley. Minneapolis: University of Minnesota Press, 1965.
7. *Seven Plays by Bertolt Brecht.* Ed., introd. Eric Bentley. New York: Grove Press, 1961. [*In the Swamp; A Man's a Man; Saint Joan of the Stockyards; Mother Courage; Galileo; The Good Woman of Setzuan; The Caucasian Chalk Circle.*]

II. Individual Plays

1. *The Baden Play for Learning.* Trans. Lee Baxandall. DR, 4/4 (May 1960), 118-33. Reprinted in *Brecht* (M), 177-97.
2. *The Caucasian Chalk Circle.* Rev. English version and introd. Eric Bentley. New York: Grove Press, 1966.
3. *The Caucasian Chalk Circle.* Trans. James and Tania Stern, with W.H. Auden. London: Methuen, 1963.
4. *The Days of the Commune.* Trans. Leonard J. Lehrman. *Dunster Drama Review,* 10/2 (1971).
5. *Edward II. A Chronicle Play.* Trans., introd. Eric Bentley. New York: Grove Press, 1966.
6. *Galileo.* Trans. Charles Laughton, ed., introd. Eric Bentley. New York: Grove Press, 1966. [Included also: "Writing the Truth: Five Difficulties."]
7. *The Good Person of Szechwan.* Trans. John Willett. London: Methuen, 1965.
8. *The Good Woman of Setzuan.* Rev. English version and introd. Eric Bentley. New York: Grove Press, 1966.
9. *The Guns of Carrar.* Trans. George Tabori. New York: S. French, 1971.
10. *He Who Said Yes.* Trans. Gerhard Nellhaus. *Accent,* 7/2 (Autumn 1946).
11. *The Life of Galileo.* Trans. Desmond I. Vesey. London: Methuen, 1963.
12. *The Mother.* Trans. Lee Baxandall. New York: Grove Press, 1965.
13. *Mother Courage and Her Children.* Trans. Eric Bentley. New York: Grove Press, 1966.
15. *The Private Life of the Master Race.* Trans., introd. Eric Russell Bentley. New York: New Directions, 1944.
14. *Puntila and His Hired Man.* Trans. G. Nellhaus. New York: G. Nellhaus, c1960.
16. *The Resistible Rise of Arturo Ui. A Gangster Spectacle.* Adapted by George Tabori. Music by Hans-Dieter Hosalla. New York: S. French, 1972.
17. *Rise and Fall of the City of Mahagonny.* Trans. with recording U.S. Columbia KL 5271-73.
18. *Saint Joan of the Stockyards.* Trans. Frank Jones. Bloomington: Indiana University Press, 1969.
19. *Schweyk in the Second World War.* Music by Hanns Eisler. Trans. Peter M. Sander. Waltham, Mass.: Brandeis University, 1967.
20. *Senora Carrar's Rifles.* Trans. Keene Wallis. *Theatre Workshop,* 2/1 (April-June 1938), 30-50.
21. *The Seven Deadly Sins of the Lower Middle Class.* Trans. W.H. Auden and Chester Kallmann. DR, 6/1 (September 1961), 123-29.

22. *The Threepenny Opera*. Trans. Desmond Vesey and Eric Bentley. New York: Grove Press, 1964.
23. *The Trial of Lucullus. A Play for the Radio*. Trans. H.R. Hays. New York: New Directions, 1943. Reproduced, Ann Arbor: University Microfilms, 1972.
24. (with Lion Feuchtwanger). *The Visions of Simone Machard*. Trans. Carl Richard Mueller. New York: Grove Press, 1965.

III. Poems, Songs

1. *Bertolt Brecht's Hauspostille*. Introd. and selected trans. Sidney Hillger Bremer. Stanford: Stanford University Press, 1967.
2. *The Brecht-Eisler Song-Book*. (*German and English*). Ed. Eric Bentley and Earl Robinson. New York: Quick Fox, 1966.
3. *The Great Art of Living Together: Poems on the Theatre*. Trans. John Berger and Anna Bostock. Bingley: Granville Press, 1972. [Seven poems from *Der Messingkauf*; new ed. of III/5.]
4. *Manual of Piety. A Bilingual Edition*. Trans. Eric Bentley, notes Hugo Schmidt. New York: Grove Press, 1966.
5. *Poems on the Theatre*. Trans. John Berger and Anna Bostock. London: Scorpion Press, 1961. [Poems from *Der Messingkauf*.]
6. *Selected Poems*. Trans., introd. H.R. Hays. Evergreen Books. New York, London: Grove Press, 1959. [Bilingual ed. Selections from *Manual of Piety; Songs, Poems, Choruses; Svendborg Poems*.]

IV. Prose Writings

1. *A Little Organum for the Theatre*. Trans. Beatrice Gottlieb. *Accent*, 11/1 (Winter 1951), 13-40.
2. *The Messingkauf Dialogues*. Trans. John Willett. London: Methuen, 1965.
3. "On Chinese Acting." Trans. Eric Bentley. DR, 6/1 (September 1961), 130-36.
4. "On the Experimental Theatre." Trans. Carl Richard Mueller. DR, 6/1 (September 1961), 3-17.
5. *Tales from the Calendar*. Prose trans. Yvonne Kapp, verse trans. Michael Hamburger. London: Methuen, 1961.
6. "Theatre for Learning." Trans. Edith Anderson. DR, 6/1 (September 1961), 18-25.
7. *Three-Penny Novel*. Trans. Desmond I. Vesey, verse trans. Christopher Isherwood. Harmondsworth: Penguin, 1965, 1972.
8. *Brecht on Theatre. The Development of an Aesthetic*. Ed., trans. John Willett. New York: Hill and Wang, 1964.
9. "Writing the Truth: Five Difficulties." Trans. Richard Winston. Cf. II/6.

INDEX TO BRECHT'S WORKS

All of Brecht's writings mentioned in the preceding essays, except those volumes included either in the list of Abbreviations (p. x) or the Select Bibliography (pp. 227-29), have been listed by both English title(s) and German original. English titles are followed by page references; references to notes have been given only in cases where the work in question is not mentioned in the text. For the German originals the bibliographic information for the texts used here has been added. To indicate the type of work the following abbreviations have been used:

E   Essays and notes (on art, society, politics)

F   Films and film projects

N   Narrative prose

P   Individual poems, ballads, songs (given by title and/or first line)

PP   Collections or cycles of poems

S   Stage works (plays, projects, adaptations)

No separate references to individual characters in Brecht's works have been provided; references to them have been listed under the title of the play in question.

UNIVERSITY OF NORTH CAROLINA
STUDIES IN THE GERMANIC LANGUAGES
AND LITERATURES

Initiated by RICHARD JENTE (1949-1952), *established by* F. E. COENEN (1952-1968)

Publication Committee

SIEGFRIED MEWS, EDITOR   JOHN G. KUNSTMANN   GEORGE S. LANE

HERBERT W. REICHERT   CHRISTOPH E. SCHWEITZER   SIDNEY R. SMITH

For other volumes in the "Studies" see page ii and following pages.

Send orders to: (U.S. and Canada)
The University of North Carolina Press, P.O. Box 2288
Chapel Hill, N.C. 27514
(All other countries) Feffer and Simons, Inc., 31 Union Square, New York, N.Y. 10003

UNIVERSITY OF NORTH CAROLINA
STUDIES IN THE GERMANIC LANGUAGES
AND LITERATURES

Initiated by RICHARD JENTE (1949-1952), *established by* F. E. COENEN (1952-1968)

Publication Committee

SIEGFRIED MEWS, EDITOR   JOHN G. KUNSTMANN   GEORGE S. LANE

HERBERT W. REICHERT   CHRISTOPH E. SCHWEITZER   SIDNEY R. SMITH

For other volumes in the "Studies" see preceding and following pages and p. ii

Order reprinted books from: AMS PRESS, Inc.,
56 East 13th Street, New York, N.Y. 10003

UNIVERSITY OF NORTH CAROLINA
STUDIES IN THE GERMANIC LANGUAGES
AND LITERATURES

Initiated by RICHARD JENTE (1949-1952), *established by* F. E. COENEN (1952-1968)

Publication Committee

SIEGFRIED MEWS, EDITOR   JOHN G. KUNSTMANN   GEORGE S. LANE

HERBERT W. REICHERT   CHRISTOPH E. SCHWEITZER   SIDNEY R. SMITH

For other volumes in the "Studies" see preceding pages and p. ii

Order reprinted books from: AMS PRESS, Inc.,
56 East 13th Street, New York, N.Y. 10003